Robert Ethol Welsh, Frederick George Edwards

Romance of Psalter and Hymnal

Authors and Composers

Robert Ethol Welsh, Frederick George Edwards

Romance of Psalter and Hymnal
Authors and Composers

ISBN/EAN: 9783337345372

Printed in Europe, USA, Canada, Australia, Japan

Cover: Foto ©Thomas Meinert / pixelio.de

More available books at **www.hansebooks.com**

ROMAN

OF

PSALTER AND HYMNAL:

Authors and Composers.

BY THE REV.
R. E. WELSH, M.A.,
AND
F. G. EDWARDS,
Author of " United Praise."

New York:
JAMES POTT & CO.,
ASTOR PLACE.
1889.

PREFACE.

THE past thirty years have witnessed the issue of a host of Hymnals, each having its own special feature or guiding purpose. The Tractarian Movement and, at an earlier period, the Methodist Revival, awakened emotions and left tastes and tendencies which contributed largely to this outburst of the Churches into song. Roundell Palmer's *Book of Praise*, and *Hymns Ancient and Modern*, published in 1860, of which a million copies have been sold every year, are significant landmarks.

This multiplication of Hymnals has naturally excited a new and keener curiosity regarding the makers and the historic associations of the Hymns and Psalms with which our lips have become so familiar.

The present volume seeks to meet and guide this new curiosity ; takes some of our choicest sacred verse and endeavours to throw around it the living interest of curious origin, personal incident, and historic episode, which weave for us a veritable romance, the Romance of Sacred Praise.

The scope of the book is too wide to leave room for much literary criticism or exhaustive detail. It makes no claim to be a Dictionary of Hymnology, or complete book of reference. Specialists must go elsewhere. It perhaps attempts to cover too wide a field, and, in consequence, much that was written has had to be excluded; but its object is to be a companion to the entire Praise, literary and musical, of the Christian Church, giving to well-known Psalms, Hymns, and Tunes the charm of having a history.

The facts have been gleaned from many fields. For the story of the Psalter I have been under great obligations to Dean Stanley, *Four Friends* (Ewald), Maclaren, Van Dyke, and Dr. Ker. I have also to thank Dean Perowne for courteous and cordial permission to make frequent use of his vivid translation of *The Psalms*.

Although this work is not critical, the conclusions of Professor Robertson Smith and Canon

PREFACE.

Cheyne on the one hand, and of Canon Fausset on the other, have not been overlooked. The historic setting of many of the Psalms is a matter of probability only; and some of my positions I assume with considerable diffidence.

In relating the story of the Hymnal, I have made large use of the biographies of many of the Hymn-writers; and, whilst making fresh additions to modern Hymnology, I owe much to Duffield, King, and other previous workers in the same field.

This Companion would be incomplete without some account of the makers of the Music to which our best-loved hymns are wedded; and this part of the work has been committed to the hands of my musical friend the author of *United Praise*.

R. E. W.

St. George's, Brondesbury,
London, N.W.

The biographical sketches of representative modern hymn-tune composers, forming Part III. (p. 273) of this book, have been prepared at the suggestion of my friend the Rev. R. E. Welsh, M.A.

Like much other biographical matter, the material

for them has been gathered from various sources, largely from periodical literature. I must express my indebtedness to my friend Mr. J. Spencer Curwen (whose books *Studies in Worship Music*, First and Second Series, are invaluable to all who take an interest in Church Music) for much information contained in his writings; and to Mrs. Gauntlett for kindly giving me some interesting details relating to her late husband, Dr. Gauntlett.

F. G. E.

South Hampstead,
    Midsummer Day, 1889.

CONTENTS.

PART I.—*PSALTER.*

		PAGE
I.	GENERAL SURVEY: CHRIST'S HYMNAL; THE PSALMS IN HISTORY	3
II.	SONGS OF A SHEPHERD	15
III.	CAVE SONGS: IMPRECATORY	31
IV.	CORONATION AND PROCESSIONAL HYMNS	38
V.	A ROYAL PENITENT'S WAIL	47
VI.	PSALMS OF A ROYAL FUGITIVE	58
VII.	SONGS OF SOLOMON	67
VIII.	ODES OF VICTORY	79
IX.	SONGS IN A STRANGE LAND	86
X.	PILGRIM SONGS	99

PART II.—*HYMNAL.*

I. GENERAL SURVEY.

1. Nilometer of the Church 113
2. The Church Universal 116
3. Children's Hymns 118
4. Sermonic Hymns 123
5. Introspective Hymns 123
6. Sensuous Hymns 125
7. Hymns or Soliloquies? 125
8. Rejected Hymns 127

CONTENTS.

II. EARLY CHRISTIAN HYMNS:

    PAGE

1. Primitive Church Praise: "Tersanctus"; "Gloria in Excelsis"; "Gloria Patri"; "Lamp-lighting Hymn" 129
2. Hymns of Heresy and Orthodoxy: "Bardesan"; "Ephrem"; "Synesius" 131
3. Ambrosian Hymns: "Te Deum" 134
4. Ambrose 135
5. Prudentius and Anatolius 136
6. Gregory the Great: Gregorian Music . . . 137

III. HYMNS FROM THE CLOISTERS:

1. Monks of Mar Saba 140
2. Monks of the Studium 143
3. The Two Bernards 143
4. From a Prison and a Palace 146
5. "Dies Iræ" 148

IV. HYMNS OF THE REFORMATION:

1. Martin Luther 150
2. Nicolai 153
3. Gustavus Adolphus 153
4. Rinckart 154

V. CLASSIC ENGLISH POETS:

1. Milton 158
2. Dryden 158
3. Addison 159
4. Sir Walter Scott 161
5. Kirke White 161

VI. CLASSIC EVENING HYMNS:

1. Lyte 163
2. Ken 166

VII. PURITAN HYMNS:

1. Watts 170
2. Doddridge 176

VIII. METHODIST REVIVAL HYMNS.

		PAGE
1. Toplady	. . . .	. 181
2. Wesley .	. . .	. 186

IX. OLNEY HYMNS:

| 1. Cowper . | . . . | . 195 |
| 2. Newton . | . . . . | . 200 |

X. CLASSIC MISSIONARY HYMNS:

| 1. Heber . | . . . . | . 207 |
| 2. Montgomery . | . . . . | . 210 |

XI. EVANGELICAL HYMNS:

1. Charlotte Elliott .	. . .	. 215
2. Bonar .	. . . . .	. 218
3. Ray Palmer .	. . . .	. 220
4. Havergal	. . . .	. 221

XII. OXFORD HYMNS:

1. Newman	. . . . . .	. 228
2. Faber .	. . . . . .	. 233
3. Keble .	. . . . . .	. 238

XIII. HYMNS OF FOUR BROAD CHURCH DEANS:

1. Stanley .	. . . . .	. 241
2. Milman .	. . . . . .	. 242
3. Alford .	. . . . .	. 243
4. Plumptre	. . . .	. 244

XIV. HYMNS OF THREE BISHOPS:

1. Bickersteth .	. . . . .	. 245
2. Wordsworth .	. . . . .	. 246
3. Walsham How	. .	. 247

XV. HYMNS OF THREE POET-VICARS:

1. Monsell .	. . . . .	. 248
2. Ellerton .	. . . . .	. 249
3. Stone .	. . . . .	. 250

XVI. HYMNS OF AMERICAN POETS:

PAGE
1. Oliver Wendell Holmes 253
2. J. G. Whittier 255
3. W. C. Bryant 258

XVII. HYMNS OF THREE FEMALE SINGERS:
1. Adelaide A. Procter 261
2. Jean Ingelow 264
3. Harriet Auber 264

XVIII. LAST, BUT NOT LEAST:
1. T. T. Lynch 266
2. Adams 269
3. Palgrave 270

XIX. RETROSPECT 272

PART III.—SOME HYMN-TUNE COMPOSERS.

I. DR. H. J. GAUNTLETT 277
II. HENRY SMART 285
III. DR. E. J. HOPKINS 295
IV. REV. J. B. DYKES, Mus. Doc. . . . 302
V. DR. W. H. MONK 310
VI. SIR JOHN STAINER 317
VII. SIR ARTHUR SULLIVAN . . . 327
VIII. MR. JOSEPH BARNBY 332

INDEX I. Psalms Mentioned . . 341
II. Hymns Mentioned 342
III. Hymn-Writers Mentioned . . . 348
IV. Hymn-Tune Composers Mentioned . 350
V. Hymn-Tunes Mentioned . . . 351

PART I.

ROMANCE OF THE PSALTER.

I.

GENERAL SURVEY OF THE PSALTER.

1. Christ's Book of Praise.

THE Bible, like each separate Book in it, has a natural history. It was not always a bound volume. Its sixty-six Books sprang from distinct human experiences, and cover a period as long as the Christian era. We are, perhaps, prepared to believe that the historical Books were the product of natural circumstances as truly as were Homer's *Odyssey* and Bunyan's *Pilgrim's Progress;* but to one Book we have not been in the habit of applying this conception.

The Psalter has been to some a sort of Melchisedec in the Bible, "without father, without mother, without descent, having neither beginning of days nor end of life." Others have always had the vague idea that to David belonged the entire Book. Are they not called "The Psalms of David"?

It is wonderful how devoutly we have read and loved them, how profitably we have used them, and yet how little curiosity we have shown as to the lives and histories and experiences which they crystallize.

Who collected them? Are the inscriptions prefixed to most of them of the same date as the Psalms themselves? How can we understand and use the Psalms of Cursing? What are the Songs of Degrees? Why that clause at the end of Ps. lxxii., "The prayers of David the Son of Jesse are ended," while, later, several Psalms bearing his name are given? What is the reference in "Lift up your heads, O ye gates"?

These and scores of questions like these we have been content to leave in nebulous mystery. It would add greatly to the charm and living interest of the Psalms if we could give the Romance of their history. It is possible to do for some of them what we can do for Lyte's "Abide with me," Newman's "Lead, kindly Light," and Havergal's "Thy life was given for me."

The former is not so easy a task. The Psalms are so ancient that fewer sidelights remain for us. But we can do much to surround them with tales of their origin, the tragic and pathetic episodes of their history.

Regard the Book for the nonce purely as a hymnal, *Christ's Hymnal*, used by the Jews as their Book of Praise. Examine it as you would examine *Hymns Ancient and Modern*.

Its name explains its contents. As the lyre gave its name to lyric poetry, the stringed instrument to which these sacred odes were sung gave its name—The Psalter—to the collection of Psalms.

The Psalter we find divided into five distinct books, a second Pentateuch: as has repeatedly been pointed out, the fivefold word of the congregation to Jehovah, as the Pentateuch is the fivefold word of Jehovah to the congregation. It must be confessed that this parallel has the look of manufacture about it, and the keener criticism of the present time believes the fourth and fifth books to have been originally one.

The *First Book* ends with Ps. xli., concluding with the Doxology and the double Amen.

The *Second Book* begins with Ps. xlii. and closes with Ps. lxxii., ending with the Doxology and the note "The Prayers of David the Son of Jesse are ended."

The *Third Book* opens with Ps. lxxiii. and concludes with Ps. lxxxix., ending again with the Doxology—which thus separates the Books much as the "Gloria" separates the chants in a Service.

The *Fourth Book* begins with Ps. xc. and closes with Ps. cvi., with the Doxology, Amen, and Hallelujah.

The *Fifth Book* contains the rest of the Psalms, the last being one long Doxology with Hallelujahs.

Why these five Books? The division points clearly to the fact that the Psalter comprises different collections of Hymns. It is not the "Higher Criticism" that has found this out. One confirmation patent to all is the fact that certain Psalms are found in more than one of the five compilations. The fourteenth and the fifty-third are almost identical; the latter part of the fortieth and the seventieth; the fifty-seventh and one hundred and eighth have close resemblances.

The *First Hymnal* contained forty-one pieces, all, with few exceptions, written by David. A little later an Appendix or *Second* collection was formed, many of them by the "Sons of Korah," and others by David. Still again a *Third Selection* was made, one set by "Asaph" (*i.e.* the Guild of Asaph), and another by the "Sons of Korah." Similarly with the others —or other.

When the second compilation was completed with Ps. lxxii., a note was appended to the effect that no more of David's songs were known to exist, although others were found at a later point—"The prayers of David the son of Jesse are ended."

Then followed some editor who combined the five (or four) successive collections into one. The Inscriptions and the Doxologies are no doubt the work of the editor or editors, and hence did not stand part of the Psalms as originally written. Like the notes affixed to the New Testament Epistles, the Inscriptions which are prefixed to one hundred and twenty-six of the Psalms are not decisive, but "are entitled to a general respect as ancient editorial annotations." The thirty-four anonymous Psalms, called "Orphans" by the Jews, are none the less authoritative because they have no editorial authorship prefixed.

These Psalms cover a period of at least a thousand years, as long as that covered by our Hymnal collections. At one extremity stands the Song of Moses, Ps. xc.,—if indeed it be his; at the other the Psalms of the Captivity, a period corresponding to that which lies between Stephen the Sabaite's "Art thou weary?" written a hundred years prior to King Alfred's reign, and Bonar's "I heard the voice of Jesus say."

The Reformation, the Evangelical revival of the Wesleys, the Olney history, the Tractarian Movement, have all left their impress on our hymn books. After the same fashion, the great movements in Hebrew history left their high water mark in the Psalms. These periodic outbursts of praise are quite distinguishable.

The tragic deliverance at the Red Sea produced the great "Ode to Liberty" of ancient times, the triumphal song of Moses.

The pathetic retrospect of Moses as he resigned himself to death without entering the promised land gave us, if the tradition may be believed, Ps. xc., "Lord, Thou hast been our dwelling place in all generations."

The eventful story of Deborah is crystallized in her bold and fiery ode in Judges.

It was David, however, whose poetic genius, fed by his dramatic history, enriched the Psalter with the loftiest lyrics. It was during his reign that sacred praise sprang into maturity, as it did again at the Reformation. In addition to writing so many Psalms, he founded a School of Sacred Poetry, many fruits of which are contained in the Psalter. During one part of his reign there were twenty-four bands of Levite musicians taking turn in public worship, each band consisting of one hundred and sixty-six musicians.

The reign of Jehoshaphat, the reign of Hezekiah, and lastly the Captivity and Restoration, left separate and large deposits of Sacred Song. These two kings devoted their energies to the restoration and improvement of the musical service at the Temple.

Jehoshaphat established public instructors in every part of his kingdom. Hezekiah organized a sort of Literary Antiquarian Society, "a society of learned men whose duty it was to collect and preserve all the scattered remains of the earlier literature" (Perowne). They probably saved numerous Psalms from perishing. That royal reformer, also, revived the ancient Hebrew music, and restored the singing of the Psalms of David and his school. He himself wrote sacred songs, as witness the plaintive lines composed on his recovery from his nearly fatal illness (Isa. xxxviii. 9). The Korahite singers, "Sons of Korah," during his reign, also wrote several Psalms.

As in the case of the Hymnal, the Psalter is thus an epitome of the history of the Jewish Church. The great personal and national events, the religious revivals, the social movements, are registered here in the sacred lyrics called into existence by these awakenings and deliverances. Periods that permitted sacred praise to languish were periods of languishing religious life. New outbursts of song were the immediate product of new advances in piety.

The later Psalms are less passionate, less lofty and poetic, and more didactic and formal. Ps. cxix.—which, as an acrostic, is evidently of late origin—is full of proverbial lines about the glory of the law, and has the antithetic formality of its late creation.* It was in David's time that sacred poetry had reached its purest and divinest tones.

The *Inscriptions* prefixed to most of the Psalms cannot all be satisfactorily explained. Some of them are musical directions. *"To the chief Musician"* would be, in modern dress, "For the Precentor" or "Choir Conductor," meaning that the Choir-master or Organist was to set these Hymns to music for the Temple Service. Indeed the name of one choir-master is prefixed to three of the Psalms; namely, Jeduthun or Ethan, one of the three famous Choir-leaders of David's time.

This Inscription serves to illustrate the fact that not all of the Psalms were written with the Temple Service in view. Just as the Olney Hymns were private and personal expressions of devotion, so some of the Psalms were written no doubt first of all for private use.

Other musical directions are given. Some Psalms were to be accompanied by flutes, others by stringed

---

* Some of the later Psalms were evidently composed for liturgical services in the second Temple, and compiled from earlier Psalms.

instruments. That word *Selah*, that has been a mystery to so many young (and some old) minds, is some musical instruction or poetic break. Most probably it marks the place where a pause was made in the Hymn.

Sometimes the name of the tune is prefixed, anticipating the fashion in modern Hymnals. Ps. xxii. is to be sung to the "Hind of the Dawn;" Ps. lvi. to the "Silent Dove in far off lands."

Other titles indicate the aim of the Psalms: "For Teaching" (Ps. lx.); "For Thanksgiving" (Ps. c.). One is called "A Prayer," another a "Song of Loves" (xlv.), and others are described as "Songs of Ascents."

2. THE PSALMS IN HISTORY.

The Psalter has been the Prayer and Praise Book of the Church Universal. It has moulded the very language and desires of all devout spirits, binding Ancient and Modern, Eastern and Western, in a brotherhood of common praise. It has been the liturgy of the Jewish as well as of the Christian, of the Protestant as well as of the Greek and Romanist Churches. In creeds and forms they differ, but in devotion they are alike.

We may guess how deeply the Psalms had sunk into the Jewish Church of our Lord's time from the fact that of the two hundred and eighty-three quotations in the New Testament from the Old, one hundred and sixteen are from the Psalms.

It was the Hymn Book of the primitive Christian Church. Christ at the last Supper, along with His disciples, sang the Hallel Psalms, cxiii.—cxviii. This was the "hymn" they sang before starting for the Garden of Gethsemane.

In the early centuries of the Christian Church the Psalter was the book put into the hands of young Christians as their *vade mecum;* and "no man was admitted to the superior orders of the clergy unless, among other prerequisites, he could say all the Psalter by heart.

They formed an essential part of the service. "After the reading from the Epistle, a whole Psalm was sung, or partly read and partly sung, and then followed the reading of the Gospel." "Sometimes they were sung by the whole congregation; at other times they were recited by one individual, who was followed by the rest." It was a very early practice also to sing them, as they were sung in the Temple, antiphonally. They sang either the verses or the two halves of each verse alternately, the decani and cantoris responding to each other.

How these Psalms have rung not only through the Jewish temples, but through the centuries! It fills us with awe to think that David sang them; that Isaiah, Nehemiah, Gamaliel, chanted them; that, more than all, our Divine Lord sang them the night before He embraced the cruel cross, that He consoled His spirit as He expired with the words of the Psalms; that Paul and Silas sang them while their feet were held fast in the stocks, and praised God in such vigorous tones that their fellow-prisoners heard them.

"Jerome tells us that in his day the Psalms were to be heard in the fields and the vineyards of Palestine. The ploughman, as he guided his plough, chanted the Hallelujah, and the reaper, the vinedresser, and the shepherd sang the songs of David." Gallic boatmen, as they urged their heavily-laden barges up stream, sang the Psalms till the river banks echoed with the Hallelujah.

Augustine at his conversion burst into a Psalm, and a Psalm consoled him as he died. Chrysostom in exile, Bernard on his death-bed, Huss and Jerome of Prague in the midst of the martyr-fire, Xavier and Savonarola in persecution, sang comfort to their souls in Psalms.* At his execution, Wallace had the Psalter suspended before his eyes.

Gustavus Adolphus marched to victory, Martin Luther went to "meet all possible devils at Worms," George Wishart dared the perils of the plague at Dundee, Bunyan waked the echoes in his prison cell, singing Psalms.

Cromwell's troops, true Ironsides, went to the battle of Dunbar singing the sixty-eighth Psalm: "Let God arise, and let His enemies be scattered." When the Huguenots were crowding the French prisons to overflowing, they were beaten and dragged

---

* Stanley's *Jewish Church*, vol. ii.

by their hair for persisting in singing Psalms. They sang them in the ships which bore them into banishment beyond the seas. "Women and young girls were mixed with the vilest criminals, and the Psalms were their defence against oaths and foulness. Meeting among the mountains and forests of the 'Desert,' the sound of Psalm-singing guided their friends to their assemblies; but sometimes also brought on them the sudden fire of the enemy. When at last madness drove them to arms, the Psalms became their battle-songs, and their opponents speak of their singing as wild and fierce like a trumpet."

In many a glen, on many a moss and moor, by many a lonely stream, have the Scottish Covenanters worshipped God with Psalms, with the blue sky as roof, and the mist as sole shelter.

"What a wonderful story they could tell," says Dr. Ker, "if we could gather it all from lonely chambers, from suffering sick-beds, from the brink of the valley of the shadow of death, from scaffold and fiery piles, and from moors and mountains." "What a history, if we could discover the place this book has occupied in the inner life of the heroes of the kingdom" (Tholuck). "When we sing them we join with a multitude which no man can number, a long line of pilgrims in the most distant ages, who drew from them strength for their journey and solace for their hardships. There is no river of melody which has made glad so many generations in the city of God." Herein is the Communion of Saints.

The Psalms give shape and intensity to all those delicate, lurking instincts and cravings which lie unformed in our hearts. They meet the soul, not in its lighter moods, but in its secret and unspeakable experiences, in its great crucial moments. They gather all our wide, profound existence, our better and worse selves, up into the searching, beneficent presence and pity of God. Not only do they hold a mirror to our hearts, give an "anatomy" of all its parts, but they

"Sing God's comfort through our soul."

The Psalter is "not for an age, but for all time;" a modern book, defying its two thousand years of existence. Compare the songs of a later period in Greek or Latin literature. The ancient classics remain as standard examples of literary culture and genius. But while they sing of bloody battles, of wine and passion, the Hebrew psalmists, in sublime vision of the Father Spirit, sing of His moral purity, His holiness, His supreme majesty, His tender compassion; and come so close to the very thoughts of God that their songs have absorbed into themselves the highest conceptions of the Gospel.

II.

SONGS OF A SHEPHERD.

1. The Hebrew Poet King.

IT is a remarkable fact that no Psalm celebrates the fame of any Hebrew hero. Not only was the body of Moses buried out of the sight and out of the ken of men, but his generalship, his statesmanship, his moral grandeur, are never rehearsed in song. The poets of Greece and Rome sang the praise of their national heroes, but the Hebrew poets sang the glories of Jehovah and Jehovah alone.

Even David, whose life of stirring incident, of light and shadow, of swift change and sudden tragedy, would have supplied material for a noble epic, remains unsung.

A better memorial of him than an Epic exists in the Lyrics into which he poured his heart. They write his life-history, transcribe the thoughts, the passions that throbbed within him as he watched his sheep or studied the night-sky, as he fled before the blind fury and mad jealousy of Saul, as he sank into sin and shame and endured the dread Nemesis of his dark past.

The historical books construct the scaffolding of his life: his Psalms raise the real man, give shape and colour and expression to the true personality. They are the mirror of his mind. They reveal a character distinguished for noble aims and warm-hearted enthusiasms, a spirit fervid with great loves and hates, and torn with conflicting passions. We can almost tell which Psalms are his by their intensity of feeling, their poetic elevation, their creative freshness. They stand in strong contrast to the dogmatic lines, proverbial sayings of later singers.

Seventy-three Psalms are attributed to David by the Inscriptions. But no one accepts their authority as decisive. The destructive critic Ewald allows only fifteen to pass muster. Probably the truth lies somewhere between these two extremes; and we are not far from the truth when, with Maclaren, we set down forty-three as the contribution of the " sweet singer of Israel."

Some twenty-three of these can, with approximate accuracy, be classified according to the succeeding stages of his history.

2. Songs of a Shepherd.

Psalms viii., xix., xxiii., xxix.

The Romance of David's lyrics begins with the *Making of the Poet.*

His home lay in Bethlehem, six miles from Jerusalem, at that time Jebus. The scene was a sloping ridge, with a deep valley in front and another behind, in which the cornfields were so rich that they gave its name to the village, "Beth-lehem," "The House of Bread." Beyond lay a wilderness broken with bare limestone hills sheltering deep rugged ravines.

It was on these slopes, through these valleys, and beside these limestone gorges that the future poet and king kept his father's sheep.

Like Sir Walter Scott, he was surrounded by scenes which nourished his poetic soul.

Yonder, close by, was the grave of Rachel, memorial of Jacob's sorrows. On those very cornfields Ruth gleaned after the reapers. This very house was probably the home to which came his great-grandparents, Boaz and Ruth, when the alien woman became the ancestress, not only of David, but of David's greater Son.

Homestead and field alike served to quicken his imagination: and no doubt he heard the romantic story as embodied in *Ruth*, as well as many another incident about her told by aged people. Other influences, too, must have moulded his character.

The memory of Samson was still fresh in people's minds, and stories of that Hebrew Hercules, of his daring exploits and wild riddles, must have fired the soul and kindled the eye of one who was a warrior and a poet in the making.

Possibly a deeper spiritual cast was given to his awaking mind by the revival which Samuel had inaugurated at his School of the Prophets, or Religious

Training School for Young Men at Ramah, a few miles off. Like Wycliffe and his poor preachers, Samuel had formed Theological Schools, where godly young men were prepared to be sent out to different places as preachers.

It was a time of awakening, and what more likely than that the earnest youth David should have been influenced by the spiritual teaching of Samuel? It is certain that he was brought into contact with these Sons of the Prophets, who were not only Divinity students, but also students of poetry and music. The school was a college of sacred song and music, as well as of religion. By these students, young men like himself, he was made familiar with the treasures of sacred poetry, the odes of Moses and Deborah, and with the music of the harp and the lyre. Under such influences his devotional, musical, and poetic tastes were cultivated.

Like so many who have afterwards risen to fame as authors, he appears to have stood alone in his family, who saw nothing in him. This is betrayed in the dramatic story of his consecration by Samuel.

Samuel appears at Jesse's door, calls on the sons of the house to appear, rejects one after another until apparently all have been set aside.

"Are these all your children?"

"There remaineth yet the youngest, and behold he keepeth the sheep"—as if his father had scarcely ranked this dreamy shepherd lad beside his other, seven, stalwart sons.

"Send and fetch him."

And when they have brought him in from the sheep runs, we see him, pictured with a few strokes of the brush, a youth of some sixteen or eighteen.

Here he comes with shepherd staff in his hand, of fair complexion, with auburn hair remarkable among the raven-locked Syrians, and "of a beautiful countenance," or rather with keen, bright, deep eyes, in which shone the light of genius and the warmth of a fervid heart.

In this youth of thoughtful face, manly bearing, liquid eye, Samuel recognises the future king, and pours the sacred oil on his head.

Whether he was told the meaning of the act we do not know. But it must at any rate have marked an era in his history, must have given him *the sense of coming responsibility*, and waked him to deeper meditation and self-mastery. This symbol of a call to some large service would ripen his mind and mature his character.

The fascination that was felt by Samuel was felt by all who met him. Some irresistible charm in him won, in later years, the devoted attachment of the brave young Jonathan; captivated Saul's daughter, who confessed her love unasked; drew around him loyal retainers; and gained the admiration of his very foes the Philistines. He was always "David," "The Beloved."

But as yet he was keeping his father's flocks. With no companion save his dumb sheep, he was thrown in upon himself and out upon God.

One companion he had, his harp, with which he was yet to soothe the madness of King Saul, and which was to be the solace of all his years of royal eminence and of exile wanderings.

His calling developed daring and strength. A shepherd's life there and then, unlike the quiet pastoral life on British hillsides, was full of perils and hardships. Bedouin tribes swept down upon the flocks at intervals; lions, wolves, bears, made the sheep their prey. It required courage and strength, firm nerve and presence of mind, to deal with such dangers. And these David displayed, as when he smote a lion, and caught a bear by the beard and, as it was rising to give him the fatal hug, slew it.

There are Shepherd Songs which are the poetical transcript of these years of pastoral life. Such are Psalms viii., xix., xxiii., and xxix. That they were composed while he was still with his flocks cannot be demonstrated, although it is highly probable. They are certainly the product of his early manhood, full of high hope, and of wild delight in nature, God, and truth.

They do not bear the scars of sorrow, the brand of his fall. He has not yet done battle with the problems of successful sin, the perplexity of life's inequalities and misfortunes, the strange contradiction of saints suffering.

His questions are those of an opening mind. His are the thoughts of a young thinker. Even if written subsequently to his pastoral life, these Psalms are the reminiscences of his life among the sheep, under the sky, among nature's varied scenes.

Persians were still worshipping the stars as divinities; Greek imagination was yet to people the hills and glades with varied gods.

David makes all nature praise its Creator, every star and mountain acknowledge Jehovah.

Whence this clear perception of the unity, supremacy, majestic and holy personality of God, while elsewhere polytheism and astrology flourished without protest?

Psalm XXIX.

is a dramatic picture of a thunder-storm. Such a thing was rare in Palestine, and, when it did come, must have impressed the shepherd-poet as he watched it from his rocky shelter.

The Psalm consists of five parts:—

1. A prelude, in which the poet, as he sees the gathering thunder-clouds, bids the "sons of God," the angels, in the holy attire of worship, bow before the approaching Jehovah. We can almost catch the hush of nature, the ominous stillness that awaits the voice of God.

2. Then follows the body of the Psalm in three equal strophes, each of five lines, and each marking a new phase of the storm:

(i) The distant muttering is heard, the gathering bellow; and, as the first peal bursts on the ear, he exclaims:—

> "HARK! Jehovah is above the waters (clouds),
> The God of Glory thundered,
> JEHOVAH! above the water floods."

And each new "Hark!" seems to follow a pause, a fresh peal:

> "HARK! *Jehovah*—is in power,
> HARK! *Jehovah*—is in majesty."

(ii) Then, after a pause, the storm breaks on the northern mountains, crashing the cedars of Lebanon, leaping across to Hermon (Sirion) to shatter its peaks and make its trees skip like young buffaloes, and the awe-struck poet is blinded with the flash of fire.

(iii) Then a slight pause, and once again a long peal rolls across the sky, shaking the solid earth underfoot; and the storm sweeps southwards to spend its fury on the trembling wilderness of Kadesh.

It has bowed the very beasts in labour, "made the hinds to calve," stripped the leaves off the trees, and, as it dies away, the heavenly host are heard "shouting GLORY!"

3. The conclusion follows, containing the poet's musings on the storm: that the Jehovah who wakes cloud and flood to uproar sits as King, in royal power above them all, and can still them; that He is the same God who gives strength to His people and blesses them with peace.

The storm has gone and left delicious calm, a softened freshened atmosphere, and dew-covered grass; and the calm seems to be God's promise of peace after tempest, of quiet after strife.

How David must, like a select number still, have revelled in the grandeur of the thunder-storm! The very structure of the language echoes the rugged thunder-peals! It gives him one overwhelming thought: Jehovah revealing His grandeur and waking worship in man.

Psalm XIX.

is a nature-psalm, but of a very different kind.

Many a time has the young shepherd seen what he describes.

Already in the fields before day-dawn he sees the first flush of the Eastern sunrise. Ere the sun has leaped into the sky, nature is hushed and silent:

> " There is no speech and no word,
>   Their voice is not heard."

But quickly the sun lifts himself into sight :

> " He goes forth as a bridegroom out of his chamber ; "

and emerging, not through long twilight as in these northern zones, but with sudden energy, he climbs the skies:

> " He rejoiceth as a mighty man to run his race ;
>   From one end of the heaven is his going forth,
> And his circuit as far as the ends thereof,
>   Neither is anything hid from his heat."

Day and night "utter speech," come in succession, singing as it were strophe and antistrophe, answering each other like decani and cantoris in a grand nature-cathedral. All " declare the glory of God." They proceed in silence; no speech! no language! Yet their silent testimony to Jehovah goes round the world afresh with the throb and glory of each new morning's light.

Then comes a sudden transition from the glory of God's round heaven to the glory of God's dome of truth. The change in style and subject is so complete that some critics are disposed to break the Psalm into two parts, and to ascribe the second to a later writer. But this sudden transition is meant to give dramatic force to the comparison of God's truth to God's sky.

There in the Law, David's Bible, is a revelation of God more glorious than the revelation in the heavens. God's words, His statutes, His precepts, are perfect, pure as the stars, refresh the soul like the light, heal the wounds of the heart which nature cannot cure.

The heavens have beauty for the eye but little balm for the sin-bruised and abashed soul. Only Thou, O God, canst cleanse me from these stains; and so the poet's heart reaches out to grasp that pity of which nature's gift of beauty was the foregleam.

Psalm nineteen is a study of the heavens by day:

Psalm VIII.

is a study of the same heavens by night.

Like other Eastern shepherds, he had spent many a night with his sheep; and he had wandered alone, gazing on the colossal dome over-arching the earth, and studded with the brilliant gem-like stars, and with the clear moon. All were of surpassing splendour in that Eastern sky.

His first exclamation is: what majestic glory it reveals in God:

"Thy glory is high above the heavens!"

What is he, a mere shepherd youth, a mere babe of yesterday? Yet even from his, a babe's, lips can come the acknowledgment of glory.

Compared with that mysterious immensity above, with the moon and the stars:

"What is man, that Thou art mindful of him?
And the son of man, that Thou visitest him?"

The problem that baffled the mind of the shepherd-poet is the same as perplexes earnest and thoughtful minds three thousand years later. It is the young man's question in all time.

Only, it has gathered force with the discoveries of the astronomers and the geologists. David could have had no conception of the bewildering vastness of creation: that our earth would make merely a mound on the surface of the sun; that our sun is but one of millions of suns, and one of the smallest of them; that there are some stars so far distant in the depths of space that the light of our earth, though it has travelled one hundred and eighty-six thousand miles per second since the world first gave light, has not yet reached them. It would take fifty thousand years to reach even the nearest fixed star.

And geology has done for time what astronomy has done for space—stretched it into infinite depths.

Before the illimitable sweep of creation, we shrink into unspeakable insignificance. *What is man*, that the Almighty Being who presides over all this should give a thought to him, to a mere speck of dust in the infinite palace of His universe? Who can believe that He ever came to dwell among men?

These are the questions that stagger the eager, earnest minds of men to-day; and the answer is the same as quieted the shepherd-poet of yore.

He swiftly thinks again—referring no doubt to the story of creation in Genesis which he had often read—

" Thou hast made him a little lower than God (the angels),"

a little lower because in the image of God.

" Thou hast crowned him with glory,"

the glory of Thine own attributes, with mind and soul, and power to commune with Thee. Earth's creatures are His servants.

All these stupendous discoveries of science only point the more convincingly to the superior greatness of man's mind, which can hold all these stars and constellations in the hollow of its thoughts.

Man is not measured by the yardstick. Quantity of atoms cannot compete with spirit.

There is a second universe, namely, the spirit-universe, of which the soul is a denizen. With all its intellectual, moral, and spiritual powers, it stands higher than a galaxy of stars, for *it is like God in kind.*

The endless sweep of creation proves Him to be infinite. But His infinity must reach down to the infinitely little as well as rise to the infinitely great. A straight line is not infinite which only stretches up without limit; it must stretch down as far.

God is not infinite unless He reach down to the infinitesimally small. His power is infinite, as astronomy proves. If He is love, His love must be infinite too. Enlarge the universe and you only enlarge God; and His Godhood widens down as well as up.

Psalm XXIII.

contemplates the same question, the minute Divine care, in another light and mood.

It is *the* great shepherd song, which has sung itself into the holy of holies of our souls, and has become the heart's great comforter and companion.

It is a transcript of David's life. It was written perhaps after he had risen to the throne, as he looks down on those valleys and ridges where he has kept his sheep, and thinks of all the care he had spent on them.

"The Lord is *my* shepherd."

When the fierce sun had burnt up the vegetation,

and the sheep had been panting and exhausted with the heat, he had often gone ahead of them, and led them down into the green strips of meadow-land beside the quiet-flowing stream that made the grass fresh and cool. My shepherd

"Maketh me to lie down in green pastures;
He leadeth me beside the still waters."

Many a time he had rescued the careless sheep that had fallen into the ravines; from many a prowling wild beast had he rescued them. Many a time had he gone after them, when they had strayed away out to the pathless, rough heights and thickets, and had restored them to the familiar and safer ground.

"He restoreth my soul:
He leadeth me in paths of righteousness."

He had often led his sheep through the rocky gorges, through the narrow defiles where the Bedouin lurked ready to kill the shepherd and seize the flock.

"Yea, though I walk through the valley of the shadow of death,
I will fear no evil, for Thou art with me."

And when they wandered into perilous positions, were in danger of falling over cliffs, or of becoming the prey of prowling wild beasts, he had used his rod to smite the wolf, or lion, or bear,—a rod of wood, as in India to-day, with a spiral piece of iron at the end,—and, with his staff, his crook, he had drawn them back and gently chastened them, and guided them out into safety again.

"Thy rod and Thy staff, they comfort me."

In presence of these watching enemies, beasts and brigands, he had shielded them and fed them with abundance.

> "Thou preparest a table for me,
> presence of mine enemies."

From his flocks he had one day been called in to be confronted with Samuel, who poured the holy oil over him, and his heart had overflowed with hope; and the recollection winds itself into his shepherd-memories:

> "Thou anointest my head with oil,
> My cup runneth over."

Then thinking of all the strong ties that bound him to his flock, how he kept them all the day and then gently folded them at night, he exclaims in deep confidence:

> "Assuredly goodness and mercy shall follow me all the days of my life,
> And I will dwell in the house of Jehovah for evermore."

At last He will gather us into His fold, will be with us all through life's day, and at eventide will fold us in His safe Home for evermore.

A thousand years later, other shepherds were keeping watch over their flocks by night on the same hills of Bethlehem, while the same stars looked down upon them. "And lo! the angel of the Lord came upon them, and the glory of the Lord shone round about them." It was the message of "good tidings of great joy." And there at Bethlehem a new sun rose, a new glory in God surpassing the glory of the heavens; and feeble man found God mindful of him, visiting him with His salvation, proving that the Infinite Creator is the Shepherd who knows each separate life among His charge, and "gives His life for the sheep," till at last He will fold them in peaceful security.

III.

CAVE SONGS.

Psalms vii., lvi.

THE next group of Psalms marks a new epoch in David's history. They are no longer weavings of speculation. He finds himself suddenly drawn into the maelstrom of life's fierce wrongs and stern duties. This new period is linked with Saul.

King Saul, who had in him the materials for a splendid man, had destroyed himself. Brooding over his predicted downfall, vindictive, gloomy, he seemed to lose his moral and mental balance.

Browning's dramatic description ("Saul") of the young shepherd-harpist flinging out his ravishing music and stealing away the king's moody passion pictures with surpassing skill David's loyal love—

"And oh! all my heart, how it loved him!"

Every one remembers how the young shepherd's slaughter of the Philistine giant and the people's song in his honour woke the king to jealousy; how as David tried again the medicine — the therapeutic power—of music, a swift spear grazed the agile harper as he sprang aside; how the hand of the eldest princess was first promised and then mockingly withdrawn, Michal being given instead; how the courtiers and even Prince Jonathan received secret orders to assassinate David; how the former advocated his bosom friend's innocence; how a new victory renewed the vengeful jealousy, and the spear again whizzed past him; how he escaped to his house, the "lurking dogs" (Ps. lix.) after him; how his wife let him down in a basket, placing a figure ("teraphim") in his bed as a blind to detain his pursuers.

The title of Psalm lix. ascribes it to this narrow escape, but without much authority.

We see him next at Nob, a hungry refugee, eating the priest's consecrated bread, watched by the bronzed face of Saul's sneaking, spying herdsman, Doeg.

He seizes Goliath's sword, and flees to the hills, taking refuge at last in Gath, the very capital of the Philistines. To escape recognition—for he is viewed with suspicion he stoops to a demeaning trick,—feigns madness, and acts like a slavering idiot.

At the first opportunity he escapes to the hills again.

In the deep caves, many of them excavations, of Adullam, he is joined by some six hundred outlaws like himself, driven to the mountains by Saul's mad tyranny.

Then, like Robin Hood, we find him in the woods. With the forest for covert, Jonathan and he

"lived one day of parting love."

Listen to the two friends. Jonathan speaks: "Fear not; for the hand of Saul, my father, shall not find thee; and thou shalt be king over Israel, and I shall be next to thee." It was their last meeting: for Jonathan was fated to fall with his father.

Engedi is his next refuge, high up among the hills, under cliffs that hide deep natural caves. These caverns are dark as night. The motley band of followers are enjoying themselves; but David retires to the extreme end of the cave.

Saul's regiments, three thousand strong, are on his track again. Not knowing the outlaw's hiding-place, in the heat of the day the malignant but wearied king turns into a cave for shelter from the sun. In the darkness he sees nothing, but throws himself down and falls into a deep sleep.

Now is David's chance! How easy to lift his sharp javelin and pin the king to the ground, and then claim the throne! Now we shall see the real mettle of the man.

He refuses to touch the God-anointed king. He will not force the hand of Providence. He will bide God's time. Were he to stab the king and claim the crown, it would be said that he had been a rebel all the time. Though in the Psalms he calls down curses on his pursuers, he is at heart no hater of his persecutor. With difficulty but determination he holds back his men thirsting for revenge.

It is a striking picture: these outlaws looking in that dim cave on the sleeping form of the man who has hunted them, and David, the chief sufferer, restraining them! The king has slept his sleep, and leaves the cave all unconscious of the situation.

David will venture it: perhaps it may restore friendly relations, and end the conflict.

"My lord the king!" he calls; holds up the strip of cloth he had cut off from the king's skirt; appeals to it in proof of his loyalty and love for the king. We can almost see the awestruck king, tears falling down his cheeks, as he calls: "Is this thy voice, my son David? Thou hast rewarded me good: whereas I have rewarded thee evil."

The marks of this period are numerous in the Psalms.

Psalm VII.

points to this occasion. He protests his innocence of any evil design on King Saul. He calls down the curse of God on himself if he has been guilty of any such sinister scheme:

> "If I have rewarded evil unto him that was at peace with me,—
> *Yea, rather, I have delivered him that without cause was my enemy,—*
> Let the enemy persecute my soul and take it."

At Engedi he had asked Saul: "Wherefore hearest thou men's words, saying, 'Behold, David seeketh thy hurt.'" The poor, half-mad king was evidently the tool of intriguers and slanderers, who were always poisoning his mind against David.

This is clear from
PSALM LVI.,
if it belongs to this period:

> "All the day long they wrest my words:
>   All their thoughts are evil against me.
> They gather together, they lie in wait,
>   As they have hoped to take away my life."

But

> "Thou tellest all my wanderings:
>   O put Thou my tears into Thy bottle."
> "In God have I put my trust; I am not afraid;
>   What can man do unto me?"

It is against these false-hearted counsellors that he utters his imprecations. These are the lies, the bitter opponents so often denounced in the Psalms. No wonder the hunted outlaw, half in despair, pours out indignant appeals to God's retributive justice.

Many a man's lips refuse to sing Psalms so full of withering anathemas. The curses uttered make us tremble as we read them.

How are we to interpret the Imprecatory Psalms?

The story already told supplies the chief part of the answer.

These Psalms have to be interpreted, not as if they were written in a Christian country by a pious man seated in a cosy study, but by a brave, noble-hearted, passionate, but innocent man, who was marked for assassination, exiled from home, pursued as an outlaw, hunted from hill to hill, from forest to forest, from cave to cave.

He was conscious of his integrity,—and hence the bold claims of innocence before God,—and I do not wonder that he put hot, burning words into his songs at the time, that he denounced the men who dogged him with malignant falsehoods. We do not look for fine forgiving phrases from such pre-Christian times, and from men under such persecutions: we find the natural, unchristianized language of a heart that resents slanders.

Indeed, David was magnanimous, in spite of his denunciations. When he had the chance of putting Saul to death, his heart failed him.

Here is the progress of revelation. There is but broken, partial light at first; there are but half-truths. We do not look for Christ's loftiest teaching in Deborah, Samson, David, Solomon.

Let the Book finish its story: read it all: it reveals the truth when we have heard it out.

Besides, we are in danger of losing all moral indignation against sin. We would take Christ aside and rebuke Him for speaking of a hell. No man loves God who does not hate the devil.

The Imprecatory Psalms have a basis in God's character, and in man's nature.

"The poet Wordsworth was once walking on the sands of Morecambe Bay when a courier passed him on the gallop. As he raced by, waving the flag of England in the air, he announced the fall of Robespierre, which had taken place two days before. 'Immediately,' says the poet, 'a passion seized me, a transport of almost epileptic fervour.' He reverently lifted his hat; and there, alone, under the open heavens, he shouted forth 'anthems of thanksgiving for the vindication of eternal justice.' His biographer, in relating the incident, grows eloquent in sympathy. Did not the whole civilised world respond in like passion of retributive gladness? Yet what has the Hebrew poet sung in Psalms of imprecation more offensive to the ethical instincts of modern culture than the poet-laureate of England shouted on the sands of Morecambe Bay?"

IV.

CORONATION AND PROCESSIONAL HYMNS.

Psalms xviii., xxiv., lxviii., ci., cxxxii.

DAVID is no longer an outlaw, chased from cave to cave. His pursuer is dead, and he is king.

When a swift runner brought the news of Saul's sad and lonely end to David at Ziklag, all his pity for the once noble king, all his love for his true and tried friend Jonathan, broke into passionate lamentations. Like Tennyson's sorrow for A. H. Hallam, his grief grew into a touching "In Memoriam," a pathetic dirge called "The Song of the Bow" (in reference probably to Jonathan's great skill as an archer).

He apostrophises (2 Sam. i.) the mighty fallen and the dewy mountains of Gilboa.

"Saul and Jonathan were lovely and pleasant in their lives,
And in their death they were not divided.

. . . . . .

I am distressed for thee, my brother Jonathan;
Very pleasant hast thou been unto me."

"The king is dead! Long live the king!"

But a new capital must be selected. Many a time

he had looked across those six miles that intervened between his home at Bethlehem and that stronghold, Jebus, that had thus far stood impregnable. David saw his opportunity. Here were thousands of warriors gathered for his coronation. He would utilize at once the ardour of such an army, and would lead them to the capture of the lofty fortress.

So impregnable had their city been that the Jebusites mocked the besieging troops below with taunts and gibes. The blind and lame could defend the place, they said in scorn.

David offered to make the first man who scaled the cliffs and took the fortress his commander-in-chief. Joab it was who, like Wolfe at Quebec, climbed the precipitous heights; and the place was in David's hands.

The strong citadel, a very Edinburgh Castle, became the city of David, the city of wonderful history and of most hallowed associations. But as yet it was a rude fortress. Much must be done to it ere this rocky castle would be a fit capital for the king. Among other things, a palace must be built.

More important still, God must be enthroned in the very citadel of the nation, making it a true theocracy; the Ark, the symbol of His presence, must be brought and enshrined in a house of the Lord in Zion. Saul had sunk into semi-heathenism; David, whose confidence had always been in Jehovah, is resolved to set Him in the throne above the throne.

Coronation Hymn.

Psalm ci.

was probably written at this point. It contains "the godly purposes and resolves of a king." It is language natural to David, as he enters on his reign with gratitude to God and with devout resolutions for his future action. It is full of royal vows.

It begins with adoring praise of God and His loving-kindness and judgment in all David's past career. Awed by God's evident care of him and by his grave responsibilities, he vows that he will conduct himself in an upright, godly, "perfect" manner.

"When wilt Thou come unto me?" (ver. 2).

When wilt Thou, Thine ark, come to my capital? I will keep my court clear of all unfaithful men (vv. 3, 4). Then, as if he went back in thought to Saul's slandering, cunning courtiers and resolved to make his court a contrast to his predecessor's, he proclaims (ver. 5):—

"He that worketh deceit shall not dwell within my house;
   He that speaketh falsehood shall not be established in my sight."

It was a splendid coronation oath, a high-toned commencement of his reign.

The Philistines, however, were roused to jealousy by the sudden success of David. They took the field against him, carrying their idols with them in the hope of surer victory. But David's troops swept them down the valley with irresistible force. He seized their idols, and burnt them. Ere long they made a second attack; and David, after again inquiring of God and receiving His command, marches to a second, a decisive and glorious, victory.

These were but the beginnings of numerous conquests. Neighbouring nations began to recognize the strength and wide sway of this new monarch, and some came to do him homage. All these conquests he ascribes to Jehovah and His goodness.

Hymn of Providence.

Psalm XVIII.

is a retrospective survey taken at this point. It is an outburst of adoring praise in view of all the "hairbreadth 'scapes" of his past history, of all his perils in caves, perils in forests, perils in battles, perils of spies and traitors, and also in view of Divine protecting care and favour that had led him safely and brought him to the throne.

But the king cannot rest till the Ark has been installed in the royal city. A chest of locust-wood covered with gold, the Ark contained the stone slabs on which the Ten Commandments had been written on Mount Sinai, also the golden pot of manna, and the rod of Aaron which blossomed, memorials of the migration. Its lid was the mercy-seat, on which the blood of atonement was annually sprinkled. Over this mercy-seat cherubim spread their wings. It was the symbol of Jehovah's presence, the Jewish palladium. It had been carried round Jericho till the city walls crashed to the ground. It had become a fetish to the wicked sons of Eli, who took it out to battle, trusting to its magical protection, but ignorant of its God; and in the defeat it had been captured by the Philistines.

Every one remembers how it had been placed as a trophy in the temple of Dagon; how that image fell to the ground before it; how it carried pestilence and death to the Philistines wherever it went, until they were glad to get rid of it.

Irreverent curiosity had led the men of Bethshemesh to lift the lid and peep in, when they were instantly struck dead. For nearly seventy years it had lain neglected in its forest home at Kirjath-jearim ("forest town"). Both it and the God symbolized had been forgotten or ignored by Saul and his son.

David remembers it, resolves to restore it to its central place in the national life. The Tabernacle which had sheltered it had been separated from it; so he erects a new tabernacle or tent for it on his hill capital.

He sets out with thirty thousand men to accompany the Ark in state procession. Among these are nine hundred and sixty-two priests and Levites. Under David's fostering care, the choral service has been reorganized; trained singers compose large choruses, and, accompanied by instruments, form the musical service on this state occasion. Thus prepared, that vast body of people sets out.

Reminiscences of this great desire of David are given, written perhaps after the event is over, in these

Processional Hymns:

Psalm cxxxii.

He had sworn unto Jehovah (ver. 2, etc.)—

> "I will not give sleep to mine eyes,
>   Nor slumber to mine eyelids,
> Until I find out a place for Jehovah,
>   A dwelling-place for the Mighty One of Jacob."

At Ephrathah (ver. 6) he had heard of the neglected ark, and in the fields of the wood (Kirjath-jearim) he had found it.

> "Arise, O Lord,"—

and perhaps these words were sung by the priests as they bore it to the Holy City,—

> "Arise, O Jehovah, into Thy resting-place,
>   Thou and the ark of Thy strength" (ver. 8).
> "Let Thy priests be clothed with righteousness,
>   And let Thy saints shout for joy" (ver. 9).
>   .   .   .   .
> "For Jehovah hath chosen Zion" (ver. 13);
>   "Here will I abide, for I have desired it."

The Ark is lifted to the shoulders of the Levites, and the triumphal march begins with the sound of the trumpet, and as these thirty thousand people move on and up toward the new capital the choruses and orchestra ring out the nation's rejoicing.

Psalm LXVIII.

is commonly believed to belong to this period. It certainly celebrates the triumphal entry of the Ark into Jerusalem. It is too long to be treated in detail here. Enough to say that it touches on the historic episodes in the nation's past, and in ver. 16 apostrophises the hills as if jealous of God's special choice of Zion :—

> " Why look ye enviously, ye many-peaked mountains,
>   Upon the mountain which God hath desired to dwell in ?
> They have seen Thy goings, O God, into the sanctuary"
>   (ver. 24).
> "Before went the singers, behind the players on stringed instruments,
>   In the midst the maidens playing with timbrels."

It is a triumphal Processional Psalm.

Psalm XXIV.

is positively known to have been sung by that colossal procession.

They have now come to the foot of the steep gradient up to the fortress city. David, who leads the procession, begins the ascent with the proclamation :—

> . " The earth is the Lord's, and the fulness thereof:
>   The world, and they that dwell therein."

Not only the royal city, not only the chosen land, but, as he already sees with prophetic eye, the whole earth and its people are Jehovah's.

Then one of the singers chants the thrilling challenge :—

"Who shall ascend into the hill of God?
And who shall stand in His holy place?"

Then one half of the chorus, the decani, answer in clear, full tones :—

"He that is of clean hands and pure of heart,
Who hath not lifted up his soul unto vanity,
And hath not sworn deceitfully."

The other half of the chorus, the cantoris, respond :—

"He shall receive a blessing from the Lord,
And righteousness from the God of his salvation."

The full chorus takes up the theme, and the valley of Jehoshaphat resounds with the shout :—

"Such are they that worship Him,
That seek Thy face, [O God of] Jacob."

Then a considerable pause, "Selah," during which the instruments play till the procession reaches the closed gate of the city, when the whole host halts. These gateways were here perhaps when Melchisedec entered the ancient town; they are, as it were, from everlasting.

The king again raises his voice in ringing strains :—

"Lift up your heads, O ye gates;
And be ye lifted up, ye everlasting doors,
That the King of glory may come in."

The semi-choral response asks :—

"Who is this King of glory?"

The rushing answer comes from the other semi-chorus :—

"Jehovah, strong and mighty,
 Jehovah, mighty in battle."

The whole choir catches up the king's command, and pours out in full volume :—

"Lift up your heads, O ye gates,
 Yea, lift them up, ye everlasting doors,
That the King of glory may come in."

Once more the question, now intensified, is asked—some think by those within the closed gates—

'Who is this King of glory?"

And as the one triumphant choral shout peals out,

"Jehovah of hosts,
 He is the King of glory,"

the heavy gate is drawn open, and the Levites bear in the Ark, followed by the procession. The curtains of the tent are rolled aside ; and in presence of the joyful, reverent thousands, the sacred emblem passes in to its rest, to remain there till the Temple should be erected to contain it. Then burnt-offerings are presented, and the glorious event is over.

Jehovah is once more installed in the throne.

V.

A ROYAL PENITENT'S WAIL.

Psalms xxxii., li.

SOME ten years have elapsed since the triumphal removal of the Ark to Jerusalem amid the people's rejoicings. That decade had its successful wars, and was the most prosperous period in all David's reign. His palace was built, his pro-Temple service improved, his army organized more thoroughly, and the national life consolidated.

We no doubt have Psalms which were written during these years; and some of these it might be possible to distinguish. But little fresh light and interest are thrown upon them by contemporaneous history.

Ten years have passed, and now we find the king under a dark shadow. I do not recount the facts; every one knows the story.

"How are the mighty fallen!"

David's shame seems almost to compromise the Book that tells it. We have been so long accustomed to look on Bible characters as if they were set up as models that any stain on their reputation is felt to imperil the sanctity of Scripture.

But we are learning that the Bible teaches us, not by painting immaculate saints on the one hand and incarnate demons on the other, but by picturing the mixed character of all human life, by revealing the struggle between good and evil such as we ourselves experience. It is left to religious novelists to create angelic heroes.

True to life, the Bible reveals the war of passion, the mixture of motive, the light and shadow in its characters; and they teach us better thus.

When sitting for his portrait, Alexander the Great, as every one knows, leaned his head on his hand and rested his fingers on his face as if deep in thought, but in reality for the purpose of hiding a scar.

If the Bible were a concocted book, it would place a finger on every scar in its favourite characters. But it paints them as they were: the drunkenness of Noah, the falsehood of Abraham to Pharaoh, the deceit of Jacob, and the cowardice of Peter. And it does not spare David. It tells the whole black tale without the faintest attempt to soften the sin or screen the sinner. It speaks with impartial justice. It is a true Book.

Moreover, the story is the key to all that follows.

David seems to fall suddenly from heaven to hell. But a great sin never comes suddenly. Hints are given of a hidden decadence, a weakening of moral fibre, that had been stealthily preparing for the king's sudden fall.

Why was he not at the head of his army, as he used to be, in his expedition against the Ammonites? Why did he "tarry at Jerusalem," and this "at a time when kings go forth to battle"? He was still in his prime. Why was he idling at home when a bitter struggle was going on at Rabbah with a powerful enemy? Clearly success, ease, luxury, had sapped away much of his old heroism, and had helped to make him self-indulgent and effeminate.

Some great change has taken place; for the man who at one time had scruples about cutting off a piece from the skirt of his sleeping persecutor, Saul, now plunges into sin after sin of the basest kind. We think of only one sin, but we never find a solitary sin. One sin brings a train of others.

After his first great transgression, he orders Uriah home from the war in order to hide his sin. Stooping to the most despicable shifts, he even makes his brave general drunk in order to effect his purpose of concealment. When that fails, and Uriah hastens to the front again, he makes him—daring wickedness!—the unsuspecting bearer of a message to Joab plotting the general's death. Joab exposes him in the forefront of the battle; Uriah falls; and the once pure shepherd-poet, the once tender fugitive, is a cold-blooded murderer; and the crafty Joab knows his guilty secret.

Sin drags sin after it, as link drags link in a chain.

David, strange to say, has a long period of insensibility to his sin. A year wears away, and he shows no visible sign of having revolted from his sin. No avenging angel may disturb a bad man's sleep. The worst of all consequences of sin is to be blinded to it. The man one of whose arms may be pricked without causing him any pain is scarcely to be congratulated on his impunity. It is paralysis. To sin away all sense of sin is the unpardonable sin, because it is unfelt.

Yet, under his mask, David was evidently ill at ease. Although carrying out his policy with unblushing effrontery, he was irritable under the horrid shadow. That is evident in the cruel treatment to which he subjected the prisoners taken at Rabbah. Joab had sent to Jerusalem bidding the king come and finish the siege, and take the town in person. He had come, and on the surrender of the city he had put the prisoners under saws and harrows, and into brick-kilns. Such deeds—if we are to accept the common interpretation of the language—are utterly unlike the man. He is evidently violent and cruel because of the torture of concealed sin. A conscience that is sullen and ill at ease makes its possessor harsh and savage.

David had been glad to be called out to battle. It is a relief to a sin-tracked man to lose himself in exciting events, to forget the foul thing in some absorbing interest. Some men have plunged into a busy life and made a fortune all in order to escape a dark memory.

There are two **Psalms**, li. and xxxii., which tell us how it fared with him during these months of seeming insensibility. In

Psalm XXXII.

we see behind the mask he wore.

"While I kept silence, my bones waxed old" (ver. 3).

His obstinate refusal to see and own his sins sent them in and aged his very bones, as sin has made many another man feel aged. He had no music left in him; his harp was unwelcome; his heart shrunk and his lips closed. He "roared" or groaned all day long.

Day and night (ver. 4) God's heavy hand lay like a burden on him. There were no tears; emotion, fresh feeling, tender regrets—all were dried up, evaporated. The natural moisture of feeling had turned into the drought of summer.

He may well call sin a "missing of the mark," a blunder. It wears out the heart, ages the face, and lies like hot iron in the hand. Sin *burns*—that is hell-fire—and burn it must. God has in mercy joined burning anguish to sin that He may, if possible, force us to fling it from us. As pain is the warning of disease that, unheralded by suffering, would kill us before we knew of its existence, so compunction mercifully forewarns of moral death. But the sin that burns may also *scar*, so that it can be carried hot in the palm without pain. See how David can look on a good man and listen to his significant parable without a pang.

He has returned from his successful war; Nathan, the prophet, goes in to pay a visit to the king. He lays before him a tale of cruel wrong that calls for the king's interference, the exquisite parable of the ewe lamb, so simple, so direct in its quick power, so artless and pathetic.

"There were two men in one city; the one rich, and the other poor. The rich man had exceeding many flocks and herds; but the poor man had nothing save one little ewe lamb, which he had bought and nourished up; and it grew up together with him and with his children; it did eat of his own meat, and drank of his own cup, and lay in his bosom, and was unto him as a daughter.

"And there came a traveller unto the rich man, and he spared to take of his own flock and of his own herd to dress for the wayfaring man that was come unto him; but took the poor man's lamb, and dressed it for the man that was come to him" (2 Sam. xii.).

It is a clever plot of Nathan's. He gives no names, getting conscience to give a verdict on its own case slightly disguised. A significant fact. Self-love blinds to sin in oneself. We require to see it in another before we can give an impartial judgment. Who knows his own heart? "Search me, O God, and know my heart; see if there be any wicked way in me."

The tale of cruel robbery wakes the king to an

outburst of honest indignation; and he swears that the man who stole the poor man's ewe lamb shall die for it. Then, with swift but calm, brave thrust, Nathan says: "Thou art the man!"

For a moment he is stunned and amazed; and then the sudden, searching light bursts in on the soul, and the whole black affair lies before his opened eyes in its naked ugliness, and he breaks into the confession: "I have sinned against the Lord."

What a lifetime was crowded into that minute! Men in the act of drowning have seen the whole of their past life flung at once on the screen of memory—have lived forty years in a minute. May not the crisis of the Judgment recall all the past in a moment by touching memory thus? This was David's judgment hour, and how he felt he tells us in the two Psalms of this period.

Psalm li.

is the earlier of the two. It is, as Maclaren says, "all blotted with tears as he sobbed out his penitence."

Aye, and how many sinning, overwhelmed hearts since then have used its language to pour out their sorrowful shame! He has only one cry:

> "Have mercy upon me, O God, according to Thy lovingkindness;
> According to the multitude of Thy tender mercies blot out my transgressions."

Here is the difference between remorse and repentance; the former a bitter gnawing of the heart on itself such as David had during his year of sullen silence, the latter a sorrowing hope that God's mercy will forgive the shameful sin.

Then, as if revolting from the foul thing:

"Wash me thoroughly from my iniquity."

" For "—not as a claim, but as an admission justifying God's condemnation—

"For I acknowledge my transgressions,
And my sin is ever before me."
"Against Thee, Thee only have I sinned."

Inasmuch as he has done it unto these, he has done it unto God.

He finds not only a few acts of sin, but a tainted nature, a deep root of sin. The discovery of one act has revealed a luxuriant undergrowth of sin. To use Maclaren's metaphor, a great mass of knotted weeds growing by a stagnant pool is dragged towards you as you drag one filament. Draw out one sin, and it brings with it a whole matted nature of sin.

"Behold, in iniquity I was brought forth."

He does not throw the blame on heredity, but discovers that he has been sheltering sin from the beginning.

God will have truth within (ver. 7), truth and not a mask of peace, not a veil of pretence.

Then comes again and again (vv. 7-9) the cry to be purged with hyssop, to be washed whiter than snow, to have the joy of pardon, to feel youth come back to the aged bones. It seems as if he could not forgive himself, as if his sin was ever before him, for still (ver. 9) he cries :

> "Hide Thy face from my sins,
> And blot out all my iniquities."

Such a warm and passionate nature, that had sinned with such intensity, repents with equal intensity.

We are told that " Voltaire once attempted to burlesque this Psalm. While carefully perusing it, that he might familiarize himself with the train of sentiment he designed to caricature, he became so oppressed and overawed by its solemn, devotional tone, that he threw down the pen, and fell back senseless on his couch in an agony of remorse."

Only a man with noble strains in his nature could make confessions and utter laments characterized by such generous frankness and such passionate emotion.

Psalm xxxii.

is a fit sequel to Ps. li., marking another stage in the story.

Ps. li. opened with a moan of shame; Ps. xxxii. opens with a burst of joy in God's pardon :

> "O the blessedness of the man whose transgression is taken away, whose sin is covered."

In Ps. li. he used various synonyms for sin, "a missing of the mark," or "blunder," "transgression," etc. ; here he uses various phrases to exhibit the various sides of the blessedness of pardon. In Ps. li. the utmost stretch of his hope was that perhaps God would have pity on the contrite heart. Here he has grasped with eager delight the Divine forgiveness.

But the horrid nightmare of his sin is ever before him (ver. 3). He recalls (ver. 5) how he was glad to fling out the whole horrid thing, glad to cast out the gnawing secret, the serpent that he had kept warm only to sting him the more.

"I said, I will confess."

"Faults!" says Carlyle in his *Heroes*, "Faults! the greatest of faults, I should say, is to be conscious of none. Readers of the Bible above all, one would think, might know better. Who is called there the man according to God's own heart? David, the Hebrew king, had fallen into sins enough: blackest crimes: there was no want of sins. And thereupon unbelievers sneer and ask, 'Is this your man according to God's own heart?' The sneer, I must say, seems to me but a shallow one. What are faults? What are the outward details of a life if the inner secret of it—the remorse, temptations, true, often-baffled, never-ending struggle of it—be forgotten? . . .

"Of all acts, is not, for a man, repentance the most divine? The deadliest sin, I say, were that same supercilious consciousness of no sin. That is death. The heart so conscious is divorced from sincerity, humility, and fact: is dead."

After ignoble sin, David did the only noble thing that he could now do—made frank and shame-struck confession; and God sent the swift answer of pardon through the same messenger, Nathan. He cannot forgive himself, the shame ever comes back, but (ver. 5)

"Thou tookest away the iniquity of my sin."

No man must cover his own sin; only the One against whom we have sinned can cover it.

The same messenger brought the charge and the pardon. Christ is God's Nathan, and brings with Him both dismay and peace. His holy, searching eye smites with conviction, and then to the humbled heart utters the warm assurance of pardon. The Cross is the great charge against mankind, the supreme proof, lifted up before all time, of human hatred of goodness. Yet the Cross proclaims pardon and peace, and stands for ever as the proof and means of Divine redemption.

God will make your sin burn you; in mercy He will make it too hot for you to hold it. But confess it, and the wrong is half undone. Confess it, and you have divided yourself from it in heart. Give God your eye, and be led by the language of His eye; but if not (vv. 8-10) He will hold you with bit and bridle, and make sorrows sober you. What a patient, persistent love in God! "Thou art my hiding-place." Such grace fills us with "songs of deliverance."

VI.

PSALMS OF A ROYAL FUGITIVE.

Psalms iii., iv., xli., lv.

DAVID'S children have been quick to follow in their father's self-indulgent and vicious ways; and with unutterable anguish he sees them repeat his own sins. Now, after ten years of gathering sorrows, his very throne is threatened.

It makes terrible reading, the story of his Nemesis. His son Amnon outrages his daughter, and the vile criminal is allowed to go unpunished. How can David carry out the law upon his son, when he himself had incurred the penalty of death by his sin? This ties his hands.

But Absalom, who is bound to revenge his sister's insult, decoys Amnon to his distant sheep-farm, and, during the excesses of a feast, hired assassins kill the ravisher.

Poor David! three of his own family repeating in blacker colours his own sins of vice and murder! And his own past robs him of all moral power to punish any crime, and Absalom is finally restored and forgiven This is the beginning of the decline.

A handsome young fellow, with flowing hair that yielded an enormous yearly crop, inheriting his father's charms of beauty and gracefulness, Absalom captivated the people's hearts as he moved about among them. Like the Jacobite Pretender, he won as many by his personal attractions as by the worth of his cause. He made a princely show as he drove his chariots and horses, attended by his fifty guardsmen.

The king seems to have become passive, apathetic. The sins and sorrows of the past decade had probably unmanned him. It was his duty to "sit at the gate" to act as judge in his people's disputes. But he withdrew from public life.

London grumbles if the Sovereign lives too private and retired a life. Even the English people love State pageantry.

The fickle populace of Jerusalem were captivated by the State splendour and personal graces of Prince Absalom; and he took advantage of the retired and sad life of his father to win over, by crafty tricks, the affections of the people.

This dashing young Pretender frequented the "gates," and fanned the slumbering feeling of disaffection. "O that I were made judge!" he would say, "that every man which hath any suit might come to me and I would do him justice." So he became the idol of the army, and the hope of the disloyal, and laid plots to displace the heir-apparent, Solomon.

No doubt David was aware of the change, heard echoes of the taunts flung at his feeble government.

But heart and arm were broken. All bold sense of righteousness was lost. His misery under the shadow of the past, and the threatening changes of the present, must have been most poignant. May God have mercy on him!

Psalm XLI.

gives us a glimpse of his sorrows at this time. He pronounces his blessing on the man who considers and pities the miserable, the unfortunate sufferers.

"Blessed is he that considereth the miserable."
"Heal my soul; for I have sinned against Thee."

He complains of the popular discontent and of disloyal subjects:

"Mine enemies say evil of me:
When will he die and his name have perished?"

Already some of his trusted counsellors have broken off from him. Perhaps it is Ahithophel; for whenever Absalom gives the signal of insurrection, Ahithophel—once one of David's closest friends and advisers—is found to have left Jerusalem, and forthwith joins the Pretender's cause.

This trusted but treacherous counsellor has hidden his disloyalty under fair and fawning words (ver. 6).

"And if he come to see me he speaketh vanity;
When he goeth abroad he speaketh of it" (of his condition).
"Together against me do all they that hate me whisper,
Against me do they devise evil for me."

There is good reason for believing that all these

years David was suffering from some serious illness that hindered him from performing his kingly functions. Perhaps it was this disease that prevented him from sitting at the gate, and accounted for his feeble government. At any rate his enemies made capital out of it, predicting and hoping for his speedy death.

> "A thing of Belial" (*i.e.*, some shocking thing) "they say is
>   poured out upon him;
> And now that he lieth he shall rise up no more."
> "Yea, mine own familiar friend, whom I trusted,
>   Who did eat of my bread,
>   Hath lifted up his heel against me."
>   "But Thou, O Jehovah, be gracious unto me."

The fact that he fled whenever his son raised the standard of rebellion shows that he had known how powerful Absalom's party was. He knew the mine was laid and ready for the match. How he wished he could escape from it all!

It is all written (*pace* Robertson Smith) in the agonizings of

Psalm LV.

Tired of all the vigilance and strife of party, he cries—

> "Oh that I had wings like the dove,
>   Then would I fly away and be at rest.
>   Lo, then would I flee afar off,
>   I would lodge in the wilderness.

Again, referring, probably, to the fawning but false loyalty of Ahithophel, he declares (ver. 12)—

"It is not an enemy that reproacheth me;
   Then I might bear it:
  But thou art a man mine equal,
   My familiar and well known friend;
  We were wont to take sweet counsel together,
   To walk to the house of God among the festal throng."

Then addressing himself, he calls upon his heart to (ver. 22)—

"Cast thy burden upon Jehovah,
  And He shall sustain thee."

Spies are in every town, ready for Absalom's signal. He pretends to have a religious vow which requires him to go to Hebron, and immediately sets up his standard as king.

The evil news soon reaches Jerusalem, and at once, discouraged, broken-hearted, forsaken, David gives it all up without striking a blow. Now he will take wings as a dove, will fly away and be at rest.

The story of his flight is told with great pathos and tenderness. He hurries away out of the city with his bodyguard, his regiment of six hundred men.

The fugitive procession hastens across the brook Kedron, up the slopes of Olivet, with all the signs of woe and grief; the king barefooted, his head covered with the mantle of sorrow, and tears falling hot and fast—a faint forecast of David's greater Son, who, one thousand years later, looked down from the summit of this path, and wept over the city that rejected Him.

Hushai, one of his privy councillors, is sent back to feign allegiance to the Pretender and delay the rebel army's pursuit of the fugitives. They have rounded the shoulder of the hill, when Ziba comes from the stronghold of Mephibosheth with the present of supplies of food and fruit. As they hurry along a ridge with a deep gorge on one side and a higher ridge on the other, Shimei, a still bitter remnant of Saul's family, keeps pace with him, from the heights flings down stones and curses at the head of the exiled king. He curses him as only an Oriental can curse. Abishai would make short work of him, but, with a strange humility and submissive meekness, David says, "Let him curse;" as if these curses were partially merited, as if David felt their justice.

It was a dreary march—the saddest journey in all David's life—a march away from home and throne and a nation's allegiance, away to his old haunts in the wilderness, to be chased and hunted by his own son, the ungrateful usurper, as he had been by Saul of yore.

Absalom has hurried to Jerusalem, has called a council, and asked advice. Ahithophel would press on in the track of the fugitives and catch them weak and helpless. Hushai, the secret agent of David, advises delay, on the plea of organizing a more powerful force; and his advice is taken. A secret and swift message is sent in hot haste to David, to bid him hurry forward across the Jordan. The message reaches him at night, and he speeds on, never resting till he gets to Mahanaim across the Jordan—a famous spot in Jacob's life, and now a fortified city.

Psalms III. and IV.

belong to this period. The one is a Morning and the other an Evening Hymn. Psalm iii. is probably the product of one of those mornings after he had fled from his son, and before the fatal battle at Ephraim. In

Psalm III.

David pours out his sorrows in humble trust:

> " Lord, how numerous are mine adversaries!
>   Many are they that rise up against me."

Many there are who fling the malicious gibe at him:

> "' *There is no help for him in God.*'
>   " But Thou, O Jehovah, art a shield about me.

He has travelled with bowed head:

> "But Thou art the lifter up of mine head."
> " Even from His holy mountain He will send help.'

He had encamped the previous night among the hills, amid many perils—perils of pursuers, perils of spies, perils of traitors (ver. 5). The unsleeping God had been his only protection.

> " I laid me down and slept:
>   I waked, for Jehovah sustaineth me."

This security gives him courage:

> " I will not be afraid of ten thousand of the people
>   Which have set themselves against me round about."

Psalm IV.

begins with an appeal to God for some response, some sign of care:

> "When I cry, answer me, O God of my righteousness.
> Thou hast enlarged me in distress."

In my sorrows and misfortunes, in my flight and sufferings, Thou hast waked me from my horrid slumber of soul. As Richter says: "The canary-bird sings sweeter the longer it has been trained in a darkened cage."

Then he recalls the persecutions he had suffered, the treacherous Ahithophel, the curses of Shimei, and, in imagination, he addresses them and remonstrates with them:

> "Ye sons of men" [a phrase applied only to men of rank and power], "how long will ye turn my glory to shame?"

How long will ye blacken my character with slander and falsehoods?

Perhaps addressing himself, or possibly his fainting followers:

> "Stand in awe and sin not:
> Commune with your heart on your bed and be still."

Trust in God and do the right.

> "Many say, '*Who will show us any good?*'"

His followers are half despairing, are ready to give up the struggle. "*What's the good of it all?*" many of them say. His answer is a mighty prayer—a prayer that bids the faint hearts look up higher than man and seek God's favour. There is good *there*.

> "Lift Thou upon us the light of Thy countenance, O Jehovah."

The gladness which he feels (ver. 7) now that God's loving presence has been restored to him, this gladness is better than his gratification when Ziba brought large supplies of corn and wine to the royal fugitives.

It is evening:

> "In peace, at once will I lay me down and sleep:
> For Thou, Jehovah, alone makest me to dwell in safety."

And so again, in the midst of pursuing perils, he casts all his care on Jehovah, pillows his head on the Divine providence, and, committing himself to the unslumbering God, lies down to a peaceful sleep.

When his forces meet the rebel army, the latter are utterly routed, the Pretender caught in a tree in the forest and then slain. David returns to Jerusalem, and to his throne; and his heart is made happy in the thought that his son Solomon is to succeed him, happy in that son's wisdom, and happy that Solomon will build the Temple which he himself had longed to erect for God.

VII.

SONGS OF SOLOMON.

Psalms lxxii., xlv.

SOLOMON does not seem to have inherited his father's poetic gifts. The age of heroic enterprise, which always bursts into song, passed now into a period of quiet and reflection. Not a little literature is ascribed to Solomon; but little or none of it has any touch of David's poetic fire. The son's special literary gift was the creation of proverbs, proverbs that contain tit-bits of wisdom, that are the compressed results of experience.

He is said to have composed and collected three thousand of these proverbs, and of that number we have a fraction in our Book of Proverbs. His proverbs can scarcely be called poetry, although they are composed in rhythmic form. They are, like Pope's *Essay on Man*, didactic lines arranged antithetically, without fire and passion, and aiming only at moral effect.

We hear of him having composed a thousand and five songs, but of these, whatever they may have been, we have only two or three. His fame rests, not on any poetic gifts, but on his knowledge and wisdom.

Psalm LXXII.

crystallizes a great amount of Solomon's life. We shall find, as we study it, that "a greater than Solomon is here" in dim prophetic outline; that the Ideal King who was yet to come hovers above and beyond the figure of Solomon. But Solomon is evidently the first subject of the Psalm. The writer is probably some sacred Psalmist of his reign who celebrates the far-reaching sway, the wisdom, and the magnificence of Solomon. It is a "Song of Solomon," although perhaps not composed by him. It is arranged in couplets, which are balanced and formal, after the manner of the Book of Proverbs. Every verse is radiant with allusions to the glories of Solomon's reign.

" O God, give Thy judgments unto the king,
 And Thy righteousness unto the king's son,"

calls us back to a memorable and dramatic incident in Solomon's reign.

It was at his great coronation ceremonial, when he marched to the sacred Gibeon, and offered an enormous sacrifice.

There, in a night vision, God comes to him and bids the young king make a choice of any great gift he desires. "*Ask what I shall give thee.*" "I am but a little child," he says—and he is only twenty; "I know not how to go out or come in. Give, therefore, Thy servant an understanding heart to judge Thy people, that I may discern between good and bad."

It is a noble prayer for a young man to make, and his very asking for wisdom shows that he already had wisdom in embryo.

God commends the wish, and, seeing he has not asked riches, as he might have done, or long life, as he might have done, wisdom will be liberally bestowed, and, in its train, riches and long life too. He has sought first of all God's kingdom; wisdom and all else will be added to it.

Here in ver. 1 of this Psalm we have the echo of that young king's coronation prayer:

"O God, give Thy judgments unto the king,
   And Thy righteousness unto the king's son."

In ver. 2—

" May he judge Thy people with righteousness,
   And Thine afflicted with judgment "—

we are reminded of a striking instance of the sagacity which he displayed while still so young.

Two women appealed to him as he sat at his court at the gate. Each brought an infant boy, one living, and the other dead; born about the same time, and in the same house. One charged the other with having overlain her child, and, finding it dead, with having exchanged it for the living baby by stealth. Both claimed the living one: who was to be believed? It was a splendid stroke of sagacity to apply a test which would reveal the true mother's heart.

He bade one of his soldiers divide the living child in two, and give a half to each. In an instant the true mother's love showed itself. "O my lord, give her the living child, and by no means slay it." Solomon's device had served its purpose; that was the mother who spoke, and, using her own words, but now about herself, he says to his soldiers, "Give *her* the living child, and in no wise slay it: she is the mother thereof."

This was an instance of the prayer of the second verse of the Psalm:

> "May he decide the cause of Thy people with righteousness,
> And of Thine afflicted with judgment;"

and again ver. 4:

> "May he judge the afflicted of the people,
> Save the sons of the poor,
> And crush the oppressor;"

and then in ver. 5,—as if referring to the effect of his sagacious decision about the two children, when, as we are told, "all Israel heard of the judgment, and they feared the king"—

> "(So that) they fear Thee as long as the sun endureth.

Solomon's reign was a period of peace and prosperity. He had no long wars like David's; and his commercial success combined with the thirty or more years' peace to make the people happy and prosperous.

> "May the mountains bring forth peace to the people."
> "Let him be as rain coming down upon the mown grass."

His rule was to come to the war-wearied nation like rain on mown grass, like showers that water the earth.

He had extended the realm as left by his father until now his rule was acknowledged from the Mediterranean on the west, to the bank of the great river Euphrates on the east; and from Damascus on the north, to the "stream of Egypt" on the south. These seemed to the Jews almost the utmost ends of the earth. Hence the prayer:

"Let him have dominion from sea to sea."
"Before him let the inhabitants of the wilderness bow."

In the first clause of ver. 10—

"Let the kings of Tarshish and the isles render gifts"—

we are reminded of the great commercial enterprises in which Solomon engaged.

The Phœnicians had always been the great seafaring race of the Mediterranean, had built up an immense shipping trade. Besides being sailors, they were also skilful artisans. David had drawn his skilled workmen from Tyre when he built his palace. And this relation between the two countries became more intimate under Solomon.

The Jews thus far had been purely an agricultural people, forbidden to engage in commerce. But now Solomon joined with Hiram, King of Tyre, in his shipping enterprises. A numerous fleet of merchantmen traded with Cyprus, Sicily, Malta, and the north of Africa. A new country, also, had been discovered, which excited the Phœnician merchants with visions of wealth and pleasure, much as the discovery of America inspired and enriched the Old World.

It was Tarshish, a southern section of Spain, where they founded a colony, and from which they shipped precious metals, the richest ores, gold, silver, iron, lead, even the anchors being sometimes made of silver to save freight. These ships of Hiram and Solomon sailed through the "Pillars of Hercules" at Gibraltar out into the Atlantic, up to the mouth of the Tartessus or Guadalquivir. Some conjecture that the Phœnician ships may have come across the Bay of Biscay and as far as the shores of Britain, but such is nothing better than a speculation. From the south of Spain, and then from Sicily, Malta, Cyprus,—from "Tarshish and the Isles,"—rich gifts and precious products were shipped, and the palaces of Tyre and Jerusalem grew gorgeous with the gold and silver, the woods and spices from the West.

Solomon had also a harbour opened in the Red Sea, which he visited in person, and from which voyages were made to the far-distant Ophir. Ophir is now generally believed to be, not where Rider Haggard has placed *King Solomon's Mines*, but at the mouth of the Indus. The imports they brought back were of Indian origin, and bore Indian (Sanskrit) names. They included ivory, apes, peacocks, and the almug wood. Besides these, immense quantities of gold—four hundred and twenty talents—were transferred to Jerusalem to adorn palace and Temple and add to the gorgeous magnificence of Solomon's court.

Besides his shipping enterprises, he carried on a land traffic with Arabia. It was from this country that he received his supplies of spices, of cassia (a sort of cinnamon), of aloe, of myrrh, of spikenard, and of other aromatic spicery, to which we find frequent reference in the Solomonic writings.

With Egypt also he carried on a brisk trade, purchasing many horses and chariots, for which that country was famous. Huge caravans transported them across the desert. At his zenith Solomon had four thousand two hundred horses, and one thousand four hundred chariots (three horses in each). In those richly-chased and splendidly-coloured chariots he was carried by swift horses, attended by a train of archers remarkable for handsome looks.

In such luxurious style he drove to his well-watered garden at Etam, or in gorgeous palanquin was carried to his summer retreats in the cool hills of wooded Lebanon. Elsewhere we have allusions to his houses and vineyards, his orchards and pools, his men-singers and women-singers. By sea and by land, by a fleet of ships and by long lines of camels, the precious products of Spain, Sicily, Egypt, Arabia, and India, were brought to enrich and beautify Solomon's palaces. Hence the line:

"Let the Kings of Tarshish and the Isles render gifts."

But the second part of ver. 10 points to the outstanding proof of his fame.

"Let the Kings of Sheba and Saba offer presents."

Rumours of his wisdom and of his magnificence had spread far and near, and had reached Sheba, in the south of Arabia. The Queen of Sheba had heard of Solomon's brilliant wit, of his refined wisdom, of his wise sayings and sagacious answers to deep questions. This Arabian queen, evidently a woman of exceptional earnestness, courage, and capacity, resolved to break through the seclusion of her royal home, and brave the dangers of a desert journey, in order to see this paragon of wisdom and of splendour at Jerusalem. "She came to Jerusalem with a very great train, with camels that bare spices and very much gold and precious stones."

He showed her his palace and lion-throne of ivory and gold, his hall of cedar where he sat as judge, his harps framed in aromatic wood, his goblets and vessels of pure gold, his Egyptian chariots and his noble guardsmen. She also tested his wisdom by intellectual riddles, by hard questions, and he "told her all her questions." She opened out her mind, "communed with him of all that was in her heart;" and "there was not anything which he told her not."

When she discovered all his wisdom, saw the splendours of his palace and capital, she said that the reports she had heard she had not credited, but now she finds half had not been told her. She was so amazed that "there was no more spirit left in her." Happy, she said, happy were the servants and subjects and councillors around such a king: blessed the God that delighted in him.

Solomon gave her on her departure the best presents

from his stores, in return for the gifts of gold and spices and precious stones which she had brought with her.

Hence the sentence,

> "Let the Sovereigns of Sheba and Saba offer presents.
> Let all nations serve him."

Then, in succeeding verses, follows a picture of a land where royal beneficence (ver. 12) rescues the poor, helps the helpless and afflicted; (ver. 13) spares the weak; (ver. 14) rights the wrongs of the oppressed, and values the blood of the injured.

So that (ver. 15) many another offers gifts of gratitude to this beneficent king, as gold came to him from Sheba, and men pray for him and bless him all the day. There are (ver. 16) abundant harvests, fields of corn on the mountain terraces that wave and rustle like the forests of Lebanon under the breeze. It is a picture of fertility, peace, and prosperity, while the people multiply and grow strong; and (ver. 17) the fame of the illustrious king promises to last for ever, to go down through the endless generations to come.

(What follows, "Blessed be Jehovah," etc., is added by the editor at the end of the second book of Psalms.)

Psalm XLV.

is called a "Song of loves," and is to be sung to a tune entitled "Lilies." It is a Marriage Song, and celebrates the espousals of a Jewish king with a princess of some foreign country. There is no one whom it suits so well as Solomon; and—while of course not written by him—was no doubt composed in honour of his marriage with the daughter of a Pharaoh, King of Egypt (or perhaps with the daughter of the King of Tyre). It was a splendid alliance for him, helping to raise him to a position of equality with other Oriental potentates.

The writer (ver. 1) delights to have such a good theme for his song, a royal ode, that makes his pen run swift. He refers (ver. 2) to Solomon's beauty beyond the rest of men, and to his eloquent lips and golden, gracious speech. Then he glances at his military eminence and wide sway:

> "Gird thy sword upon thy thigh, O mighty one;
>   Yea, in thy majesty ride prosperously.
> Thine arrows are sharp—people fall under thee,
>   They are sharp in the heart of the king's enemies.
> Thy throne, O God, is for ever and ever,
>   A sceptre of righteousness is the sceptre of Thy kingdom."

Myrrh and aloes and cassia perfume all his garments (ver. 8), and music steals on the ear out of the ivory palaces.

Kings' daughters (ver. 9)—Pharaoh's and Hiram's—are among his loved ones, and the queen-consort stands richly clad in robes gilt with the gold brought from the Indian Ophir.

In ver. 10 he bids her forget her own native country:

"Forget also thine own people, and thy father's house,
   That the king may desire thy beauty."
"And the daughter of Tyre shall come with a gift;
   And the rich among the people shall seek thy favour.
All glorious is the king's daughter in the inner palace,
   Of thread of gold is her clothing.
On tapestry of divers colours is she conducted unto the king;
   The virgins in her train, her companions, are brought unto thee.
They are conducted with joy and exultation;
   They enter into the king's palace."

Instead of her father and relatives, she is to take her children.

"Let me make thy name known through all generations:
   Therefore shall the people give thee thanks for ever and ever."

But though Solomon is the first subject of these Psalms, he does not fill all the splendid outlines. There is history in these Songs, but there is prophecy too. We know that the Jews looked for centuries for a glorious sovereign who would fulfil all their hopes. These hopes are rising and taking shape here. They are painting the ideal portrait, but Solomon does not fill it. He rose to magnificence and far-famed wisdom, but both his splendour and wisdom were shattered by folly, idolatry, polygamy—and he fell, and in his fall showed that these ideals of a perfectly wise, perfectly noble, perfectly beneficent, perfectly glorious and everlasting king were not to be realized by any common human being. Hovering behind the real king of the time rose in dim outline the coming Ideal, the longed-for Deliverer, the Messiah that would fulfil all their conceptions and aspirations.

I do not mean that these seers had clear notions who their Messiah King would be. At this stage the vision was shadowy, yet it was there.

Round the sufferings of David, round his sorrows and his solitude, rose the vision of the sufferings of the coming Ideal Man ; and the rapt language of the half-conscious prophet transcends David and fits only the Man of Sorrows ; and Christ Himself applies the words to Himself:

"My God, my God, why hast Thou forsaken Me?"

So of Solomon as king. The words that took their rise in the glory and splendour and vast dominion of Solomon far transcend the first subject, rise to an Ideal King, and are true only of one King, Christ. He is fairer than the sons of men, reigns in righteousness and peace. He comes down like showers, etc. All men come to Him and bow before Him.

"Thy throne is for ever and ever."

VIII.

ODES OF VICTORY.

Psalms xlvi., xlviii., lxxvi.

WE leap across an interval of three hundred years, to about 700 B.C.

Solomon's sumptuous luxury had sapped away the vital force of the nation, which had split into two, and had sunk under godless kings into idolatry, strife, and bloody war. Hezekiah on his accession had to dethrone paganism and restore the service of God.

The Eastern horizon had been growing dark with the hosts of the Assyrians as they swept, tide after tide, westwards to Palestine and Egypt. Swaying between alliance with Egypt and submission to Assyria, the Jews were "between the devil and the deep sea."

Sennacherib despatches an army, led by two officers and his cup-bearer Rabshakeh, to capture Jerusalem and spoil it of its remaining wealth. They send a blasphemous and mocking call to surrender. Rabshakeh sarcastically offers Hezekiah two thousand horses if, indeed, he can find men enough to ride them. Now with jeers at their religious confidence, now with threats and again with promises, the Assyrian general demands surrender.

Hezekiah, rending his clothes and wearing sackcloth, sends a message to Isaiah, telling him his trouble and fear, and bidding him cry to God for deliverance. True to his unflinching courage, Isaiah bids the king be brave and firm, for the enemy will be diverted by the rumour of rebellion in their own Babylon.

Now Sennacherib sends an insolent letter to Hezekiah, asking whether he expects his God to protect him when so many other cities have fallen trusting in their gods. Has he not heard of the fate of Haran and Sepharvaim and others?

"And Hezekiah received the letter and read it; and Hezekiah went up into the house of the Lord, and spread it before the Lord."

Then comes the reply that God has heard the prayer, and Isaiah stands forward to hurl defiance at the enemy around the walls of the city. With dauntless eloquence and confidence in God he asks, Do they know whom they have been reproaching, that they have been blaspheming the true God? They have besieged the city in their pride of conquest, but they shall not shoot an arrow, nor use a shield, nor raise a defence; and they shall return by the way they came.

These were brave words, for Hezekiah had but a few infantry, and no cavalry. The city battlements were weak, its treasure exhausted, while below the walls were gathered mighty bearded warriors. There were ranks of bowmen, and regiments of cavalry with chariots and horses, all fearless with past victories. If ever resistance seemed hopeless, it was the resistance of the besieged within the ancient capital of Solomon and David.

When night fell, it brought little sleep to the besieged, you may be sure. Next day these well-armed and irresistible Assyrians would scale the crumbling walls and sack the sacred city.

When the sun rose and looked upon the place where yesterday stood an irresistible army, the whole host, one hundred and eighty-five thousand, lay dead on the ground!

> "Like the leaves of the forest when Summer is green,
>   That host with their banners at sunset were seen;
> Like the leaves of the forest when Autumn hath blown,
>   That host on the morrow lay wither'd and strown.
>
> "For the Angel of Death spread his wings on the blast,
>   And breathed in the face of the foe as he passed;
> And the eyes of the sleepers wax'd deadly and chill,
>   And their hearts but once heaved, and for ever grew still!"

We do not know, we can only conjecture, what that natural agent was. One thinks it was the poisoning of the waters; another suggests a storm; some suppose a simoom; others pestilent vapours from a volcanic eruption; but Josephus, followed by the vast majority, believes it to have been a pestilence. Whatever it was, it terrified Sennacherib, who, we know, fled precipitately to his own eastern home at Nineveh. And the mysterious and sudden destruction of the invader struck awe into the hearts of Hezekiah and his people. What sensations they must have had of mingled fear and triumph as daybreak revealed the armed thousands lying stiffened in the sleep of death!

No wonder if this event fired the devout imagination of the Jewish poets, produced sacred Odes of Triumph, and crystallized in Hymns of Praise. It was evidently this event which gave shape to

Psalm LXXVI.

This Psalm, written probably some little time after the destruction of Sennacherib, and after he had withdrawn his dreaded forces to Assyria again, begins by celebrating Jerusalem as the sacred abode of Jehovah. There He is known and there is His tabernacle. Then ver. 3:

> "There brake He the arrows of the bow,
>   Shield and sword and battle;
> The stout-hearted have been spoiled,
>   They have sunk into their sleep,
> And none of the men of valour have found their hands.

That is, those who stretched out their hands in mocking defiance of God's city have not been able to use or raise them.

> "At Thy rebuke, O God of Jacob,
>   *Both chariot and horses were cast into a dead sleep*"

—overpowered by the languor and lassitude of death. The event, no doubt, struck awe into all the surrounding nations:

> "Thou, even Thou, art to be feared."
> "From heaven didst Thou cause judgment to be heard.
> 　The earth feared and was still.
> For the wrath of man must praise Thee."

That is, every angry attempt of men to defeat God's will is turned to their own overthrow, and is used for His glorious ends. And these last feeble, impotent acts of resistance are overruled and made an instrument for a Divine work.

Then the Psalmist closes with another call to hushed awe:

> "He is to be feared by the kings of the earth."

Psalms XLVI.—XLVIII.

are also the product of this event. The first of these is the chief and most memorable one. The other two are bursts of triumph, with few direct references to the event, and yet coloured by the glorious deliverance. Psalm xlvii. is one repeated shout of thanksgiving. There is reason to think that Psalm xlviii. was meant to be used in the Temple service.

Psalm XLVI.

is particularly rich in reminiscences of the event.

> "God is our refuge and stronghold,
> 　A very present help in trouble."

In vv. 2 and 3 we have a reflection of the shaking of the nations before the sweep of the invading Assyrians. It is in metaphorical language: the earth changing, the mountains removed to the seas, the floods roaring and rising—yet in all "we will not fear."

"There is a river whose streams shall make glad the city of God;"

referring to the fact that a supply of water had been brought within the walls by the construction of an aqueduct hidden underground.

"God is in the midst of her: she shall not be moved.
God shall help her *when the morning dawns;*"

i.e., at early daybreak, the hour of the discovery of the dread slaughter.

"Nations roared: the kingdoms were moved;
He uttered His voice—the earth melteth.
Come, behold the deeds of Jehovah,
Who hath done terrible things in the earth;
Who stilleth wars to the ends of the earth."
"Be still, and know that I am God."

This Psalm was paraphrased by Luther in his "Ein feste Burg," which is translated for us in the well-known lines, "A safe stronghold," etc. This was the "Marseillaise of the Reformation." In the dark Reformation times Luther would say to Melanchthon, "Come, Philip, let us sing the forty-sixth Psalm." When the Protestant cause seemed to be losing ground, "he sang it to the lute every day, standing at the window and looking up to heaven."

When he and Melanchthon and others were sent into banishment, and were entering Weimar in great despondency, they heard a girl singing this Psalm. "Sing on, dear daughter mine," Melanchthon said, "thou knowest not what comfort thou bringest to our hearts."

Gustavus Adolphus prepared for the battle of Leipsic by singing this Psalm along with his whole army. Wesley preached on it when a shock of earthquake threw London into terror last century. The people of Moscow used this Psalm as their memorial song of triumph for that night on which twenty thousand of Napoleon's horses perished by frost, and the French army were driven back by an unseen hand into its disastrous retreat. It has nourished the Christian heroes of the world, and may well nourish us.

IX.

SONGS IN A STRANGE LAND.

Psalms xlii., xliii., lxxxiv., cii., cxxxvii.

A HUNDRED years have passed since the tragic destruction of Sennacherib's host beside the walls of Jerusalem, and during that period the Assyrian Empire has crumbled to insignificance.

The Babylonian Empire has sprung up into power and splendour in its place, and now casts its dark shadow over surrounding nations. Nebuchadnezzar sweeps westwards like an irresistible flood. Egypt is his aim, but Palestine lies on the highway to the Nile, is in league with the King of Egypt, and must be subdued in passing.

The Egyptian host anticipates the attack, speeds eastwards to meet the army of Nebuchadnezzar, and not far from the Euphrates is driven back in defeat by the Assyrians.

Like a pitiless tide they roll on. The people everywhere flee to their fortified cities, and even the Bedouins take refuge within the walls of Jerusalem. King after king among the Jews had cast off God and God's laws, and now doom is at the gate.

Jeremiah foresees that submission to Babylon is inevitable, and urged, but urges in vain, that terms of peace should be made with Nebuchadnezzar. The invaders enter the city, fling the king, Jehoiakim, into fetters, and rifle the Temple, from which many of the sacred vessels are carried as plunder to deck Babylonian palaces.

Upon the untimely death of Jehoiakim, Jehoiachin (or Jeconiah) is enthroned; but he has reigned only three months when the Babylonian forces for some reason make a second attack, sack the city, hack off the golden ornaments from the Temple, take away extensive and precious booty, and carry off the king, his wives, the queen-mother, the princes, priests and minstrels, seven thousand warriors, and one thousand skilled workmen. Altogether, according to the best account, some ten thousand captives were carried off to Babylon at this time.

Over those that were left in Palestine Zedekiah was set king as vassal to Nebuchadnezzar. He made a journey to Babylon to take the oath of allegiance; but scarcely had he returned, when he set up a flag of rebellion, in company with neighbouring nations, and formed an alliance with Egypt. It was against the warnings of Jeremiah that this fatal step had been taken, and that prophet might have been seen in the streets of Jerusalem wearing a wooden collar round his neck, such as prisoners were compelled to wear. This was Jeremiah's dramatic way of foreshadowing the approaching captivity.

That type, the wooden collar, was soon fulfilled. Nebuchadnezzar marched in person to lay siege to Jerusalem. It was a crisis so terrible and so momentous that it has been commemorated ever since by a Jewish fast. Forts were reared beside the city, and from them the assailants discharged their missiles. Battering rams shattered the walls. Troops hemmed in the people.

The siege lasted for a year and a half. Within the city famine and disease turned the fair princes and proud people into walking skeletons. Jewish ladies might have been seen sitting in splendid robes on the refuse heaps, glad if they could pick up a morsel of food. The siege of Paris had no horrors to equal those of the siege and fall of Jerusalem. Hunger turned fathers and mothers into brutish cannibals, as they devoured their own starving children.

Yet all the while, in the very Temple erected for the worship of Jehovah, might have been seen priests prostrate before the rising sun; and in underground chambers * the base Egyptian idols were receiving offerings of incense from the Jewish elders. The people seem to have become utterly demoralized and demented.

One midnight in July 587 B.C., under the covering of the darkness, the Babylonian forces made a breach in the walls, stole into the very Temple itself, and, ere morning broke, killed the occupants of the sacred

---

* Stanley's *Jewish Church*, sect. xl.

courts, the false priests and prophets and princes, so that "the virgin marble ran red like a rocky winepress in the vintage."

In the twilight of daybreak, the king and his harem, in muffled disguise, escaped by a secret exit, and made for those very scenes beyond Jordan to which David had hastened at the rebellion of Absalom. But he was overtaken and carried to Nebuchadnezzar, who, according to the savage Oriental custom, killed his sons in their father's presence, put out the captive king's eyes and took him to Babylon, where, according to tradition, he was forced to toil in a mill as a slave.

Now had come the destruction of Jerusalem. All the sacred vessels that were left from other devastations, the brazen laver, even the two famous pillars with their ornaments, were collected and removed; the captives were secured; and then the whole city, Temple, palace, public buildings, all were deliberately fired, and Jerusalem was in flames. The savage cruelty of the spoilers is beyond description, and makes terrible reading. We are told that even the royal tombs were rifled, and the dead kings given to the birds of prey, and soon jackals were wandering even over the sacred hill of Zion.

And as the captive host were conducted to their foreign home, the Ammonite and Moabite flung at them derisive shouts of delight. Even their nearest kinsmen, the descendants of Esau, the Edomites, had gloated over the siege of Jerusalem, crying, " Down with it! Raze it even to the ground." They caught any Jewish fugitive that attempted to escape, and held wild revels on the ashes of the fallen city. Then and ever after the curses of the Jews fell on these Edomites the very songs of the captives in Babylon break out as do the prophets, into denunciations of them. The second Isaiah pictures the Messiah Conqueror as coming "knee-deep in Edomite blood."

This was the second or third band of captives that had been marched off to Babylon. The present one was smaller and less important, for the previous deportation had taken away most of the nobles and skilled workmen: and amongst the melancholy band had been Ezekiel, and Daniel with his three companions.

We can well imagine these captive hosts lingering on the heights of Hermon, on the ridge of Mizar, and looking back with unutterable grief and yearning on their beloved city and Temple and home, now blackened ruins, and now seen for the last time. We can well imagine their idolatrous captors, or the insulting Edomites, taunting the pious with the derisive question, "Where is your God now?" "What can He do for you now?"

It was this scene which probably gave us

PSALMS XLII. AND XLIII.

which are really one Psalm.

It is composed by one of the "Sons of Korah," one of the leaders of sacred song, one of the Temple Psalmists. It crystallizes his emotions as he pauses on the eastern hills and takes his farewell look at his darling city. Whether or not it was written there and then, it pictures the scene and the thoughts of the pious minstrel as he looks back from the Hermon hills. It falls into three sections or strophes, each passing through the same ebb and flow of faith, and each ending with the singer's assurance to his own heart :

> "Why art thou cast down, O my soul ?
> Hope in God."

It begins with the picture of the wild gazelle of the forests, panting in the summer heat for the fresh, cool water of Jordan. He may have seen it as he passed across the river.

> "As the hart panteth after the water-brooks,
> So panteth my soul after Thee, O God,"

after God's house and city and immediate presence.

> "When shall I come back and appear before God ?"

He has mourned and wept day and night, but his captors ask, derisively, "Where is thy God now?" Then (ver. 4) he recalls in his grief how he used to go with the crowd of worshippers to the Temple.

> "How I passed with the (festal) throng,
> How I led them in procession to the House of God,
> A multitude keeping Holy Day."

He looks back from the eastern hills (ver. 6) :

> "I remember thee from the land of Jordan,
> And from the Hermons, from the mountain Mizar."

His misfortunes, descending upon him in quick succession, he likens to the torrents (ver. 7), to the floods that answer each other with their rush and roar. Yet (ver. 8) Jehovah is with him, and gives him a song in the night. Why go in sorrow, then (ver. 9)? And again hope triumphs in the power of faith.

He prays, in the third strophe, that God will judge between him and the cruel conquerors, that He will not cast him off (xliii. 2), that He will send out light and truth, and bring the captives back to the holy mountain, to the holy altar, to the harp and the song of God in His House. Three times he cries:

"Why art thou cast down, O my soul?
Hope in God: for I shall yet praise Him,
The Health of my countenance and my God."

Now we pass with these captive bands to the banks of the Euphrates, leaving a few inhabitants in the sacred land to till the soil and keep the vineyards. We are now in Babylon the great, in the centre of a vast plain, and beside the fourth river of the Garden of Eden. The city is fifty-six miles in circumference (according to Herodotus), larger even than London. The wall surrounding it, three hundred feet high, is a broad terrace on its summit, as wide as Westminster Bridge. Its streets are rectangular (like American cities) and abut on the river. It has ten brazen gates, and two hundred and eighty towers, ranged at intervals round the walls. Its Great Palace is, "a city within a city," seven miles round, has mountain gardens, "hanging gardens," constructed for the delectation of the Median princess who is now the queen.

The gigantic temple of Bel, or Baal, rose as high

and square as the Pyramids. The name of Nebuchadnezzar, who built both temple and palace, may still be seen on the bricks and sculptured fragments that are found among the ruins.

It must have been a strange scene to these Jewish captives. Their own court and buildings at Jerusalem were as children's playthings compared to Babylon. All were strange: the gorgeous cavalry, the chariots-and-four, the soldiers' scarlet costumes and shields and burnished helmets, the pomp and luxury, the science and art, the magicians' and astrologers' lore, the idolatrous worship, the King Nebuchadnezzar, who spoke with pride of "this great Babylon which I have built."

The Euphrates ran through the city, and was divided into canals for the purpose of irrigation, forming a "network of watercourses." Lofty poplars lined their banks and cast their sheltering shadows on the captive people as they clustered together to cheer each other in their foreign land. Their harps, their music, they had carried with them; and often when by themselves they sang for their own comfort the songs of Zion.

Here is one, composed probably by some Levite Psalmist:

PSALM CXXXVII.

"By the rivers of Babylon, there we sat down; yea, we wept
When we remembered Zion."

It is the "Home, Sweet Home" of the Jewish captives:

> " 'Mid pleasures and palaces
>   Though we may roam,
> Be it ever so homely,
>   There's no place like home."
>
> *   *   *   *   *
>
> "An exile from home,
>   Splendour dazzles in vain."

But not only are they patriotic songs; they are Psalms sacred to Jehovah; and to sing them for the amusement and mirth of their heathen captors would be to degrade and desecrate them and to trifle with their God. As well sing "Abide with me" at a mayor's banquet, or recite a prayer for the entertainment of a company of sceptics. Before the idolaters they will suspend their harps (ver. 2, etc.):

> " Upon the willows in the midst thereof
>   We hanged up our harps."

And as the singer broods over his wrongs, recalls the ruined city and Temple, and the taunts of the Edomites, he bursts into a terrible storm of indignation, foresees—what actually took place—the destruction of the Babylonian captors (ver. 7):

> "Remember, O Lord, the children of Edom,
>   In the day of Jerusalem,
> Who said, 'Down with it! Down with it, even to the
>   ground!'
> O daughter of Babylon, thou shalt be destroyed.
> Happy shall he be that rewardeth thee
>   As thou hast served us."
>
> "Happy shall he be that taketh thy little ones
>   And dasheth them against the rock."

It is a terrible cry for vengeance, true to the times. There is progress in revelation. We do not look for an anticipation in the Old Testament of Christ's Sermon on the Mount.

> "We sate down and wept by the waters
>   Of Babel, and thought of the day
> When our foe, in the hue of his slaughters,
>   Made Salem's high places his prey;
> And ye, O her desolate daughters!
>   Were scattered all weeping away.
>
> "While sadly we gazed on the river
>   Which roll'd on in freedom below,
> They demanded the song; but, oh never
>   That triumph the stranger shall know!
> May this right hand be wither'd for ever,
>   Ere it string our high harp for the foe!
>
> "On the willow that harp is suspended,
>   O Salem! its sound should be free;
> And the hour when thy glories were ended
>   But left me that token of thee;
> And ne'er shall its soft tones be blended
>   With the voice of the spoiler by me!"

True, they were not treated as slaves. There were few cruelties practised on them such as the negroes suffered when shipped to America. Jeremiah wrote and advised them to make the best of their subjection, to build houses and plant gardens, and to prove themselves loyal. Some of them rose to positions of influence and wealth. Daniel, for example, rose to a high and responsible post. Yet the command that he should not pray to his God, his refusal to comply, and the tragic consequences in the lions' den; and the treatment of Shadrach, Meshach, and Abed-nego; show that pagan despotism rode roughshod over the liberties and religious convictions of the captives.

Not only the heathen worship, but the heathen food, was repugnant to the Jews, and some, like Daniel, refused to eat anything but pulse. They suffered many indignities, and were made the butt for the contempt of their masters.

Psalm CII.

is also a cry of the captives. It describes their bitter lot:

> "I have forgotten to eat my bread.
>   Because of the voice of my sighing
> My bones have cleaved to my flesh.
>   I am like a pelican in the wilderness,
> I am become an owl of the ruins."

They have "eaten bread like ashes and mingled their drink with weeping." But

> "Thou wilt arise, and have compassion on Zion,
>   For it is time to be gracious unto her,
> For the set time is come,"—

the time set by the prophets in their predictions.

> "Thy servants find pleasure in her stones (Zion's ruins),
>   And are gracious unto her dust."

But God will

> "Hear the sighing of the prisoner,
>   And set at liberty those that are doomed to death."

In the course of years the captivity was made easier: the captives earned greater privileges, and a few were permitted to pay a visit to their own land and home.

Psalm LXXXIV.

expresses the yearning of the exiles for the return, their envy of those who can go up to the festivals and see the sacred courts so dear to them.

> "How lovely are Thy dwellings, O Jehovah of Hosts!
> My soul longeth, yea, even fainteth for the courts of Jehovah."

He envies the very sparrows and swallows, which are free to build their nests in the sacred eaves and walls:

> "Yea, the sparrow hath found a house,
> And the swallow a nest for herself, where she hath laid her young,
> Even Thine altars, O Jehovah of Hosts."

Happy are they that have access to God's House!

Then he thinks of those who have gone to visit Jerusalem, or he recalls the caravans of pilgrims that go up to Jerusalem at the great festivals: and he envies those (ver. 6)

> "Who, passing through the valley of Baca"

(the vale of weeping—some sorrowful valley),

> "Make it a place of springs;"

i.e., who forget the trials of the journey for the joy of reaching the holy city; and who (ver. 7)

> "Go from strength to strength"

(as they go from station to station, becoming more buoyant as they come nearer the sacred place),

> " Till each one appeareth before God in Zion."
> "For a day in Thy courts is better than a thousand (elsewhere) ;
> I had rather be a doorkeeper in the House of my God
> Than dwell in the tents of wickedness (Babylon).
> Blessed is the man that trusteth in Thee."

X.

PILGRIM SONGS.

Psalms cxv., cxviii., cxx.—cxxxiv.

THE inscription, "Songs of Degrees," prefixed to Psalms cxx. to cxxxiv., has bewildered young minds—and old ones too—almost as much as the mystic "Selah."

These are literally "Songs of Ascents," or "Songs of the Upgoings." Some have supposed they were sung by the Levites as they ascended the steps of the Temple. Others think they were chanted by the caravans of pilgrims as they gathered at Jerusalem for the great festivals. And others believe they were sung by the pilgrim bands as they returned from Babylonian captivity.

The second and third interpretations must be combined as the true explanation. Some of these Psalms point to the return from captivity; and all of them were sung by the companies who ascended to Jerusalem for the yearly holy days. They accordingly connect themselves with two different sets of scenes.

For the first set of scenes we must return to Babylon.

The captive Hebrews are no longer weeping hopeless tears. For years the prophets have foreseen the overthrow of Babylon. "Comfort ye! comfort ye!"—these words, which have come like soothing music to countless weary hearts since then, were first addressed as a message of good cheer to the captives in Babylon foretelling speedy release: "*Comfort ye My people*, saith your God. Speak ye comfortably to Jerusalem, and cry unto her, that her warfare is accomplished, that her iniquity is pardoned: for she hath received of the Lord's hand double for all her sins."

Cyrus had become King of Persia, had overrun one territory after another, carrying his conquest as far as the Himalayas. The prophet, with far-sighted wisdom, pointed to Cyrus as the coming deliverer. At length the seventy years' predicted captivity were finished.

All remember how Belshazzar, now on the throne of Nebuchadnezzar, was giving a great feast to his princes and nobles and generals; how the cups once used in the Temple at Jerusalem were here to grace this scene of luxurious revelry; how in the midst of it there creeps forth a hand; how the proud king turns pale as he sees the finger move and write——but, O ye gods, write what? The court scholars, the astrologers and magicians fail to read it; but a Jew, one of the captives, Daniel, is called, and foretells immediate doom to Babylon—and, indeed, already doom is at the door.

For Cyrus has diverted a branch of the Euphrates

from its course, and has stealthily stolen up the half-dry river-bed and emerged with his army within the wall; and these revelling, half-drunken Babylonians are struck with consternation more tragic than that at Brussels before Waterloo. The winecups slip from their hands; the tread of heavy feet, the clang of approaching troops is heard. "In that night was Belshazzar the King of the Chaldeans slain."

It was a terrible night. The Persian invaders met with no resistance, cut down the young men, set fire to the houses, heedless of their treasures, hunted the terror-stricken population like chased deer, and actually carried out the vengeful wish of the Hebrew captive singer in Psalm cxxxvii., for they literally took the little children and hurled them against the ground.* "Babylon the great is fallen!" The news echoed through the whole land, and many hearts woke to liberty.

Ere long Cyrus, with generous spirit, gave permission to the Jewish captives to return to their own native land and city. To this they had looked forward for years with restless impatience. Now the day had come. Far and near heralds proclaimed the decree of Cyrus.

All know how, when the abolition of slavery was declared in the West Indies, to take effect at sunrise on a certain day, the slaves climbed the hills the night before and waited and watched for the morning rays;

---

* Dean Stanley's *Jewish Church*, iii., 59.

how they kept their eyes on the eastern horizon to catch the first streaks of daylight, and as the sun peeped into sight these slaves sprang to their feet with the cry, "We are free! we are free!" and the cry rang down the valleys and among the huts of the emancipated.

It was with such overflowing gladness that these Hebrew captives greeted the day that was to see them on the way back to the Holy City and Holy Land.

Psalm cxxvi.

pictures their feelings.

> "When Jehovah brought back the returned of Zion,
> We were like unto them that dream."

It was like a happy dream, from which one wakes afraid lest it be only a dream, too good to be true.

> "Then was our mouth filled with laughter,
> And our tongues with songs of joy."

The heathen no longer mock at their God-forsaken lot, no longer cry, "Where is your God?"

> "Then said they among the nations (the heathen),
> 'Jehovah hath done great things for them.'
> Yea, Jehovah *hath* done great things for us,
> Whereof we were glad."

So also

Psalm cxxiv.

celebrates the liberation of the captives.

> "If Jehovah had not been on our side
> —Israel may now say—

> If Jehovah had not been on our side,
>   When men rose up against us;
>   Then they had swallowed us up alive."
> "Our soul is escaped as a bird from the snare of the
>   fowlers:
>   The snare is broken and we are escaped."

This emancipation was a second exodus, and they themselves compared their deliverance to the escape of the Israelites from Egypt.

It is true, many, indeed the majority, of the Jews chose to remain in their new homes. Some had prospered, others had succumbed to idolatry. But the best of them had sung:

> "If I forget thee, O Jerusalem,
>   Let my right hand forget her cunning,"

and hastened to return.

By order of Cyrus, the vessels of gold and silver which had been taken from the Temple on Zion were handed back to the Jewish priests among the pilgrims. There were thousands of them, cups, salvers, etc., many of which had graced the fatal feast of Belshazzar. So generous was their liberator that he even provided beasts of burden and supplies for the four months' journey.

They set out under the leadership of Zerubbabel, and the mustering of so many released captives, all aglow with patriotic enthusiasm, must have been an impressive sight. The pilgrim host consisted of over forty-two thousand persons, male and female, adults and children above twelve, besides more than seven thousand slaves. There were two hundred singers, and one hundred and twenty-eight trained musicians of the clan of Asaph.

Tradition describes the enthusiasm of the start. We are told that "an escort of a thousand cavalry accompanied them for protection against the desert Arabs, and they started at the sound of tabrets and flutes."[*] The old and infirm were placed on camels; a few rich people were able to ride on horseback—a luxury in those days,—while two hundred and seventy asses carried the supplies and baggage. But, as there was only one animal to every seven pilgrims, by far the greater portion of them must have done the journey on foot.

But their enthusiasm and courage were all required. The journey was a long and dreary one, occupying four months. Over the rough gravel plains, one monotonous level stretch, with but few if any springs, they trudged on resolutely. No doubt the minstrels and singers relieved the weary marches and the evening rests with the songs of Zion.

They were returning to a land that lay in ruins. When they had passed through all the perils of robbers and of beasts of prey, they found almost all their land occupied by Edomites and others, and only a narrow strip, including Jerusalem, open to them. That sacred city itself was still a heap of ruins, and the dream of all their captivity had been to restore it to its former

---

[*] Geikie's *Hours with the Bible.*

and even to greater glory. It was the work of long years. It was this in

Psalm cxxvi.

that made the writer say :

"They that sow in tears shall reap in joy."

Though they go back in tears and trouble, there will be a time of joy and prosperity by-and-bye. They may go along weeping, bearing a handful of seed, but they shall by-and-bye come again with songs of rejoicing, bringing their sheaves with them.

Their first task was to erect the new altar, twice the size of Solomon's. This was accomplished in face of the sallies and taunts of the wild hordes that roved round Jerusalem. When the day fixed for its consecration—the great Feast of Tabernacles—arrived, it saw a vast gathering of people who had looked forward to this occasion for many long years gone by. It was an impressive ceremony. Once more, after Zion had lain dismantled and profaned, the smoke of sacrifices ascended to heaven, and Levite singers and musicians raised songs of thanksgiving. It is believed that some of the Jubilant Psalms at the end of the Psalter (cxliv. to cxlviii.), so full of Hallelujahs, also such psalms as Ps. cvii., were composed for or sung upon this occasion.

Ewald believes that

Psalm cxv.

was intended to be sung while the sacrifices were being

presented. (And, as said already, this was one of the Psalms sung at the Passover Feast. That night when Christ instituted the Lord's Supper, He sang, as usual in the early part of the Passover, Psalms cxiii. and cxiv.; at the close, cxv. to cxviii. This was the "hymn" which we are told He sang before going out to the Garden of Gethsemane.)

Psalm cxv.

shows how they felt the taunts of the marauders, and how they now looked with scorn on the idols of their recent captivity.

> "Their idols are silver and gold,
>   The work of men's hands.
> A mouth have they, but they speak not;
>   Eyes have they, but they see not," etc.

But

> "Our God is in the Heavens:
>   He hath done whatsoever He pleased."

The deliverance has come from God, and the praise shall be His:

> "Not unto us, O Jehovah, not unto us,
>   But to Thy name give glory."

It would take too long to tell how, in course of time, other bands of captives returned from Babylon under Ezra and Nehemiah; how they built the walls, under the constant attacks of the hostile races and brigand hordes that resented their return; how they built with one hand and held their weapons with the other; how some worked while others watched; how at last the whole city was restored, and the jubilations of the people burst forth in such Psalms as

Psalm CXVIII.:

"O give thanks unto Jehovah, for He is good,
    For His mercy endureth for ever."

These verses were shared by priests and congregation, the priests reading the first clause and the people answering:

"For His mercy endureth for ever."
"Let Israel now say
    That His mercy endureth for ever."

As the procession enters the city:

"Open to me the gates of righteousness,
    I will go into them, and give thanks unto Jehovah."
"Bind the sacrifice with cords, even unto the horns of the altar."

Now we turn to another set of scenes. Years have gone by, and the Jews are settled throughout the land, coming up to the holy city to the great annual holy festivals. It will help our imagination if we remember how Jesus was brought up from Nazareth to Jerusalem when twelve years of age, and how in the crowd of caravans and pilgrims on the return journey His absence was not missed until different companies took different roads.

Josephus calculates that over two millions were in Jerusalem at the Passover time. Philo says: "Many thousands from many thousand towns and cities make a pilgrimage to the Temple at every feast; some by land, others by sea, from the east and the west and the north and the south." The whole landscape and highways were dotted with companies of travellers to the holy city, the Mecca of the Jews. Pious bands from villages gather and travel together for protection against the robbers and wild beasts. "Veiled women and venerable men ride on camels or mules; younger men walk alongside, staff in hand;" children play and romp by the side of the slow-moving cavalcade.

I have seen bands of Buddhist pilgrims in Japan on their way to their sacred places. They carried long staffs with tinkling bells. Some walked on one side of the road, others on the other side; and as they trudged along, one company exchanged a sort of plaintive chant with the other, each answering each in turn.

These bands of Jewish pilgrims had tabret and flute, singers and players with them, and sang as they travelled.

Psalms cxx. to cxxxiv. were sung as "Songs of Degrees," "Songs of Ascents," and probably at one time formed a separate collection, afterwards incorporated within the Psalter: "A Psalter within the Psalter."

They are characterized by allusions to the captivity, intense affection for the holy city, references to domestic life, the blessings of families and the delights of the pilgrims to the feasts.

Psalm CXXI.

pictures the pleasure the pilgrims felt when the first sight of Jerusalem burst on them—

> "I will lift up mine eyes unto the mountains:
> From whence should my help come?"

It pictures, in ver. 3 and onwards, the perils of the night and of the rough road, the perils of the pilgrims from brigands and beasts of prey, requiring them to travel in armed companies.

> "He that keepeth thee will not slumber.
> Behold, He doth neither slumber nor sleep
> That keepeth Israel.
> By day the sun shall not smite thee,
> Nor the moon by night.
> Jehovah shall keep thy going out and thy coming in,
> From this time forth and for evermore."

Psalm CXXII.

opens with the recollection of the pleasure of the call to the feast.

> "I was glad when they said unto me,
> Let us go unto the House of Jehovah."

It describes the pride they felt in standing within the gates of the sacred city, the impression the country people got of the grandeur and stateliness of the capital.

> "Jerusalem, that art built
> As a city which is compactly built together;
> Whither the tribes go up, the tribes of Jehovah,
> Even the tribes of the Lord."

Then a prayer of loyalty, a prayer for prosperous peace:

> "O pray for the peace of Jerusalem:
> They shall prosper that love thee.
> Peace be within thy bulwarks,
> Prosperity within thy palaces."

Jerusalem is profaned; the Holy City is now a Turkish town; and we have no Mecca remaining to-day. None here on earth. Here we have no continuing city, but we seek one above, where Christ is sitting. We are pilgrims; our life is a Pilgrim's Progress to the Celestial City. The way is full of perils and discouragements. But Christ has been a Pilgrim too, and He knows every step of the way. We are not alone, for He is with us. We are not alone, for we go together in bands, and we need Christian communion to give cheer to each other and encourage the faint-hearted and feeble. We have the Songs of Zion for our pilgrimage.

> "Onward we go, for still we hear them singing,
> 'Come, weary souls, for Jesus bids you come;'
> And through the dark, its echoes sweetly ringing,
> The music of the Gospel leads us home."

PART II.

ROMANCE OF THE HYMNAL.

I.

GENERAL SURVEY.

1. THE NILOMETER OF THE CHURCH'S HISTORY.

THERE is an instrument called the Nilometer, which is used to register the height to which the Nile rises each year in its inundations.

Hymns are the Nilometer of the Christian Church. Each rise and fall in its spiritual condition is registered in the hymns of the period.

The Advent of the Christ is marked by the outburst of adoring gratitude in the "Benedictus," the "Magnificat," the "Nunc Dimittis."

The desperate state of the world at the time is reflected in the hymns of the *Middle Ages*, in their "other-worldliness," in the heaven-hunger, the contempt of man's "brief life," in the longing for "Jerusalem the Golden," in Bernard of Cluny and Bernard of Clairvaux.

During the unhistoric intervals the Church was almost without sacred song. The Dark Ages were silent ages.

Luther found the Church almost songless. He resolved to remedy this deficiency, and secure not only liberty of conscience but liberty of praise. Himself an ardent flute player, he provided music for the young and prepared a hymn book for schools. In those schools which he and Melanchthon established nearly one-fourth of the time was devoted to musical tuition. What the "*Theses*" declared in dogma was sung into the hearts of the people in hymns. The truth was carried into every corner of the country on the wings of praise, until whole villages resounded with hymns at the time of morning and evening family worship.

Luther marching to Worms, singing "Ein feste Burg" is typical of the *Reformation*, which marched singing to victory.

Then during the succeeding *era of unbelief* there was a comparative lull in hymn-writing.

But, again, in the great *Evangelical Revival* of the eighteenth century, there came a mighty outburst of song. Charles Wesley is the representative name from among many—Olivers, Anne Steele, Cowper, Newton. People went singing to their meetings in great companies, and made the streets echo with their hymns on the way home.

The beginning of the *Missionary Movement* is clearly marked in the praise of the Church. Heber and Montgomery's hymns proclaim the opening of the mission era.

"From Greenland's icy mountains"

and kindred hymns are a landmark in the history of Christ's cause.

The revival of Ritualism inaugurated by the *Tractarians* produced, and in turn was aided by, Keble's *Christian Year* and Faber and Newman's hymns.

The Evangelical and *Evangelistic Revivals* of the present half-century have left their imprint on our praise. The awakenings that gave us Sankey's *Sacred Songs* were only part of a far wider movement. The religious life of individuals and of Churches has experienced a deepening of faith and consecration. Bonar, Miss Havergal, Ray Palmer, are a few of the names that mark this movement. Their lyrics are the ex-pressed juice in song of a Gospel *Renaissance* which has been advancing without din or strife.

The great work among the students of English and Scotch and American Universities, the flood of student volunteers for foreign missionary labour, the frequent Conferences for the deepening of the spiritual life, such as the Keswick Convention, all witness to the existence of a religious renewal.

Hymnals have, therefore, a historic value and interest. The story of Church praise is the story of all the great movements which have stirred the Christian Church. Church praise is the essence of Church History.

Hymns are thus the "high-water mark" of the Church's spirituality. The songless periods have been stagnant periods. During the dark ages the clergy sang for the people as well as prayed for them. And to-day the songless Churches are the stagnant ones. Where there is priestcraft, there the service of praise is *performed for* the congregation, and there it is still night.

Progress and power have always gone hand in hand with praise. Men sneeringly called Cromwell's Ironsides "Psalm-singers;"* but, if history proves anything, it proves that "Psalm-singers" are likely to be "Ironsides."

2. The Church Universal.

A hymn book is a *miniature of the Church Universal*. It laughs to scorn the claim of any single Church to be the one true Church of Christ. It proves the true unity of Christians in spite of the absence of uniformity.

Roman Catholics—Faber, Xavier, St. Bernard—stand side by side with Protestants,—Luther, Gerhardt. Ritualists—Keble, Neale—associate with Evangelicals—Lyte, Cowper, Havergal; and both are compelled to mix with Baxter the Puritan, Watts and Doddridge the Congregationalists, Wesley and Olivers the Methodists, and Bonar and McCheyne the Presbyterians.

The Arminian Wesley and the Calvinist Toplady no longer dispute and wrangle, but dwell together in peace.

Even the Unitarian's yearning—Adams' "Nearer, my God, to Thee"—is called into the service of God, along with Heber's Trinity Hymn, "Holy, Holy, Holy, Lord God Almighty."

All are here, and all are needed. Without the rest, no Church's praise would be perfect. Hymn

---

* *The Study*, 1873, p. 103.

books remind Romanists and Ritualists and all bigots of Christ's words: "Other sheep I have which are not of this fold." Each sings his part; all combine to produce that Harmonized Anthem which the Christian Church is learning here, and which it will sing perfectly hereafter.

When men sing hymns and offer prayers, no one can tell their theological differences. Toplady and Wesley angrily disputed upon points of theology. We sing their hymns, and cannot discover which is the Arminian and which the Calvinist. Indeed, the Calvinist's "Rock of Ages" was attributed to the Arminian—and that by an Arminian!

It seems difficult to put cold dogma into hymn or prayer. In devotion, before God, all are one, although in controversy, towards each other, they may stand opposed.

This is the true Catholic Church, or Christian Union, or Evangelical Alliance, forecast of the One Church above.

Hymn books contain and teach the theology of the people. Creeds are for controversialists, Confessions of Faith for ecclesiastics: but neither contributes much to the theology of average Christians. Hymnals are the people's creeds: hymns their religious teachers. What has set itself to music, what we sing, becomes part of ourselves. It is always with us. Prose has not the same capacity as Song to shape thought and belief. Our hymns have been among the most potent preachers.

They have been Evangelists. They have put words into the lips that have helped the heart to believe. They have enabled many to take the decisive step. We cannot doubt that numbers, as they have sung the song, "Just as I am," have seen the truth and found rest in Christ.

They have also been the Comforter's chosen channels of peace and consolation.

Hearts that could not enjoy prayer have often found relief in holy song. Hymns have given wings to their thoughts.

3. Children's Hymns.

Until the days of Watts, no hymn-writer seems to have recognized the need of hymns specially adapted to children. It appears to have been taken for granted that if the young were not able to sing ordinary hymns with interest and intelligence, it was merely one of the disadvantages of youth which they must endure till their minds had developed. Meanwhile, the little folks must commit to memory the words of ordinary hymns, and discover their meaning by-and-bye.

What a change since the days of Watts! To-day every Hymnal has its section for "The Young," and no Morning Service is complete without its hymn for the children. The benefit for the little folks is incalculable.

At first the hymns written for the young were solemn, dry, doctrinal, and threatening. They expressed sentiments impossible to any but wayworn travellers; weariness of earth, longing for Heaven, the passion of religious conflict. They embodied dogmatic theology which could, even if it were in its proper place in a hymn, be understood only by mature minds.

Still worse: they brandished punishment, death, and even hell before the eyes of the children. They sought to drive them from sin by a threat rather than win them to goodness by love. They could not but leave in young minds the impression of God as a sort of detective, with a gaol at His command; whereas hymns for the young should be like the young themselves—bright, happy, warm-hearted, winsome, inspiring.

DR. WATTS was the first to provide for the "lambs of the flock;" and we owe him a large debt for his contributions. But it is evident he was a bachelor and knew little of the real wants of children, in spite of his experience as a tutor in a family.

Here is a verse from one of his hymns meant for children; and how *wicked* is the representation given of the Gracious Father:

> "What if His dreadful anger burn,
> While I refuse His offered grace,
> And all His love to fury turn,
> And strike me dead upon the place?"

With reference to the sin of falsehood he puts these lines in young lips:

> "The Lord delights in them that speak
> The words of truth; but every liar
> Must have his portion in the lake
> That burns with brimstone and with fire."

Even more awful is the following:

> "There is a dreadful hell,
> And everlasting pains,
> Where sinners must for ever dwell
> In darkness, fire, and chains.
>
> "Can such a wretch as I
> Escape this cursèd end?
> And may I hope, whene'er I die,
> I shall to Heaven ascend?"

What can be said on behalf of putting these sentiments, however true, into a *hymn of praise;* and especially of putting them into *children's* lips? Well for the children if their love for sacred things can survive such a test!

Happily, some that Watts wrote were conceived in a more kindly vein; but such were limited in number.

In spite of the halo of respect which we throw around all we were taught at our mother's knee, we cannot fail to see the comical side of such remarks as these in a hymn fixed in everyone's memory:

> "Let dogs delight to bark and bite,
> For God has made them so;
> Let bears and lions growl and fight,
> For 'tis their nature too.
> But, children, you should never let
> Your angry passions rise;
> Your little hands were never made
> To tear each other's eyes."

CHARLES WESLEY remembered the little ones; and is sometimes very happy in his lines, as in

> "Gentle Jesus, meek and mild,
> Look upon a little child;
> Pity my simplicity,
> Suffer me to come to Thee."

ANN and JANE TAYLOR strove to meet the wants of child-worshippers. The latter received her inspiration in a peculiar way. "My method was to shut my eyes and imagine the presence of some pretty little mortal, and then endeavour to catch, as it were, the very language it would use on the subject before me. If in any instances I have succeeded, to this little imaginary being I should attribute my success. And I have failed so frequently, because so frequently I was compelled to say, 'Now you may go, my dear; I shall finish the hymn myself.'"

The origin of MRS. LUKE's well-known children's hymn,

> "I think when I read that sweet story of old,"

is interesting.

"Mrs. Luke was one day travelling in a stage-coach, when the thought struck her to write something which would be suitable for use in the village school in which her father took an interest. As the coach rattled on its way she jotted down that hymn, which has been lisped by infant voices in every land, making music on each and joy in heaven."*

---

* Edwin Hodder.

To HEBER also the children are indebted for several of their favourite hymns,—

"Brightest and best of the sons of the morning;"
"By cool Siloam's shady rill;"
"From Greenland's icy mountains."

Mrs. CECIL FRANCES ALEXANDER, wife of the Bishop of Derry, has, however, met the wants of the children better than any other writer in the present generation. Her language and her thought are alike simple. She recognises their love of incident, and in more than one hymn gives her thought a historical setting; *e.g.*—

"Once in Royal David's city;"
"There is a green hill far away."

Her sentiments befit the mind of a child; her lines express the brightness and naturalness of children, as in

"All things bright and beautiful;"
"We are but little children weak;"

and in another, which is less widely known:

"Do no sinful action,
  Speak no angry word:
 Ye belong to Jesus,
  Children of the Lord."

Among no class of hymns can we mark such progress as in those for the young. And the growth has been more remarkable in quality and suitability than even in quantity.

4. Sermonic Hymns.

Not a few of our veteran hymns were written to follow and sum up sermons.

Dr. Watts and Dr. Doddridge both adopted this method. Many of their hymns were sung at the close of their sermons. Hence they were frequently cast in a sermonic mould, declaratory, doctrinal, didactic. It is said that often the preaching was less effective and impressive than the recital of the hymn at the close. It is certain that some of our standard hymns were composed under such conditions.

Edwin Hodder tells of an extreme instance of specific hymn-writing, the case of George Wither, who made pieces for every event, public or private. The titles of some are amusing: "*A Hymn for a House-warming;*" "*For a Widower or Widow delivered from a Troublesome Yokefellow;*" "*A Hymn whilst we are washing.*" George Wither happily finds his place among the "Rejected" to-day.

5. Introspective Hymns.

The tendency in the hymns of recent times is to indulge in excessive self-analysis. This tendency is not, of course, confined to our own period. The hymns of the cloisters are often self-contemplative. But this feature is distinctive of certain writers of the present half-century.

They weigh their feelings, measure their moods,

record the fluctuations of their inner life. They accordingly become morbid and unhealthy.

FABER is specially guilty of this sin. You may open his collected "*Hymns*" at any place and find an instance, such as this, taken almost at random :—

> "My very thoughts are selfish, always building
> Mean castles in the air;
> I use my love of others for a gilding
> To make myself look fair."

His self-analysis leads to painful exaggeration. He revels in self-recrimination. He certainly holds the mirror up to human nature: but we are none the better or brighter for it. Whilst in spirit lofty and pure, his descriptions are often sensational, almost gross.

Hymn-writers who at one time were desperately wicked are liable to introspection and exaggeration. This is true of JOHN CENNICK—whose life was godless and vile—author of

> "Children of the Heavenly King," etc.

It applies still more accurately to JOSEPH HART, who abandoned himself to all sin and infidelity. When, through a companion writing a letter to him, he was brought under conviction, he was so overwhelmed with a sense of his sin that his health gave way. He happened to wander into a Moravian Chapel in Fetter Lane on a Whit Sunday, where he heard the good news of Divine pardon. His hymns embody these deep experiences of personal sin, although they do not indulge in continued self-analysis. He is best known by those lines, which have won many hearts:

> "Come, ye sinners, poor and wretched,
> Weak and wounded, sick and sore."

MISS HAVERGAL delights to express personal feelings and to describe spiritual states. The *first* personal pronoun is much on her lips. Moods and sentiments are plaintively pictured, and consequently there is a want of healthy vigour. A singer may start, as David often starts, with his own weaknesses and experiences, but he should quickly be absorbed in God, and in this contemplation of God the morbid self-analysis should be dropped.

6. SENSUOUS HYMNS.

Our praise is threatened with a deluge of amorous vapourings, sentimental effusions that verge on carnal passion and not on worship. To the emotional Mary, in the act of clasping the risen Christ, Jesus said, "Touch Me not." Many hymns, especially some from America, clasp Him with endearments, or gloat over His bodily wounds. "Touch Me not."

7. HYMNS OR SOLILOQUIES?

Some hymns included in recent collections are little more than devout meditations.

They are not *praise*, they are not *prayer*—unless by implication: they are pious reflections. They have great excellences as religious poems, but they are not hymns.

Yet, in spite of this fact, they are found to be profitable for comfort and devotion.

ADELAIDE A. PROCTER has written several pieces that a devout mind loves to repeat; but scarcely one of them is a hymn proper; *e.g.*:

> "I do not ask, O Lord, that life may be
>   A pleasant road;
> I do not ask that Thou wouldst take from me
>   Aught of its load."

A. L. WARING has written two pieces dear to our hearts, yet subject in some measure to the same criticism. Reflections occupy too much space. They are:

> " Father, I know that all my life
>   Is portioned out for me;"

and:

> " My heart is resting, O my God."

Pieces that were written first as pure literature, and not as materials for worship, are naturally more likely to be mainly meditative. Those authors whose profession is literature do not generally follow the hymn model. And it is well that we should utilize in praise matter that is unconventional and free in its form. This more liberal treatment has admitted to the latest Hymnals such writers as Whittier, Bryant, Tennyson, O. W. Holmes, Longfellow, Jean Ingelow, and George Macdonald.

8. Rejected Hymns.

When we remember that Charles Wesley wrote six thousand hymns, that other authors composed hundreds, we see that the rejected must vastly outnumber the accepted. In the "struggle for existence," the fittest have no doubt survived. The elements that constitute unfitness are very varied.

Some are rejected because they indulge in fantastic metaphors, ingenious comparisons, quips and cranks of expression, or in minuteness of detail. Such abound specially in the Elizabethan era, which is unaccountably deficient in great hymn-writers.

One by GEORGE WITHER calls upon all to join in worship with heart, and voice, and instrument. The trumpet, the lute, and the viol are the chosen instruments. The choir is arranged thus: humanity to be choirmaster; birds to sing the warbling treble:—

> "Angels and supernal powers,
> Be the noblest tenor yours.
> * * * *
> From earth's vast and hollow womb
> Music's deepest bass may come.
> * * * *
> Seas and floods from shore to shore
> Shall their counter-tenors roar."

The father of Nahum Tate, by name FAITHFUL TATE, might have figured as an approved hymn-writer to-day had he indulged less in overstrained and whimsical metaphors. The following belongs to the rejected, and no wonder!

> "O Conscience! Conscience! when I look
> Into thy register, thy book,
> What corner of my heart, what nook,
> Stands clear of sin?
>
> "And though my skin feels soft and sleek,
> Scarce can I touch my chin, my cheek,
> But I can feel Death's jawbone prick
> Even through my skin."

JOHN BERRIDGE "took up the trade of hymn-making because some jingling employment was required which might amuse and not fatigue him." He was remarkable for his humour and eccentricity, as also for his earnestness. As an example of his eccentric ways, he was buried by his own directions in that section of the churchyard where lay the suicides and the banned. His object was to remove the stigma, to *consecrate* the spot. His hymns are as eccentric as his ways.

> "Jesus, Thou art the Rose
> That blushest on the thorn;
> Thy blood the semblance shows
> When on Mount Calvary torn:
> A rugged tree Thou hadst indeed,
> But roses from a thorn proceed."

GEORGE HERBERT is almost as quaint and rich in "conceits" as Francis Quarles himself:

> "The Sundays of man's life,
> Threaded together in time's string,
> Make bracelets to adorn the wife
> Of the Eternal, glorious King."

II.

EARLY CHRISTIAN HYMNS.

1. THE primitive Christian congregations were secessions from the Jewish synagogues, and they carried the Hebrew praise with them into their services. The earliest attempts at Christian hymns were substantially compositions of the psalms of Miriam, Hannah, David. The "Magnificat" of Mary, the "Benedictus" of Zacharias, the "Nunc Dimittis" of Simeon, are all cast in the phraseology of the praise sung for long centuries previously in the Temple.

The "hymn" sung by Christ and the Twelve before leaving the Passover and first Lord's Supper to face Gethsemane's dread night was the Great Hallel (Psalms cxiii.—cxviii.)

The new faith soon demanded new expressions of its gladness. Yet for several generations the "hymns and spiritual songs" of the Christian Church rang with echoes of the sacred praise of the Temple.

The three most ancient hymns, sole remnants of the first two centuries, are the "TERSANCTUS" —

"Holy, holy, holy, Lord God of hosts"—

retained in the Communion Service of "Common Prayer;" the "GLORIA IN EXCELSIS," an expansion of the Angels' Song; and the "GLORIA PATRI," sung in various forms.

The first name that meets us, the first writer to compose hymns in metrical form, is

CLEMENT OF ALEXANDRIA.

Translated freely into modern dress, his single piece that remains appears in our Hymnals as:

> "Shepherd of tender youth,
> Guiding, in love and truth,
> Through devious ways," etc.

Clement had spent his early years at Athens, had, in spite of a Christian parentage, adopted, first the Stoic and then the Eclectic philosophy,—had been intellectually ill at ease till finally he learnt by experience the wisdom and power of the Gospel. At Alexandria he lived and laboured for years as Principal of the Catechetical College. Among his pupils was the illustrious Origen. His later years were darkened by a storm of persecution, which drove him from learned and luxurious Alexandria to distant Cappadocia. Among many works, he wrote *The Tutor*, in which appeared the hymn which, slightly recast, we sing to-day. It was a hymn for the young, written towards the close of the second century.

The

"LAMPLIGHTING" HYMN

can be traced to a date almost as early. Keble has

given it to our modern Hymnals in the rich dress so well known:

> "Hail, gladdening Light, of His pure glory poured,
> Who is the immortal Father, heavenly, blest."

It is supposed to have been sung at "Lamplighting," and hence its name.

2. Hymns of Heresy and Orthodoxy.

The next century is barren of song; and it is not till about 350 A.D. that we encounter other hymn-writers.

When we remember that Toplady wrote "Rock of Ages" partly to counteract the Arminian teaching of Wesley, we need not be surprised to find that orthodoxy defended itself in early times by means of hymns.

Heretical hymns had been composed by the Gnostic BARDESAN OF EDESSA; and with the aid of his son, Harmonius, he had wedded them to tunes so popular that the very girls and children knew them by heart and sang them at work to the accompaniment of the guitar, and at play.* Bardesan's hymns, like Luther's, were spreading his heresies as his teaching never could have done.

But he found his match in EPHRAIM THE SYRIAN, who, to counteract these heresies, wrote numerous hymns radiant with orthodox teaching, set them to Bardesan's popular tunes, and trained companies of young women, future nuns, to sing them in chorus.

---

* Smith's *Dict. of Christian Biography*.

They bewitched the people, and drowned out the heresies of Bardesan.

But controversy drove him, as it drove Wesley and Toplady, to desperate and indefensible methods of attack.

A heretic, by name Apollinaris, had written two volumes which he had left in the hands of a lady of Edessa. From her Ephraim succeeded in borrowing the books, pretending he was a disciple of the author. "Before returning them he glued the leaves together, and then challenged the heretic to a public disputation. Apollinaris accepted the challenge only so far as to consent to read from these books what he had written, declining more on account of his great age. They met; but when he endeavoured to open the books, he found the leaves so firmly fastened together that the attempt was in vain: and he withdrew mortified almost to death by his opponent's victory."

Hymns sprang from a more critical controversy, *The Arian* v. *The Athanasian*. Arius, who repudiated the Deity of Jesus, had composed sacred songs to popularize his teaching. When, seventy years after, John Chrysostom arrived at Constantinople as its bishop, he found a strange state of things. "The Arians," says Dr. Prescott, quoting Gibbon's *Decline and Fall*, "had been forbidden by the Emperor Theodosius to have places of worship within the city. But on Saturdays and Sundays and great festivals they were in the habit of assembling outside the gates, then coming into the city in procession at sunset, and all night, in the porticoes and open places, singing Arian hymns and anthems with choruses. Chrysostom feared that many of the simple and ignorant people would be drawn from the faith. He therefore organized nightly processions of orthodox hymn-singers, who carried crosses and lights, and with music and much pomp rivalled the efforts of the heretics. Riots and bloodshed were the consequence. Very soon an imperial edict put a stop to Arian hymn-singing in public. The use, however, of hymns in the nocturnal services of the Church became established."

Charles Kingsley has drawn in *Hypatia* a striking and lifelike portrait of the hunting philosopher-bishop,

SYNESIUS OF CYRENE.

Hypatia, Alexandria's great teacher of philosophy, powerfully influenced his mind; and on her he always looked with the sincerest veneration. His was more than muscular Christianity. In his North African diocese he divided his time between writing poetry, talking philosophy at midnight, and planting trees, breeding horses and training dogs for hunting. Ten of his hymns are extant, most of them amalgams of philosophical theories and Christian truths.

Of this "squire-bishop's" hymns, one is sung to-day (*Hymns Ancient and Modern*, 185):

> "Lord Jesus, think on me,
> And purge away my sin;
> From earth-born passions set me free,
> And make me pure within."

3. Ambrosian Hymns.

Various hymns are currently called Ambrosian which, however, are not from the hand of Ambrose.

Te Deum.

The "Te Deum" has been attributed to him. The story of its origin goes thus:—

On Easter night in the year 387 A.D., Ambrose stood with his convert Augustine before the principal Christian altar in Milan. The latter had just been baptized—a mighty victory over Manichean error; and the heart of Ambrose swelled with triumph as he pronounced the new name of Augustine; and perhaps he had some dim prevision of the greatness to which that name should attain in the army of the Cross. He broke forth in thanksgiving: "We praise Thee, O God! we acknowledge Thee to be the Lord!" And the newly-baptized answered in the same strain: "All the earth doth worship Thee, the Father everlasting." Thus in alternate strophes they sang, as men inspired by one Spirit, that sublime hymn of praise the "Te Deum," which has since been the voice of the Church for nearly fifteen hundred years.

It is a pity to spoil such a beautiful story, suspiciously perfect. But the facts do not support it. Ambrose was probably not the author. Parts of it may be traced to the Eastern Church and an earlier date. It is first mentioned a hundred and fifty years later, in 527, although it is then named as one among other Psalms, well known and of long standing.

It is, however, under any circumstances, one of the most ancient of Christian hymns, and, with its magnificent roll of praise, one of the grandest. Its theme is the Trinity and the redemption of man by Christ.

Probably it was originally addressed to Christ and not to the Trinity. We know from Pliny that the early Christians sang their morning hymn, "Christo quasi Deo"—"To Christ as to God;" and it is quite probable that this hymn in its first shape, before the controversies on the Trinity arose, ran: "We praise Thee *as* God: we acknowledge Thee the Lord."

It was first sung in English at Herne Church, of which Ridley was vicar from 1538 to 1549.

4. AMBROSE,

a consular magistrate at Milan, maintained order so wisely among Arian and Orthodox factions in their choice of a bishop, that the tumultuous company demanded "Ambrose for bishop!" The cry was said to have been raised by a child.

He shrank from the responsibility, but, constrained to consent, he became the most powerful bishop of his generation. Sovereigns had to bow in obedience to his will.

The Empress Justina, an Arian, resolved to depose the bishop. But the people of Milan rose *en masse* to champion his cause. They rallied round him, kept guard over his person day and night, and prepared to perish with him in case of need. To the devoted assembly he preached fervent and brave sermons. He wrote hymns and psalms to cheer and embolden them; and for some of his hymns he composed suitable tunes. Again his courageous stand was rewarded by success. So Ambrose, the John Knox of his day, beat the Empress.

Ambrose is the "Father of the Western Hymn." He did for public worship in Italy what David did for it at Jerusalem.

The hymn-singing in the Milan Basilica is described in glowing terms by Augustine. The Ambrosian chant deeply affected him. "The voices flowed in at my ears, truth was distilled into my heart, and the affection of piety overflowed in sweet tears of joy." He organized a "high" service. "Antiphons, hymns, and vigils" were sung, and he practised and advocated an ascetic life.

His reputation as a hymn-writer and composer was so great that numerous sacred pieces and chants that he never saw have been stamped with his name. The *Te Deum* and *Ambrosian Hymn* are specimens of the ninety falsely attributed to him.

Ten hymns can with moderate accuracy be ascribed to Ambrose.

5. Prudentius,

the early Spanish hymn-writer, the "Christian Pindar," celebrating the martyrs in song, wrote, about 410 A.D., one of our Christmas hymns:

> "Of the Father's love begotten."

Anatolius

was Bishop of Constantinople, but is known to us best as the author of

"The day is past and over,
All thanks, O Lord, to Thee."

Hence the name of Dykes' tune—St. Anatolius—to which the words are set. "This little hymn," says Dr. Neale, the translator, "is a great favourite in the Greek Isles. . . . It is to the scattered hamlets of Chios and Mitylene what Bishop Ken's Evening Hymn is to the villages of his own land, and its melody singularly plaintive and soothing."

6. Gregory the Great

stands on the border-land between the early Christian and the mediæval periods.

In early manhood we see him first Senator and then Prefect of the Eternal City, walking through its streets in silk robe sparkling with gems. A few years later we find him renouncing almost all his patrimony, founding monasteries, and himself becoming a monk.

When the news arrived that he was Pope Gregory, he disguised himself and fled from the city to a forest cave. He was soon discovered by the pursuing people and ordained at Rome.

He devoted himself to the reformation—improvement, shall we say, or otherwise?—of sacred music. The Ambrosian singing had been antiphonal, congregational, and melodious. Gregory regarded it as frivolous, and instituted the monotone, with only a few inflexions. This

Gregorian Music

had no bars, no measure of time, no harmonies, no rhythm, no sharps, no flats, and was sung by the choir alone. Gregorian chants, intonations, recitations, cadences have been cultivated largely in cathedrals, and have shared the popularity, or unpopularity, of the Ritualistic school.

He founded a song-school in Rome, "endowed it with some farms, built for it two habitations. There, to the present day, his couch, on which he used to recline when singing, and his whip with which he menaced the boys, are preserved with fitting reverence."

The Gregorian music was a powerful aid to the missionaries of Gregory in captivating the pagan people of Kent. The story of this mission is worth re-telling.

Ere yet he was Pope, Gregory one day saw in the Roman Forum some boys "with fair skin, comely faces, and bright flowing hair." They were to be sold as slaves. In pity for them, he asked whence they came.

" From Britain."

" Were the inhabitants of that island Christians or pagans ? "

" Pagans."

"Alas!" heaving a deep sigh, "Alas! that men of such lucid countenance should be possessed by the author of darkness, and that such grace of form should hide minds void of grace within."

Being told that they were called "Angli," "Well called so," he exclaimed, "for they have angelic faces, and should be co-heirs in heaven of angels. What is the name of the province from which they come?"

"Deiri."

"True again: de viâ Dei eruti, et ad misericordiam Christi vocati."

On hearing that the king of the province bore the name Aella, he said, "Alleluia! the praises of God the Creator must be sung in those parts."

He himself started off to evangelize the "Angli," but was brought back to fill the Papal Chair. Unable to go in person, he sent Augustine and others to the shores of southern Britain. This momentous mission was accompanied by a band of choristers, whose plaintive chanting helped to gain the Saxon people and their king, Ethelbert, to Christianity.

"Come, Holy Ghost, our souls inspire,
And lighten with celestial fire,"

is ascribed to Gregory the Great. In the Romish Church it is used at the consecration of a Pope; in the Anglican Church at the consecration of a Bishop.

Some nine hymns are attributed to Gregory, of which the above, "Veni, Creator Spiritus," is the best known.

III.

HYMNS FROM THE CLOISTERS.

1. THE MONKS OF MAR SABA.

ONE of the choicest of Christian hymns—
> "Art thou weary, art thou languid,
> Art thou sore distrest?"—

came from the lonely monastery of Mar Saba. Its history takes us into a small company of hymn-writing monks in the eighth century, somewhat resembling the Keble-Newman coterie at Oxford eleven centuries later.

There were three of them, and their lives were bound up together.

St. John Damascene,

or St. John of Damascus, was the great poet of the Eastern Church, the defender of Images or Icons. His father had adopted an orphan boy into his family, the future

St. Cosma.

These two foster-brothers played together, learned

together, composed youthful hymns in friendly competition, and retired together to the monastery at Mar Saba.

A nephew of St. John's, the future

St. Stephen, the Sabaite,

author of the hymn translated by Dr. Neale in the familiar lines already quoted,

"Art thou weary, art thou languid?"

was placed in this monastery at ten years of age. He spent the remainder of his life, sixty years, in this place along with uncle and foster-uncle, and together the three cultivated their love of sacred poetry.

Noble as are some of the hymns of the foster-brothers, those from the hand of the youngest member of the trio stand above the rest in unique simplicity and tender beauty.

The author of the admirable *Anglican Hymnology* describes a visit he paid to the scene of the writing of "*Art thou weary?*"

"The monastery stands nobly on a lofty cliff overhanging the valley of the Kedron, which here forms a deep chasm. It was founded in the beginning of the sixth century, and this secluded convent has therefore stood in the midst of savage desolation for fourteen centuries. Several times in the course of ages it has been plundered, and the inmates put to death, by Persians, Moslems, and Bedouin Arabs; and therefore, for the sake of safety, the monastery is surrounded by massive walls. Inside the gate we found chapels, chambers, and cells innumerable, for the most part cut out of the rock, perched one above the other, and connected by rocky steeps and intricate passages. The huge building seems as if it were clinging to the face of a steep precipice, so that it is difficult to distinguish man's masonry from the natural rock.

"The Sabaites at present number about forty, and their rule is very severe, being under a vow never to eat animal food. They have five religious services by day and two by night. We were shown their gaily decorated chapel, the tomb of St. Sabas, the tomb of John of Damascus, and a cave chapel containing thousands of skulls of martyred monks.

"We were led to the belfry on the roof of their little sanctuary, and saw the bells which send forth their beautiful chimes and gladden the hearts of pilgrims, who, 'weary and languid,' pursue their journey through the desolate wilderness. The bells of Mar Saba recalled to mind the soothing words:

> "'Far, far away, like bells at evening pealing,
>   The voice of Jesus sounds o'er land and sea.'

"We were then conducted to a terrace, from the dizzy height of which we looked down into the deep gorge of the Kedron, five hundred feet below. Every morning wolves and jackals assemble at the bottom of the rocks, and are fed by the monks, who cast down food to the ravenous animals. Viewed from this terrace, the scene around and below is one of stern desolation, and a sight so impressive as never to be forgotten. Here

Stephanos, eleven centuries ago, wrote the touching hymn :

> "'Art thou weary, art thou languid?'"

2. The Monks of the Studium.

At the great Abbey at Constantinople, named the Studium,

St. Joseph of the Studium

lived the life of a monk. His early manhood had been adventurous; his later life he spent in pouring out large numbers of hymns. His is the original of

> "O happy band of pilgrims,
> If onward ye will tread."

His also the inspiration of Dr. Neale's

> "Safe home, safe home in port,
> Rent cordage, shattered deck,
> Torn sails, provisions short,
> And only not a wreck :
> But oh! the joy upon the shore
> To tell our voyage perils o'er."

3. The Two Bernards.

Bernard of Clairvaux.

The Normans had conquered the Saxons and were robbing them of their lands when (1091) Bernard was born. His father, a rich baron of Burgundy, was a vassal of the Duke of Burgundy who shared in the first Crusade.

He was nineteen when his mother died, and her

pious death-bed awoke him to earnest thought, and led him three years later to devote himself to a severe monastic life. So enthusiastic was he, so strong his persuasive power, that four of his brothers were drawn by him to join the monastery of Citeaux, two of them abandoning their wives to do so. Even his father forsook his baron's castle to become a monk like his son. His sister would not desert her husband to join a convent, and he refused to see her when she came to visit him: piety could exist only in a convent, he believed. She afterwards entered one. "Mothers hid their sons, wives their husbands, companions their friends," lest they should fall under his fascinating influence.

An Englishman, Harding, was at the head of this small monastery, his rule austere. He strove to crush the bodily senses, took food only to keep himself from fainting. This excessive severity suited Bernard.

His genius as well as his devotion was soon recognised. He was chosen to lead a band of monks to found a new monastery. A well-wooded valley— afterwards named Clairvaux, "Clara Vallis," "Bright Valley"—was selected. At first it was a struggle for existence. At times they could find no food better than beechnuts and beech leaves boiled in water. Their first and only meal was taken at two o'clock in the afternoon, twelve hours after they rose,—a meal generally of vegetables and water.

Two rival Popes arose, and such was the influence which Bernard had gained, that he was called upon to advise the French king and council upon their choice.

His advice was followed, and Innocent II. became Pope. He became the greatest ecclesiastical teacher and the most noted preacher of the time. His sermons on the "Song of Solomon" and the Psalms threw their spell over knights and monks, peasants and princes alike. A band of fifteen young knights came from the University to hear him, and were so impressed that they entered the monastery. The same lot befel the son of the King of France.

His preaching was almost evangelical; although the liberal teaching of Abelard was bitterly assailed by him, and led to the great dispute of the century. Able to make Popes, he persecuted his opponent with much severity.

This austere monk and intellectual giant passed away in 1153. Luther calls him "the best monk that ever lived."

"Jesus, Thou joy of loving hearts;"
"Jesus, the very thought of Thee,"

are both taken from Bernard's poem, two hundred lines in length, beginning:

"Jesus, dulcis memoria."

The latter is a translation by Caswall, the former by Ray Palmer, the author of

"Nearer, my God, to Thee."

"O sacred Head once wounded"

is a translation, by Dr. J. W. Alexander, Professor at Princeton, of the translation of a part of Bernard's hymn into German by Gerhardt:

"O Haupt voll Blut und wunden."

Bernard of Cluny,

or Bernard of Morlaix, the latter marking his birthplace (although of English parentage), the former the scene of his life.

He lived and died a monk at the glorious abbey of Cluny. His famous poem he dedicated to Peter the Venerable, the Abbot-General of his Order. It contains about three thousand lines, and bears the title "*On the Contempt of the World,*" contrasting the world's wickedness with the blessed country above.

A translation of four hundred and forty-two lines was made by Dr. J. M. Neale, of which three portions are well known and much loved.

They may be charged with that "other-worldliness" of which George Eliot wrote. But in this they bear the marks of a century—the twelfth—when the wickedness of the world was so deep and dark as to compel earnest souls to long for a better country.

"Brief life is here our portion;"
"For thee, O dear, dear country;"
"Jerusalem the golden,"

appear in most Hymnals.

4. FROM A PRISON AND A PALACE.

"All glory, laud, and honour
To Thee, Redeemer, King,"

is in English dress the Latin hymn of

Theodulph,

Bishop of Orleans.

The story goes that the Emperor Lewis, successor to Charlemagne, suspected the bishop of conspiring against the throne, and flung him into prison at Metz. While in his cell he composed the above hymn.

As the emperor, his court, and the priests were passing the prison in solemn procession on their way to the cathedral, Theodulph, or some choristers under his orders, sang aloud:

" All glory, laud, and honour."

The emperor was so impressed with the devout song of praise that he at once gave instructions for the release of the falsely-accused bishop.

King Robert II. of France

had an unruly wife, Constantia, and a turbulent people. Whether or not he was feeble as a sovereign, he was skilful as a hymn-writer. One of his hymns, highly valued still, reflects the troubles of his reign and home:

" Come, Thou Holy Spirit, come,
And from Thy celestial throne
Shed a ray of light Divine."

At the great dispute between Luther and Ech before the Elector of Saxony, a Latin discourse was delivered, the whole company knelt at the sound of music, and this hymn,

" Come, Thou Holy Spirit, come,"

was solemnly chanted.*

---

* Dr. Prescott's *Christian Hymns.*

5. Dies Iræ.

This most dramatic and thrilling of all hymns was written in Latin about the middle of the thirteenth century by Thomas of Celano.

It is dramatic, for it is the cry of a soul struck with awe at the "Dreadful Day," the earth in ashes, the trumpet's call, the Judge seated. Then the trembling inquiry:

> "What shall I, frail man, be pleading?
> Who for me be interceding?"

With this tragic event in view, the speaker cries:

> "Grant thy gift of absolution
> Ere that reck'ning day's conclusion."

The first to translate it into English was Crashaw, but his was a free paraphrase.

Sir Walter Scott imitated the first three stanzas in his hymn at the close of "The Lay of the Last Minstrel:"

> "That day of wrath, that dreadful day
> When heaven and earth shall pass away,
> What power shall be the sinner's stay,
> How shall he meet that dreadful day?"

John Newton also made a paraphrase of this grand sequence:

> "Day of Judgment, day of wonders."

Several translations of the "Dies Iræ" exist. One is by Dean Stanley, beginning:

> "Day of wrath, O dreadful day,"

and appeared first in *Macmillan's Magazine* in 1868.

Another version appears in the *Presbyterian Hymnal*, by Dr. W. B. Robertson, of Irvine :

"Day of anger, all arresting."

But the most perfect is that by Dr. Irons, of St. Mary Woolnoth (ob. 1883):

"Day of wrath, O day of mourning."

IV.

HYMNS OF THE REFORMATION.

GERMANY more than any other country has enriched the praise of Christendom. It has produced probably not less than a hundred thousand hymns. The explanation lies in the fact that congregational singing was one of the chief features of the Reformation in Germany.

1. Martin Luther

is the father of German hymnology.

Every one remembers how as a lad he sang in the streets for alms. How as a monk he toiled and travailed in the resolute search for peace; how Staupitz guided his search to the atonement of Christ for sin; how he found and ravenously devoured a copy of the Bible, and, as he read, saw the new light; how he paid a visit to Rome; how he nailed his Theses to the church door at Wittenberg; how he burned the Papal Bull; how he gave the New Testament to the people in their own language; and how he "shook the world," every one knows.

Coleridge slightly, but only slightly, exaggerates

when he says that "Luther did as much for the Reformation by his hymns as by his translation of the Bible."

"The hymns of Luther have destroyed more souls than his writings and sermons," is the view taken by a Romanist writer. "It is my intention," says he to his friend Spalatin, "after the example of the prophets and the ancient fathers, to make German psalms for the people; that is, spiritual songs, whereby the Word of God may be kept alive among them by singing. We seek, therefore, everywhere for poets. . . .

"But I desire that all new-fangled words from the Court should be left out; that the words might be all quite plain and common, such as the common people may understand, yet pure, and skilfully handled."*

Luther wrote in all nearly forty hymns. Many he translated from Latin sources. He invited two celebrated choirmasters to live with him and assist him in recasting the Liturgy for the Reformed Church.

He and his "house-choir" ransacked the ancient stores of sacred music, and adapted for common use many chorales, Latin and German. Several he himself composed, one of lasting fame, to which his own hymn,

"A safe stronghold our God is still,"

is sung.

He kept four printers at Erfurt busy producing and publishing his hymns. "The whole people," said a Romanist with bitter dismay, "are singing themselves into this Lutheran doctrine."

---

* Miss Winkworth.

The grandest of his hymns, bidding defiance to all opposing hosts, blowing the trumpet-blast of the Reformation, is a translation of the forty-sixth Psalm—

"Ein feste Burg ist unser Gott,"

translated in rugged lines by Carlyle:

"A safe stronghold our God is still,
    A trusty shield and weapon."

There is some support for the belief that it was written on his way to Worms, to the epoch-making Diet.

The Emperor Charles V. had summoned him to appear and recant. His friends urged him not to go. His answer, sent to Spalatin, is a memorable one:— "If there were as many devils in Worms as there are tiles on the roofs, I would go and not be afraid. If Huss was burnt to ashes, the truth was not burnt with him." The resemblance of these words to the third verse of his hymn—

"And were this world all devils o'er," etc.,

gives colour to the common belief as to the occasion of its composition.

Heine has well called it "The Marseillaise of the Reformation." Over his grave at Wittenberg the first line is carved as his epitaph.

More popular even than this hymn was his second, his Gospel one. It crystallized the central truths of the Evangelical faith:

"Dear Christian people, now rejoice."

We are told that "a number of princes belonging to

the reformed religion being assembled at Frankfort, they wished to have an evangelical service in the Church of St. Bartholomew. A large congregation gathered, but the pulpit was occupied by a Roman Catholic priest, who proceeded to preach according to his own views. After listening for some time in indignant silence, the whole congregation rose and began to sing this hymn, till they fairly sang the priest out of church."

2. NICOLAI

lived through a terrible pestilence which ravaged the town in Westphalia of which he was pastor. Over a thousand of the dead passed his window to the cemetery. These saddening sights made him think much of death and heaven, and coloured his writings.

Two of his hymns have become popular, one :

"Wake, awake, the night is flying."

He composed a chorale for this hymn, which appears in Mendelssohn's *St. Paul.*

3. GUSTAVUS ADOLPHUS,

the hero of the Thirty Years' War, had come from Sweden to the rescue of the Protestant forces. Before the great battle of Leipsic he had given "God with us" to his troops as their battle-cry. When the battle was won he wrote his triumphal hymn :

"Fear not, O little flock, the foe,"

the last stanza of which points to the watchword of the day :

> "God is with us, we are His own,
> Our victory cannot fail."

A year later we find him leading on his troops to meet Wallenstein, singing his own hymn and Luther's, "A safe stronghold." It was the fatal fight of Lutzen, in which the hero, the Lion of the North, fell.

4. RINCKART.

The Thirty Years' War, with its horrors and long-drawn miseries, produced many other celebrated hymns.

One by Rinckart, pastor at Eilenburg, is introduced by Mendelssohn into his *Hymn of Praise*. It has been called the German "Te Deum":

> "Now thank we all our God,
> With hearts and hands and voices."

This great hymn had a remarkable origin. The story is told in full in *The Sunday at Home* (August 1888).

The long war with pestilence and famine had ravaged Eilenburg. Its remaining inhabitants were in despair.

Rinckart was sitting at his study window one day watching the white snow which lay thick on road and roof, and threatened to deepen the people's distress.

"Suddenly the sound of a trumpet struck his ear. 'Just God,' cried the clergyman, 'more foreign soldiers; what will become of us? We have not enough to satisfy our own hunger; and now these foreigners will take from our mouths the last morsel of bread.'

"Again the trumpet sounded, and now much nearer than before. At the same moment Rinckart's faithful wife entered the room, and in spite of her advanced age, came up to him with unwonted speed. 'You are sitting here, Martin, meditating, while out there—out in the street—all the people are hurrying and crowding round the horseman. Go and see what news the man brings. It must be something extraordinary, for the people are all rejoicing.'

"The old man now rose and placed his little satin cap on his head: 'What will it be?' he replied, with a mournful shake of the head. 'The news of some victory, of some fresh bloodshed. When will the scourge be ended? When will men leave off murdering one another? The poor victims are equally to be pitied whether the trumpeter wears the Imperial or the Swedish uniform.'

"'You are wrong, Martin. It is a Saxon soldier, probably sent by our gracious Elector from his palace at Torgau.'

"Rinckart hastened to the door. He found the street all in a state of joyful excitement, the people fell weeping into his arms. For the trumpeter had brought the news that peace had been concluded on October 24th, at Munster in Westphalia. He had been commissioned by the Elector to convey the joyful tidings to the Council and the University of Leipsic, and then to proceed to all the principal towns, to make known the great news everywhere.

"While the trumpeter, followed by the people, moved on, Rinckart returned to his study and offered up a silent prayer of thanksgiving to heaven. Then he opened his Bible, and his eye fell on the twenty-second verse of the fiftieth chapter of the apocryphal book of Ecclesiasticus, 'Nun danket alle Gott, der grosse Dinge thut an allen Enden.' *'Now, therefore, bless ye the God of all, which only doeth wondrous things everywhere, which exalteth our days from the womb, and dealeth with us according to His mercies. He grant us joyfulness of heart and that peace may be in our days in Israel for ever.'*

"Urged on, as it were, by an invisible power, he sat down at his writing table, and as though the angel of peace who had at last overcome the demon of war were whispering in his ear, verse by verse the hymn of thanksgiving rose from the very depth of his heart:

"'Nun danket alle Gott
 Mit Herzen, Mund und Händen.'

"'Now thank we all our God,
 With hearts and hands and voices,
  Who wondrous things hath done,
 In Whom His world rejoices;
  Who from our mothers' arms
  Hath blessed us on our way
  With countless gifts of love,
  And still is ours to-day.'"

And as he wrote the last line, a soft melody seemed to

strike his ear. Again he took up his pen, and in a few minutes he had committed to paper the air so simple and so wonderfully inspiriting.

"The horseman had meanwhile dismounted, but the inhabitants of the town, full of joyful emotion, gathered in front of the Pfarrhaus and waited for their minister. He came out to them in his clerical robes, and in earnest words the venerable man praised Providence for their deliverance; then with all his flock he knelt down, and drawing from his pocket the hymn he had just composed, he began to sing it. For the first time, the new-born tune sounded from the lips of the old man, and when he ended, those present, deeply moved and grateful, surrounded their faithful minister and grasped his hand."

The famine was ended, the strain relaxed; but the prolonged suffering and struggle had left him in shattered health, and within a year he was buried amidst the raining tears of the devoted population.

V.

CLASSIC ENGLISH POETS.

ENGLISH poets who have contributed to the praise of the Church — besides Cowper (p. 195) — are Milton, Dryden, Sir Walter Scott, Addison, and Kirke White.

It will be enough, in the case of such great names, to mention merely their contributions to our Hymnals.

1. MILTON

has one hymn in common use—

"Let us with a gladsome mind
Praise the Lord, for He is kind."

He wrote it when only fifteen years of age, when at St. Paul's School. It is based on Psalm cxxxvi., and, entire, consists of twenty-four stanzas.

2. DRYDEN

appears only as a translator. "Veni Creator Spiritus," attributed to Gregory the Great (p. 137), he has done into English:

"Creator Spirit, by Whose aid."

Dryden, however, contributed more to irreligion than to Christianity. He led the movement of the latter half of the seventeenth century against Puritanism and towards license and impiety.

His religious opinions, if he had any sincere opinions, may be gathered from his controversial allegory called the " Hind and Panther." The Roman Catholic Church he represents as a Hind.

> "A milk-white Hind, immortal and unchanged,
> Fed on the lawns, and in the forest ranged:
> Without unspotted, innocent within,
> She feared no danger, for she knew no sin."

The Church of England appears as the Panther:

> "The Panther, sure the noblest next the Hind,
> And fairest creature of the spotted kind;
> Oh, could her inborn stains be washed away,
> She were too good to be a beast of prey!"

The Bear is the emblem of the Independents, the Hare of the Quakers, the Ape of the Freethinkers, the Wolf of the Presbyterians.

3. ADDISON.

Joseph Addison, the greatest of English essayists, is found also among the hymn-writers. His Roman drama *Cato* contains one passage well known, on the Immortality of the Soul:

> "It must be so; Plato, thou reasonest well,
> Else whence," etc.

It was in the *Spectator*, made immortal by his essays,

that his hymns appeared. He has at least five, of which three are well known.

"When all Thy mercies, O my God,"

originally in thirteen stanzas, in connection with which Addison observes : " If gratitude is due from man to man, how much more from man to his Maker ? Any blessing we enjoy, by what means soever derived, is the gift of Him Who is the great Author of Good and the Father of Mercies."

"How are Thy servants blest, O Lord!
How sure is their defence!"

published in the *Spectator* in 1712. This piece is described as the production of "a gentleman at the conclusion of his travels."

Addison had set sail from Marseilles on a foreign tour. While near the coast of Italy, a "dreadful tempest bore him high on the broken wave." Others gave up all hope. The captain, in despair, was making confession of his sins to a Capuchin friar. Addison calmed himself with writing this hymn, partly descriptive, partly devotional. Hence these verses:

"When by the dreadful tempest borne
High on the broken wave,
They know Thou art not slow to hear,
Nor impotent to save."

Another hymn, included in those mysterious pieces which stole in at the end of the Scotch "Paraphrases," marches with a splendid tread :

> "The spacious firmament on high,
> And all the blue ethereal sky."

It is based on Ps. xix.

Addison died at Holland House, saying to the Earl of Warwick: "See in what peace a Christian can die!"

4. SIR WALTER SCOTT

has only one hymn, its subject the Pilgrimage of the Israelites:

> "When Israel, of the Lord beloved,
> Out from the land of bondage came,
> Her father's God before her moved,
> An awful Guide in smoke and flame."

The story of his life, its romance, its heroism, must be sought in the history of English literature.

5. HENRY KIRKE WHITE.

After young Kirke White's death, there was found written on the back of one of his mathematical exercise papers the celebrated war-song of the Christians:

> "Much in sorrow, oft in woe,
> Onward, Christians, onward go!
> Fight the fight though worn with strife,
> Strengthened with the bread of life."

While still a boy in a humble home in Nottingham, he exhibited poetical tastes and gifts. At fifteen he succeeded in gaining a silver medal for a translation from Horace, and at nineteen published his first volume of poems.

His parents spent themselves in the endeavour to foster his talents and give him an education. For this purpose his mother herself opened a school. Through the temporary failure of some of these schemes he had to work at a stocking loom. From that position he entered a law office in Enfield.

As an instance of the universal aptitude of this Admirable Crichton, we are told that, while a law student, he taught himself Chemistry, Astronomy, and Electricity, practised Music and Drawing, and learnt four languages.

His companions were mostly deists and infidels. One of them, however, experienced a saving change, and during walks and talks with Kirke White was led to see the truth and beauty of the Christian life. Thereafter he became anxious to study for the ministry.

Through the aid of the Rev. Charles Simeon and the illustrious missionary Henry Martyn, Kirke White was able in 1804 to go to Cambridge.

For two years he was the first man of his year. But, like so many of nature's gifted sons, excessive study and hardship proved too much for his weak constitution, and in 1806 he died of consumption.

The author of this inspiring hymn was thus only twenty-two years of age when he was removed to a higher ministry. Only ten lines of the hymn are from his hand. It was left unfinished, and has been completed by Miss Maitland. He was the writer of ten other hymns, and is best known as a poet by his epic *Christiad*.

VI.

CLASSIC EVENING HYMNS.

1. LYTE.

LYTE'S birthplace was Kelso, where another great hymn-writer—Dr. Horatius Bonar—lived and wrote and preached for about thirty years.

He was a clergyman of the Church of England for some years before he passed through any change of heart. He was suddenly sent for to stand by the death-bed of a neighbouring clergyman, who was aware that he would soon be dead, and knew as well that he was totally unprepared for the change. Both were equally in the dark, and together they turned to St. Paul's Epistles in search of peace and hope. Together they found what they sought. The one died, as his companion afterwards wrote of him,—"died happy under the belief that, though he had deeply erred, there was One Whose death and sufferings would atone for his delinquencies, and be accepted for all that he had incurred."

Lyte confesses: "I was greatly affected by the whole matter, and brought to look at life and its issue with a different eye than before; and I began to study my

Bible and preach in another manner than I had previously done."

So deeply touched was he by this loss, that he took charge of the children left by his departed friend; and thus took heavy burdens and responsibilities on a frame already too weak.

He says himself that he "was jostled from one curacy to another." It was on the south coast, at Lower Brixham in Devonshire, that his hymns were written. He "made hymns for his little ones, and hymns for his hardy fishermen, and hymns for sufferers like himself."

His people were a hardy but rough sea-faring folk, and not able to appreciate his tender yet lofty spirit. But in this he took up his cross bravely, and he was but expressing his own practice when he sang in one of his hymns:

"Jesus, I my cross have taken."

That prayerful, restful hymn,

"Abide with me! fast falls the eventide,"

was written under the following circumstances.

His health had been steadily declining, and the climate of his parish was declared to be injurious. When this was announced to him, he wrote: "I hope not, for I know no divorce I should more deprecate than from the ocean. From childhood it has been my friend and playmate, and I have never been weary of gazing on its glorious face."

He was compelled to prepare for a sojourn in a

southern and warmer climate. "The swallows," he says, "are preparing for flight, and inviting me to accompany them; and yet, alas! while I talk of flying, I am just able to crawl, and ask myself whether I shall be able to leave England at all."

Although so feeble, he sought to meet his people once more, and celebrate the Lord's Supper and leave some parting words. "I stand before you seasonably to-day, as alive from the dead, if I may hope to impress it upon you, and induce you to prepare for that solemn hour which must come to all, by a timely acquaintance with, appreciation of, and dependence on, the death of Christ."

After the Sacrament, Lyte dragged his weary frame to his room, and he remained there for a long time. The same evening he handed to a relative this hymn in its original eight stanzas. No doubt he had been at work that afternoon soothing his own mind into peace by writing this hymn. He was thinking, not of the evening hours of the day, so much as of the eventide of life, when he wrote "Fast falls the eventide," etc., "Hold Thou Thy cross," etc.

He went to Nice, and died there, pointing upward and whispering, "Peace! joy!" His was a calm and beautiful eventide.

A certain Dr. Baker, when at Nice, went to see Lyte's grave, and found a young man standing by the spot, under deep emotion, tears of gratitude falling. To Lyte he owed his hope in God, his salvation—emblem of many thousands who have been soothed and calmed even in sorrow as they sang this hymn.

He says, in a little poem called *Declining Days*:

> "Might verse of mine inspire
> One virtuous aim, one high resolve impart—
> Light in one drooping soul a hallowed fire,
> Or bind one broken heart,
>
> "Death would be sweeter then,
> More calm my slumber 'neath the silent sod;
> Might I thus live to bless my fellow-men
> Or glorify my God."

* * * * * *

> "O Thou! Whose touch can lend
> Life to the dead, Thy quickening grace supply;
> And grant me, swan-like, my last breath to spend
> In song that may not die."

He has had his wish in the immortality of "Abide with Me."

2. KEN.

BISHOP KEN is the author of the Protestant "Te Deum," distinguished as "The Doxology,"

> "Praise God from Whom all blessings flow."

These lines are sung more frequently and more widely than any other sacred stanza. They formed the close of both of his great hymns; namely, for the morning—

> "Awake, my soul, and with the sun
> Thy daily stage of duty run;"

and for the evening—

> "All praise to Thee, my God, this night,
> For all the blessings of the light.'

These hymns have an interesting history. Ken, who had been a scholar at Winchester College, after graduating at Oxford became a Fellow of Winchester, and wrote a *Manual of Prayers* for the use of its scholars. These hymns, along with another—for "midnight"—were appended to a later edition of the *Manual*. But even prior to publication, they were, it is believed, hung as broadsheets on the walls of the bedrooms of the Winchester boys.

All three—morning, evening, and midnight—can be traced to Latin sources. They are not translations, but probably are the fruit of influences received by their author at Winchester, where the college exercises included the singing of the "*Jam lucis orto sidere.*" "Awake, my soul" would thus be suggested by "*A solus ortus cardine;*" "All praise to Thee" by "*Te lucis ante terminum.*"

They are associated with the famous *Thumb Bible*,—an abstract of the Bible prepared by Jeremy Taylor for one of the royal children. In this miniature Bible, Ken's hymns are printed, with the lines, however, extended to ten syllables. The process weakened the hymns; *e.g.* :

> " Forgive me, dearest Lord, for Thy dear Son,
> The many ills that I this day have done,
> That with the world, myself, and then with Thee,
> I, ere I sleep, at perfect peace may be."

Both of his hymns were written to be sung to Tallis's Canon. He had musical skill, played on the organ, having one in his room at Winchester; every morning sang his Morning Hymn, accompanying himself on the lute.

Ken's life was an eventful one. Early left an orphan, his education was directed by his sister, afterwards the wife of Izaak Walton, author of the *Compleat Angler*. After passing through Winchester and Oxford, and enjoying various benefices, he was made chaplain to Charles II. Ken was faithful in his dealings with the king, strove to awaken his conscience, and attended him on his death-bed, urging him to receive the Sacrament.

In 1684 he was raised to the Episcopal Bench as Bishop of Bath and Wells. Seven years later he was removed from his See, and sent to the Tower for refusing to read the "Declaration of Indulgence." Queen Anne, however, relieved his later life by giving him £200 a year as a pension. Buried at his own request "under the east window of the chancel just at sun-rising," his friends appropriately sang his own favourite lines: "Awake, my soul."

Lord Houghton (Monckton Milnes), touched by the incident, has written lines upon his tomb from which the following is an extract:

> "These signs of him that slumbers there
>   The dignity betoken;
> These iron bars a heart declare
>   Hard bent, but never broken;
> This form portrays how souls like his,
>   Their pride and passion quelling,
> Preferred to earth's high palaces
>   This calm and narrow dwelling."

To relieve his weariness, the exiled bishop wrote

verses which he called *Anodynes*. They were composed during the sleepless hours of night, when pain tortured him :

> " Pain keeps me waking in the night ;
> I longing lie for morning light :
> Methinks the sluggish sun
> Forgets he this day's course must run.
> O heavenly torch ! why this delay
> In giving us our wonted day ?
> I feel my watch, I tell my clock,
> I hear each crowing of the cock."

He had his watch so constructed that by his finger he could " discern the time to half a quarter of an hour." Dryden made him his model of his "good parson " :

> " Letting down the golden chain from high,
> He drew his audience upwards to the sky :
> And oft with holy hymns he charmed their ears ;
> (A music more melodious than the spheres :)
> For David left him, when he went to rest,
> His lyre : and after him he sung the best."

VII.

PURITAN HYMNS.

1. WATTS.

ISAAC WATTS was born at Southampton in 1674, where his father was a deacon in an Independent Church, and conducted a successful boarding school. It was the age when Dissenters paid heavy penalties for their nonconformity. Both the deacon and his pastor were locked up in prison, and the deacon's wife, with the infant Isaac in her arms, used to come on sunny days, and sit on a stone near the cell where her husband was confined, to cheer him by singing to him through the bars.

But, though his father was imprisoned more than once, young Watts' education was not neglected. At four, he was learning Latin. His mother used to employ the pupils after school hours in writing verse. The reward offered was a little copper medal. Master Isaac, then eight, won a prize by this rather saucy couplet:

> "I write not for a farthing, but to try
> How I your farthing writers can outvie.

Thus early his mind was poetical; he "lisped in numbers."

At fifteen he passed through the great change, the heart change. So intensely had he studied, and so promising was his scholarship, that at sixteen a friend offered to give him a university education if he would renounce Dissent. The offer was rejected, and he studied for the Congregational ministry.

At this time some congregations had no sacred song in their services. The Southampton congregation, however, sang praise; but the jaw-breaking lines of Sternhold and Hopkins, or the jolting measures of Nahum Tate, did not please one young worshipper there, the future poet. When he complained on the subject one morning, he received the retort from one of the deacons, "Give us something better, young man." He accepted the challenge; and forthwith he produced a hymn which was sung, line by line being read, by the congregation. It was the hymn:

> "Behold the glories of the Lamb
> Amidst His Father's throne
> Prepare new honours for His name,
> And songs before unknown."

The compilers of the Scottish *Paraphrases*, in 1745, combined this hymn with another that came later from Watts' pen:

> "Come, let us join our cheerful songs
> With angels round the throne."

This combination was amended and improved by

another hand (Rev. W. Cameron, of Kirknewton), and in this shape formed the sixty-fifth Paraphrase:

"Come, let us join our cheerful songs,"

and

"Hark how the adoring host above."

Strange to say, this innovation was cordially received by the congregation, and young Watts was urged to write other hymns. For two years a new one was sung each Sunday in that church. He was thus, as the poet Montgomery has called him, "the inventor of hymns in our language." There had been occasional and solitary sacred pieces before him of intrinsic value, but "he struck the Meribah-rock of melody and the waters continued to gush forth."

His verses were published in several volumes in successive years, and won immense popularity.

In the second collection—called *Hymns and Spiritual Songs*—were many of his best; while in the third—entitled *The Psalms of David imitated in the Language of the New Testament*—amongst others was the famous version of the Hundredth Psalm. It began:

"Sing to the Lord with joyful voice,
Let every land His name adore;
The British Isles shall send the noise
Across the ocean to the shore."

John Wesley left out this verse, and altered the first lines of the next verse, which ran:

"Nations attend before His throne
With solemn fear with sacred joy,

into

"Before Jehovah's awful throne," etc.,

an alteration and improvement adopted in most Hymnals.

When Commodore Perry anchored the American fleet off Japan, and demanded the opening of the ports to commerce, Divine Service was held on the flagship, and the chaplain, within sight of thousands upon the shore, gave out this hymn to be sung. The marine band struck up the notes of *Old Hundredth*, and the natives of that empire, where Christian civilization was so soon to win such conquests, beheld and heard the worship of One Who was yet to be King of all nations.

The mechanical execution of many of his hymns is very imperfect; some of the rhymes are excruciating. The sentiment, too, is at times ascetic, monastic, as when he writes:

"Lord, what a wretched land is this,"

—a libel on nature, art, and human love, and life's delights. But the Church had not in his time rid itself of this monkish estimate of this world.

Watts had been, before entering on his ministry in Mark Lane, tutor to the children of a certain knight at Newington. It was thus that he got his knowledge of children—for he died a bachelor—and thus in later life he wrote those hymns which as children we used to sing. True, we think we have something better for our children than—

> "How doth the little busy bee
> Improve each shining hour,"

or

> "Let dogs delight to bark and bite
> For God has made them so," etc.

But they served their day and deserve honour accordingly.

Millions of copies of his *Divine Songs for Children* were circulated; they became the favourites in school and nursery; were for many years the only book of praise used in Scottish Sunday Schools, being even printed on the fly-leaves of the Catechism.

It is said that—

> "There is a land of pure delight,
> Where saints immortal reign," etc.,

was written when the author was twenty-one or twenty-two years old; that it was suggested by the view across the Southampton Water—the "narrow sea" with its "swelling flood," beyond which lie the "sweet fields" and "living green" of New Forest.

He has not given us hymns so dear to the heart as Toplady's "Rock of Ages," or Wesley's "Jesus, lover of my soul;" but he has soared to the highest regions of spiritual devotion in such hymns as:

> "When I survey the wondrous cross."

Mrs. Evans—the "Dinah Morris" of *Adam Bede*, whose prayer on the village green we all remember in George Eliot's story—was a female preacher at a place near Matlock. We are told that she lived to a great age, and in her last illness—in great pain, but in great peace and happiness—she soothed herself by singing :

> "See, from His head, His hands, His feet,
> Sorrow and love flow mingled down ;
> Did e'er such love and sorrow meet,
> Or thorns compose so rich a crown?"

Father Ignatius, preaching in a church in Lombard Street, gave out this hymn : and when it was ended, he slowly repeated the line :

> "Demands my soul, my life, my all,"

and proceeded : "Well! I *am* surprised to hear *you* sing that. Did you know that altogether you only put fifteen shillings into the collection this morning?"

> "Jesus shall reign where'er the sun"

was sung on the occasion on which King George the Sable gave a new Constitution to his people, exchanging a heathen for a Christian form of government. Under the spreading branches of the banyan trees sat some five thousand natives from Tonga, Fiji, and Samoa, on Whit Sunday, 1862, assembled for Divine worship. Foremost sat King George. Around him were ranged old chiefs and warriors, who had shared with him the dangers and fortunes of many a battle. Old and young rejoiced together in the joys of that day. It would be impossible to describe the deep feeling manifested when the solemn service began by the audience singing :

> "Jesus shall reign where'er the sun."

In the *Sunday at Home* plebiscite, Watts had a larger number—five—in the favourite hundred than had any other author. The *Paraphrases* contain twenty-two of his hymns.

Dr. Watts went to spend a week at Sir Thomas Abney's at Stoke Newington, but, instead of a week, he stayed under this kind and hospitable roof for thirty-five years. His body rests in Abney Park; and his tomb bears the simple, truthful eulogy:

" Isaac Watts, the Father of the English Hymn.'

2. Doddridge.

Philip Doddridge was a descendant of a Bohemian refugee who had found shelter in England from persecution at Prague. He was born in London nearly two centuries ago (1702). His biographer says, that at his birth "he was thrown aside as dead;" but kind and pious parents sheltered and nourished his feeble childhood. At thirteen he was left an orphan.

Hearing of his wish to enter the ministry, the Duchess of Bedford offered to educate him at her own cost, and find him a living in the Church of England. Like young Isaac Watts in a similar position, he declined the offer, being by conviction as well as upbringing a Dissenter.

Most of his ministerial life was spent at Northampton, where he was also the Principal of a Theological College. The fame of his lectures drew students from all quarters and from other countries; and the University of Aberdeen conferred the degree of D.D. upon him.

He is known to-day both as an author and as a hymn-writer.

As an author, his most famous work is his *Rise and Progress of Religion in the Soul*. It held an honoured place on the shelves of our fathers, and we may remember seeing it in our early days side by side with Boston's *Fourfold State*. A century ago it was one of the most popular volumes among earnest people.

Wilberforce read it, and became a new man in Christ, afterwards writing his *Practical View of Christianity*. Wilberforce's book found its way into the manse at Kilmany in Scotland, into the hands of a minister who was preaching, not the Gospel, but morality. God used it to open the eyes and change the heart of that preacher, by name Thomas Chalmers —afterwards, as Dr. Chalmers, to be one of the most mighty influences in the religious life of his land.

This is the true Apostolic Succession, the mantle of truth and influence passing down from one heart to another.

He is best known to us, however, as a writer of hymns.

They appear to have been first circulated in MS., and not printed till 1755. It was probably through the circulation of some of his hymns in MS. that they were embodied in the *Paraphrases*, which were firs printed in 1745.

His family crest bore the motto " Dum vivimus vivamus "—" While we live, let us *live* "—and upon it he wrote lines which Samuel Johnson called "the best epigram in the English language:"

> "'Live while you live,' the Epicure will say,
> 'And take the pleasure of the passing day;'
> 'Live while you live,' the sacred Preacher cries,
> 'And give to God each moment as it flies.'
> Lord, in my views, let both united be;
> I live in pleasure when I live to Thee."

Travelling to preach the funeral sermons of Dr. Samuel Clarke, he caught the cold that induced his death. He was too poor to go abroad at his own expense. A Church of England clergyman proposed that a subscription should be raised. The Countess of Huntingdon, ever his friend, contributed £100. He sought a warmer climate, reached Lisbon, but had been there only a fortnight when, in 1751, he died.

He wrote three hundred and seventy-four hymns. In his *Works* they are classified in the order of the books of the Bible, according to the text which supplied the theme.

One of his hymns, not in general use,

> "Awake, my soul, to meet the day,"

he repeated to himself every morning as he rose. At five o'clock he prepared to leave his bed, repeating five stanzas before doing so; at the sixth he rose and dressed!

That hymn is no longer in use. Advocating early rising, it is not likely to be widely popular in these days!

His hymns are good, sound, pious songs of praise.

But he made no claim to be a poet. They are without genius, and are of unequal merit; rising in some verses to the heights of devotion, sinking in others to prosaic statements. In his case, the menders of hymns have improved upon the original.

In the hymn—

"Hark the glad sound! the Saviour comes,"

Doddridge says that the idea in the fourth verse-

"He comes the prisoners to release"—

was borrowed from Pope's lines on the Messiah:

"Hear Him, ye deaf; and, all ye blind, behold:
He from thick films shall purge the visual ray,
And on the sightless eyeball pour the day."

The hymn—

"O happy day that fixed my choice!"

is, in some of the Church of England Hymnals, used for Confirmations. We are told that, at the request of the Queen and Prince Albert, it was sung at the confirmation of one of the royal children. A newspaper correspondent, in reporting the circumstance, stated that the hymn,

"O happy day that fixed my choice!"

was composed for the occasion by Tennyson, the Poet Laureate! and added that, if he could write nothing better than this, it was time to consider whether he should continue to receive national pay.

> " O God of Bethel, by Whose hand
> Thy people still are fed,"

was written to be sung after a sermon which Doddridge preached on " Jacob's Vow." It is found in an altered form in Logan's *Poems*, and is also among the Scotch *Paraphrases*. As written, it ran :

> " O God of Bethel, by Whose hand
> Thine Israel still is fed."

This hymn is associated with David Livingstone. He had learnt it among the *Paraphrases*, and it remained fixed in his memory. It became his favourite piece in his wanderings in Africa, and it was sung when he was buried, in April 1874, in Westminster Abbey.

VIII.

METHODIST REVIVAL HYMNS.

1. TOPLADY.

AUGUSTUS M. TOPLADY, a native of Surrey, was, like C. Wesley, educated at Westminster School. At the age of sixteen he had gone to Ireland to aid his widowed mother in claiming an estate. He strolled into a barn at Codymain, where a layman was preaching a homely sermon from the text, "Ye who sometime were afar off are made nigh by the blood of Christ."

It was a red-letter day in his soul's history. Of this occasion he wrote afterwards: "Strange that I, who had so long sat under the means of grace in England, should be brought near to God in an obscure part of Ireland, amidst a handful of God's people, met together in a barn, and under the ministry of one who could hardly spell his name."

No small encouragement to humble workers! A hymn that has been an inexpressible blessing to mankind can be traced back to a poor, stumbling, illiterate speaker in a barn in a remote Irish hamlet.

Toplady entered Trinity College, Dublin, and during his undergraduate career seems to have written numerous small pieces of verse, which he published. Only one or two of the hundred and five are remembered to-day.

At his Ordination, in subscribing to the *Articles*, *Homilies*, and *Liturgy*, he wrote his signature five times, to show his hearty acceptance of them.

It was in Devonshire, as Vicar of Broad Hembury, that he spent most of his ministerial life, "passing rich on eighty pounds a year."

But he was delicate and sickly. His mind was too active for his body; the engine too powerful for the ship. Unable for duty, he removed to London, became associated with the Countess of Huntingdon as minister of Leicester Fields, and drew such multitudes, that not a fourth part of the people could be accommodated in the chapel. At times no fewer than thirteen hundred horses used by the worshippers were turned into adjoining fields.

But consumption soon laid him low again. During his illness he wrote and sent to Lady Huntingdon the piece—not a hymn, but a sacred poem—entitled "The Dying Believer to his Soul":—

> "Deathless principle, arise:
> Soar, thou native of the skies."

When near his end, he was told that his heart was beating weaker and weaker. He replied with a smile: "Why, that is a good sign that my death is fast approaching; and, blessed be God, I can add that my heart beats every day stronger and stronger for Glory."

"It will not be long before God takes me, for no mortal can live," said he, bursting into tears, "after the glories which God has manifested to my soul."

He was only thirty-eight when he died, just about a hundred years ago.

His hymns appeared first in the *Gospel Magazine*, a magazine which espoused the cause of Calvinism. For a time he was its editor. It was here that the hymn

> "Your harps, ye trembling saints,
> Down from the willows take,"

appeared under the heading "*Weak Believers encouraged.*" Also one entitled "*Happiness found:*"

> "Object of my first desire."

The first verse of the hymn, as Toplady wrote it, is never used in hymn books. It ran thus:—

> "Happiness, thou lovely name,
> Where thy seat, oh! tell me where?
> Learning, pleasure, wealth, and fame,
> All cry out, 'It is not here,'" etc.

A bitter controversy had arisen between Toplady the stern Calvinist and Wesley the Arminian. They flung angry, almost slanderous epithets at each other. Toplady was specially indignant at the doctrine of perfection supposed to be held by Wesley.

Curious that the most precious hymn ever written should bear a reference to this controversy, namely,

"Rock of Ages,"

which appeared under the title, "*A Living or Dying Prayer for the Holiest Believer in the World.*"

This was a sly hint that even the "holiest believer" —perfectionist or not—could and must be able to use the language of this hymn; no one too holy to employ it.

It is a curious bit of irony, and a strange commentary on that angry controversy, that this hymn is to be found in every Wesleyan hymn book to-day; and its authorship was even attributed to Charles Wesley—and this by an eminent Wesleyan, Richard Watson!

When Calvinists and Arminians come to pray or write hymns of devotion, it is impossible to tell which is Calvinist and which Arminian.

"Rock of Ages" might quite well have been written by C. Wesley, and "Jesus, Lover of my soul" by Toplady. Will not the voices of all Christians of all names blend just thus above in the grand chorus sung to the Lamb that was slain?

The editors of the *Sunday at Home* issued to their readers an invitation in their January number, 1887, to send lists of the hundred best hymns. In the May number the result was tabulated. Between three thousand four hundred and three thousand five hundred lists were received, and "Rock of

Ages" topped the poll with three thousand two hundred and fifteen votes. The second in favour was "Abide with me;" the third, "Jesus, Lover of my soul;" the fourth, "Just as I am," etc.; the fifth, "How sweet the name of Jesus sounds;" the sixth, "My God, my Father, while I stray."

We are not surprised that "Rock of Ages" should be the best-loved hymn in the language. It is not by any means the most perfect in poetical form; but it directs the heart at its most critical and most anxious hour, its most momentous experience. It certainly confuses metaphors, the "pierced side" changing to "the riven rock," which is at once a "hiding-place" and a "cleansing fountain." But few notice or care to remember these peccadilloes, for we love the hymn too dearly to pick tiny holes in its phraseology.

In Mr. Gladstone's Latin translation there is no phrase corresponding to "Rock of Ages," no corresponding metaphor:

"Jesus pro me perforatus
Condar intra tuum latus."

In the best and most recent Hymnals the hymn is given much as it was written: "riven" is retained (not "wounded" substituted); "Foul" (not "vile") "I to the fountain fly;" "When I soar through *tracts* unknown" (not "to worlds unknown"). The only alteration retained is in the line, "When my eyelids close in death," which originally read,

"When my *eyestrings* break in death,"—referring to an old idea that the eyestrings snapped when a person died. But there is reason for believing that the alteration was accepted by the author.

Curious that this hymn is the only one of Toplady's that appears among the favourite hundred voted by the readers of the *Sunday at Home* (May 1887), or is widely known and loved. He has had one hour of lofty illumination; but only one: one hymn, and that the best of all in the language!

One is pleased to remember that the respected Prince Consort, when on his deathbed, turned to this hymn, repeating it constantly. "For," said he, "if in this hour I had only my worldly honours and dignities to depend upon, I should be poor indeed."

Dr. Pomeroy tells that a few years ago, when in an Arminian Church at Constantinople, he observed many weeping as they sang, and found on inquiry that they were singing a translation of this hymn. It has been translated into many languages and dialects; lately into the language spoken round Lake Nyassa, by Dr. Laws, of the Livingstonia Mission.

2. Wesley.

Charles Wesley was born into a family or succession of hymn-writers. His father, the Rector of Epworth, was the author of various hymns. One of these, written on a piece of music, was rescued from the fire which destroyed the parsonage. The infant Charles was saved from the flames at the same time. He was born into an atmosphere of poetry and music.

He had a narrow escape—what his more famous brother called a "fair escape"—from being a man of wealth and rank. A rich namesake, a landed proprietor in Ireland who was without an heir, offered to adopt him. Although only a schoolboy at Westminster, young Wesley had a life-plan, and declined the proposal. A cousin was adopted in his stead, Richard Colley Wesley, whose son became an earl and the father of the Duke of Wellington, who changed Wesley into the older form of Wellesley.

Curious to think of the influence which young Charles Wesley's refusal of the heirship had upon the history of religion in England, upon the sacred song of the Church, and upon the military glory of Britain under the great Duke. Like Moses, he refused to be the heir of a landed proprietor, and chose to suffer hardships in the poor parsonage at home, and to win his way to spiritual usefulness.

He had a long and complete classical training; was nine years at Christ Church, Oxford; became a deft master of pure English; and so was being prepared for writing some of our richest and most classic hymns.

At Oxford he began a course of such systematic study, such scrupulous regularity in the use of his time, and in attendance at the services of the Church, that he was nicknamed "Methodist."

He became the centre of a small "Society" of

pious gownsmen. This "Godly Club" was soon joined by John Wesley, whose energy and generalship gave it a wider influence. These two were the Moses and Aaron of the movement afterwards called "The Methodist Revival."

But thus far neither had learnt the simple Gospel. They were intensely religious, but their religion was one of rigorous Churchism.

The brothers went on a mission to Georgia under the "Society for the Propagation of the Gospel." The life of Charles was attempted more than once, and his efforts proved a failure. In feeble health he returned to England, during his two months' voyage experiencing a terrible storm at sea. The impression left on his mind by this voyage led him to write, in later years, the hymn to be sung at sea:

> "Throughout the deep Thy footsteps shine,
> We own Thy way is in the sea,
> O'erawed by majesty divine,
> And lost in Thy immensity."

At home he met many of the godly aristocracy. He became tutor to Peter Böhler, a Moravian who was preparing to go as a missionary to Georgia. The tutor taught his pupil English, and the pupil taught his tutor a higher subject.

Wesley seemed once "on the point to die," and the Moravian asked him, "Do you hope to be saved?" Charles answered, "Yes." "For what reason do you hope it?" "Because I have used my best endeavours to serve God." In recounting the event Charles

Wesley says, "He shook his head and said no more. I thought him very uncharitable, saying in my heart: Would he rob me of my endeavours?" But that sad, silent, significant shake of the head shattered his confidence in his "endeavours." It was left to a "poor ignorant mechanic, who knows nothing but Christ," to teach him to hope, not in endeavours, but in the merits of a perfect Saviour.

Curious that Luther *On the Galatians* was the book which brought him most light. This again is the Apostolic Succession, the succession of world-wide influence.

It does not fall within the scope of the present sketch to tell of all his work as an evangelist, and as the founder of Methodist Societies. It is as a hymn-writer that we are now studying him.

Coleridge says of Luther: "He did as much for the Reformation by his hymns as by his translation of the Bible, for in Germany the hymns are known by heart by every peasant. They advise, they argue, from the hymns."

So Charles Wesley sang the Gospel into hundreds of hearts that would never have been touched by the preaching of his brother.

George Eliot in *Adam Bede* describes Seth Bede, the village Methodist, as driving away all his griefs and perplexities as he strode across the lonely Derbyshire moors, on a bright Sunday morning, by singing Wesley's "Morning Hymn:"

"Christ, Whose glory fills the skies.'

The same author describes another Methodist, Dinah Morris (in *Adam Bede*), as singing away her sorrows with another of Wesley's hymns:

> "Eternal Beam of light divine,
> Fountain of unexhausted love;
> In Whom the Father's glories shine
> Through earth beneath and Heaven above."

Wesley had learnt a system of shorthand, and usually dashed down his hymns in this shape at first, just as they came into his mind.

It was his habit to carry small cards in his pocket-book, on which he wrote down the lines of his hymns as they arose in his mind. Many of his verses upon Prayer and Communion were composed and jotted down immediately after leaving the Prayer Meeting and the Communion Table.

"Often would he get off his horse, throwing the reins loose to let the animal graze by the roadside, while he sat upon a stone-heap or a stile, and recorded in verse the 'experiences' through which his soul had passed in some little conventicle where he had been holding forth the Word of Life."

One of his hymns, not commonly sung, interprets a scene at Land's End. There the extreme projection of the land stands two hundred feet above the boiling, seething waters of the British Channel and the Atlantic:

> "Lo! on a narrow neck of land,
> Twixt two unbounded seas I stand."

The *motif* of his

> "Oh! for a thousand tongues to sing
> My dear Redeemer's praise,"

was to commemorate his own conversion. The keynote was probably given him by a remark of the Moravian missionary, Peter Böhler: "Had I a thousand tongues I would praise Him with them all."

Of his hymns some twenty-two are in common use. The most precious, and most famous, however, is:

> "Jesus, Lover of my soul."

The traditional origin of the hymn is that "Wesley was seated at his desk when a bird, pursued by a hawk, flew in at the open window. The baffled hawk did not dare to follow, and the poet took his pen and wrote this immortal song about Christ, the Refuge of the soul."

Few hymns have been such a comfort to the weary and dying as this. One could tell many stories connected with it.

Several years ago a ship was burned in the English Channel. Among the passengers were a father, mother, and their infant daughter. When the alarm of fire was given the family became separated in the confusion. The father was rescued and taken to Liverpool; but mother and child were carried overboard, drifted out of the Channel, the mother clinging to a fragment of the wreck, her little one clasped to her breast.

A vessel bound from Newport, Wales, to America, was moving slowly on her course. Their attention was called to the floating object: there was no ship within sight, and they thought it could not be a human being. But they sent a boat. As the boat approached the floating fragment, suddenly the sound of a gentle voice was borne on the breeze, and the sailors heard these words sung:

"Jesus, Lover of my soul."

Mother and child were rescued, were afterwards conveyed to America, where they found husband and father.

Another story is told, and, although evidently "cooked," may well have had something true to cook.

A party of Northern tourists formed part of a large company gathered on the deck of an excursion steamer, that was moving slowly down the historic Potomac one beautiful evening in the summer of 1881. A gentleman had been delighting the party with his happy rendering of many familiar hymns, the last being the petition, so dear to every loving heart, "Jesus, Lover of my soul."

The singer gave the first two verses with much feeling, and a peculiar emphasis upon the concluding lines that thrilled every heart. A hush had fallen upon the listeners, that was not broken for some seconds after the musical notes had died away.

Then a gentleman made his way from the outskirts

of the crowd to the side of the singer, and accosted him with, "Beg your pardon, sir, but were you actively engaged in the late war?"

"Yes, sir," the man of song answered courteously; "I fought under General Grant."

"Well," the first speaker continued, "I did my fighting on the other side, and think—indeed am quite sure—I was very near you one bright night eighteen years ago this very month. It was much such a night as this. If I am not mistaken, you were on guard-duty. We of the South had sharp business on hand. I crept near your post of duty, my weapon in my hand; the shadows hid me. Your beat led you into the clear light. As you paced back and forth you were humming the tune of the hymn you have just sung. I raised my gun and aimed at your heart,—and I had been selected by my commander for the work because I was a sure shot. Then out upon the night floated the words:

"'Cover my defenceless head
With the shadow of Thy wing.'

Your prayer was answered. I couldn't fire after that. And there was no attack made upon your camp that night. I felt sure, when I heard you singing this evening, that you were the man whose life I was spared from taking

The singer grasped the hand of the Southerner and said, with much emotion: "I remember the night very well, and distinctly the feeling of depression and loneliness with which I went forth to my duty. I knew my post was one of great danger. I paced my lonely beat, thinking of home and friends and all that life holds dear.

"Then the thought of God's care came to me with peculiar force, and I sang the prayer of my heart, and ceased to feel alone. How the prayer was answered I never knew until this evening. 'Jesus, Lover of my soul' has been a favourite hymn; now it will be inexpressibly dear."

IX.

OLNEY HYMNS.

1. COWPER.

FROM his early years he had been a sensitive plant, and in the loss of his mother—whose portrait was in after years the theme of one of his most pathetic poems—he lost that shelter which his tender, delicate nature needed.

Yet as a young man he was active, an excellent cricketer and football-player. He started the "Nonsense Club," and wrote ballads, some of which won wide popularity. One, in particular, became famous, *John Gilpin*, the story of "how he went farther than he intended, and came safe home again."

That ballad, with its wild, sportive delight in the comical, is as unlike the hymns he wrote, so full of conflict, as two things can be

But his sun suddenly became dark at noonday.

A morbid fancy seized him that he had sought a certain official's death; and the balance of his reason was upset. The account he gives in his *Autobiography* of these ghastly times is terrible reading. He tried to take his own life in various ways—by laudanum, cord, and knife. But every attempt failed; and he felt conscience-stricken, and an outcast from Divine mercy.

Under high professional skill he was slowly restored to mental health. He became filled with religious assurance and delight in God. "Sometimes a light surprises," etc., he sings in one of his hymns. At this stage there came a "clear shining after rain."

He had several delightful and lofty friendships— with Newton, the Unwins, Lady Hesketh—which form one of the loveliest stories in literature. How he and Newton came to live beside each other at Olney, and together wrote the *Olney Hymns*, must be told when Newton's record is given.

But, under the religious strain, and swaying between assurance and despair of his own salvation, his reason began to reel. He said, "The meshes of that fine network, the brain, are composed of such spinner's threads in me, that when a long thought finds its way into them, it buzzes and twangs and bustles about at such a rate as seems to threaten the whole contexture." Attempting his own life several times again, he was taken by Newton into his own home and tenderly cared for. So deep was his despair of God, and foreboding of eternal ruin, that, when "grace" was being said, he would purposely play with knife and fork to show he had no part in it.

Strange that he whose hymns have brought thousands such tender comfort and peace was a man subject to the most melancholy moods, the darkest gloom. Of Dante his contemporaries said, "There goes a man who has been in hell." The same might be said of Cowper. And it was probably just because he knew all the heart's worst experiences that he could put so powerfully in verse the conflicts and comforts of the Christian.

His hymns bear the marks of these conflicts, as in :

"Oh, for a closer walk with God;"

"Sometimes a light surprises."

The first signs of his recovery appeared one day when, in the usual course of his gardening, some trifle made him smile. "That is the first smile for sixteen months," said Newton. Gardening and carpentering gave him gentle employment.

Everyone knows about Cowper's hares, which a friend gave him, and the "Epitaph on a Hare" which he wrote. These, as well as some other animals and birds, helped to lift the gloom off his mind; and once more he became able to write.

Among his poems are "The Task," the "Progress of Error," "Truth;" forming some of the most exquisite gems of English literature.

For seven years he was comparatively cheerful. But a foreboding of another attack of insanity haunted him. In terror of the approaching gloom, he ordered, it is said, a postchaise, and told the coachman to drive him to the River Ouse, his intention being to drown himself in it. The night was very dark: the coachman mistook the road, and they found themselves unexpectedly back in front of Cowper's house again. This strange thwarting of his purpose so affected him that he went in and wrote those lines:

"God moves in a mysterious way."

This incident probably gave him hope that God had better things in store for him than a fresh attack:

"Ye fearful saints, fresh courage take;
The clouds ye so much dread
Are big with mercy, and shall break
In blessings on your head."

The hymn—

"Jesus, where'er Thy people meet"

was written upon the occasion of the removal of the prayer-meeting at Olney from its old scene to the "Great House." Emphasis is placed on "where'er."

When escaping from his blighting malady he paid a visit to Huntingdon. Finding himself a stranger among strangers, and dreading a return of his trouble, "he wandered away, strolling quietly through lanes and fields; alone, yet not alone, for God was with him. The scene was so peaceful and calm that its spirit entered into his own soul. Coming to a grassy knoll beneath a leafy canopy, he knelt down and poured out his heart in prayer and praise. Confidence in God came back again. On the following morning he went to church for the first time since his period of insanity.

"A worshipper, whose whole soul seemed thrown

into the praise of God in the Psalm which was being sung, attracted his attention. He says: 'I looked at him, and could not help saying in my heart, with much emotion, "The Lord bless you for praising Him Whom my soul loveth."'

"When the service was over he went back to the quiet spot where he had found joy on the previous day, and there again he felt that glorious Presence which giveth life."

This was the birthplace of the hymn, included in some books:—

> " Far from the world, O Lord, I flee,
>   From strife and tumult far,
>   From scenes where Satan wages still
>   His most successful war.
>
> " The calm retreat, the silent shade,
>   With prayer and praise agree ;
>   And seem by Thy sweet bounty made
>   For those who follow Thee."

His spirit was gentle, and could be playful when healthy; not unlike Charles Lamb in his pawky humour, which, however, was of a more religious tone. In his brighter and saner moments he was not gloomy, but a delightful companion. His life was as harmless and lovely "as the lilies he loved." He had the true poet's genius—genius akin to insanity.

Strange that he, who had been a minister of grace to thousands, died in despair, saying to all the assurances of friends: "You know it is false; spare,

spare me." Yes, here again, "God moves in a mysterious way." But no one, except the dying man himself, doubted that he was a true child of God, a true saint burdened with a constitutional malady. Some bad men die without horror: their calmness does not save them. Some good men die in fear: their fear does not destroy them.

Mrs. Browning's exquisite piece on "Cowper's Grave" touches a sympathetic chord in every heart:

"O Poets! from a maniac's tongue was poured the deathless singing.
O Christians! at your cross of hope, a hopeless hand was clinging.
O Men! this man in brotherhood, your weary paths beguiling,
Groaned inly while he taught you peace, and died while ye were smiling."

2. NEWTON.

John Newton's life was an eventful one, full of desperate deeds and hairbreadth 'scapes.

His mother, a devout, godly woman, had from his infancy dedicated him to the ministry. But she "died in faith, not having received the promise."

Following his father, young Newton became a sailor. But he was reckless and vicious, and "being his own enemy he seemed determined that no one should be his friend."

He was forced into naval service on board the

Harwich man-of-war, and flung virtue and religion to the winds.

His *Narrative*, from which we learn the facts of his history, depicts these years in the blackest colours. Perhaps the picture is overdrawn. Prodigals who have returned are always tempted to exaggerate the wickedness of their godless life. But when full allowance is made for such natural exaggeration, it is clear that his life was an abandoned and vicious one.

Yet he had conscience-stricken hours. In the uttermost parts of the sea, even there God's hand found and touched him. Though a scapegrace, he occasionally fasted and prayed and read his Bible. But these whims and superstitions did not last long. He turned to infidelity for a time. He delighted to talk virtue and to practise vice.

Not every infidel is a profligate by any means; but it is equally clear that profligates are glad to be infidels. The profligates of the world are a witness to Christianity, just because they do not like, cannot endure, its light cast upon their evil deeds.

He deserted, was caught, kept in irons, publicly whipped, and was degraded from the rank of midshipman. He was in consequence filled with bitter anger and despair.

By a mere accident—a midshipman having maliciously cut his hammock, and dropped him on the deck and injured him—he was exchanged on board a merchant vessel trading with the west coast of Africa.

It was here that he landed without anything but the

clothes on his back, became practically a white slave among black ones, and, like the prodigal, in hunger was glad almost of the swine-husks for food.

Newton was an instance of the common experience that men who are morally shipwrecks are intellectually clever, the ruins of great citizens. He amused himself in his semi-slavery by studying mathematics. He mastered Euclid, drawing the figures of the first six books on the sand.

His father sent out money to ransom him; but the master of the vessel who received the commission was told that Newton had gone far inland, and so took no further trouble about him. But in reality the semi-slave was not a mile off. Following his custom, he was walking along a narrow neck of land on the beach. He saw and hailed a passing vessel: it stopped: he took a canoe and went out to it. It was the very vessel whose captain carried the ransom for Newton's emancipation.

On the homeward voyage he was treated kindly by the captain, and having little to do, took up Thomas à Kempis.

An inventory of all the earnest minds that have been influenced by the *Imitatio* would contain many great and curious names. It would include George Eliot, and others who had lost their Christian faith, indeed many of the greatest thinkers and workers of these later centuries.

Newton was affected by it. "What if these things be true?" A storm arose; the ship seemed sinking and book and storm united to arouse his conscience. The hurricane passed, but while he had been at the wheel, steering at midnight, a crisis in his heart came, when his life of sin passed before him, and he began to pray and think wistfully of Christ, Whom he used to deride. This was the "Great Deliverance."

But light did not come all at once. He desired to change. He renounced swearing and other evil habits. But it was little more than an attempt to mend himself.

He made several voyages as a captain; purchased slaves, and sold them again in the West Indies. Curious what contradictory principles can live in the same mind! His conscience did not trouble him on the slave question. We sometimes wonder if there is any question on which *our* consciences are as yet as unenlightened.

He by-and-bye met a captain who taught him the true way of faith in Christ, and he became a sincere child of God.

Through a sudden attack of illness he was compelled to leave the sea, and became a tide-surveyor or ship-inspector at Liverpool; met Whitefield, Wesley, Wilberforce; occupied spare time in studying classics; applied for Ordination, and was refused by the Archbishop of York because of some formal irregularity.

But the Bishop of London ordained him, and he became the minister of Olney Parish. Thus the Providence that had so strangely watched over his life brought Newton and Cowper together. Living close beside each other, they were scarcely twelve hours apart. They were like David and Jonathan in their friendship.

Newton, while a man of the deepest piety, was too stern and ultra-Calvinistic a companion for the sensitive Cowper, and sometimes unintentionally increased his mental troubles.

From the time of his " great deliverance" he kept a diary, of which the following passage is the opening: "I dedicate unto Thee, most blessed God, this clean, unsullied book, and at the same time renew my tender of a foul, blotted, corrupt heart."

Together they held a prayer-meeting every week, and Newton proposed that they should unitedly write a volume of hymns, partly "for the promotion and comfort of sincere Christians," and partly as a memorial of their intimacy. Many of them were written for use in these weekly prayer-meetings. The volume was not published for eight years after it was begun. It appeared under the name of *Olney Hymns*, the place giving the title to the book.

Of the *Olney Hymns* Cowper composed about sixty-eight, Newton about two hundred and eighty. Many of these are quite unsuitable for public praise. In proportion to the number that each wrote, Cowper has far more that are held dear by Christian hearts everywhere.

Newton wrote one well-known prose work—*Cardiphonia*.

When fifty-four he became Rector of St. Mary Woolnoth, in Lombard Street, in the City of London. Here his ministry was much blessed; far more popular than in his former sphere in Buckinghamshire. Many flocked to Lombard Street to get their spiritual food from him. Here he died at the age of eighty-two. His epitaph was written by himself:

> "JOHN NEWTON, Clerk,
> Once an infidel and libertine,
> A servant of slaves in Africa,
> Was by the rich mercy of our Lord and Saviour
> Jesus Christ,
> Preserved, restored, pardoned,
> And appointed to preach the Faith
> He had long laboured to destroy,
> Near 16 years at Olney, in Bucks;
> And   years in this church."

He was certainly a brand plucked from the burning; his life a study in Providence; the change in his character a witness to the transforming power of grace; the hymns he has left among the most devout and simple, full of grace and truth.

Few of his hymns appear to be drawn from episodes in his career. One, not found in most Hymnals, beginning—

> "Saviour, visit Thy plantation,"

is clearly drawn from the time when he used to plant lime and lemon trees in Africa. If his hymns have not a special history, he himself has.

Another contains a biographical metaphor :

" Begone, unbelief,
  My Saviour is near,
And for my relief
  Will surely appear :
By prayer let me wrestle,
  And He will perform ;
With Christ in the vessel
  I smile at the storm."

X.

CLASSIC MISSIONARY HYMNS.

1. HEBER.

BISHOP HEBER, a native of Cheshire, entered Brasenose College, Oxford, just when this century began. His father was a clergyman both wealthy and scholarly, and his brother had collected a hundred and fifty thousand volumes in his library: both circumstances helping to foster in young Heber a literary taste. At seven he had versified Phædrus; and at Oxford he gained, in his first year, the prize for the best Latin poem, and, two years later, the prize for the best English poem ("Palestine"). This position of honour has often since then foretold literary fame.

His brilliant career won for him a scholarship, and then he began his travels on the Continent. The path to literary fame lay open to him, but he preferred to be a minister of Christ. On his return his brother gave him the living of Hodnet in Shropshire. He became Preacher at Lincoln's Inn and Bampton Lecturer, and author of various works in prose and poetry. In his parish work he devoted himself to the welfare of his people heedless of personal danger in times of epidemics.

Twice he was offered the Bishopric of Calcutta, and twice refused the responsibility. Asked for the third time, he accepted, and sailed in 1823, and was soon actively engaged in planting churches, and visiting and cheering missionaries. His travels he described in his *Journey through India*.

But his work lasted only three years. He returned one day from a Confirmation in a heated state, and soon after was found dead in his bath, an attack of apoplexy having cut him off at the age of forty-three.

He was thus a many-sided man: observant traveller, enthusiastic missionary, scholar, and author and poet.

Thackeray, in his *Four Georges*, writes of Heber thus: "We have spoken of a good soldier and good men of letters as specimens of English gentlemen of the age just past; may we not also speak of a good divine, and mention Reginald Heber as one of the best of English gentlemen? The charming poet, the happy possessor of all sorts of gifts and accomplishments—birth, wit, fame, high character, competence—he was the beloved parish priest in his own home of Hodnet, counselling the people in their troubles, advising them in their difficulties, kneeling often at their sick-beds at the hazard of his own life; where there was strife, the peacemaker; where there was want, the free giver.

"When the Indian Bishopric was offered him he refused at first, but after communing with himself (and committing his case to the quarter whither such pious men are wont to carry their doubts), he withdrew his refusal and prepared himself for his mission and to leave his beloved parish. 'Little children, love one another and forgive one another,' were the last sacred words he said to his weeping people. Like those other good men of whom we have spoken, love and duty were his life's aim. Happy he, happy they, who were so gloriously faithful to both."

He is most widely known and will be remembered longest as a hymn-writer.

His desire was, as he says in a prefatory note, to write hymns "for the Sundays and principal Holy Days of the year, connected in some degree with their particular Collects and Gospels, and designed to be sung between the Nicene Creed and the sermon." He was not able to finish his design, but he wrote in all fifty-seven pieces, and other authors were drawn upon after his death in order to complete the Christian year.

"Holy, holy, holy, Lord God Almighty,"

meant for Trinity Sunday, is one of the loftiest expressions of devout adoration. The tune "Nicæa" was expressly composed by Rev. J. B. Dykes for this hymn, and takes its name from the Council of Nice, at which the doctrine of the Trinity was affirmed against the Arians.

"From Greenland's icy mountains"

was written by Heber when he was on a visit to his father-in-law, the Dean of St. Asaph and Vicar of Wrexham. It was Whit Sunday, and a missionary collection in aid of the "Society for the Propagation of the Gospel" was to be taken. On the Saturday the Dean asked Heber to prepare some verses to be sung at the close of the Morning Service. Seated at the vicarage window he set to work, and at a heat composed this hymn, with the exception of the lines "Waft, waft, ye winds, His story." Not thinking it complete he returned to the window and added that verse. He would have added another stanza, but the Dean pleaded that anything more would mar the unity of the whole. The MS. was shown at the great Exhibition of 1851.

2. Montgomery.

James Montgomery, a native of Ayrshire, born over a century ago (1771), belonged to a Moravian family. Of Irish parentage, he was born in Scotland, and spent his life in England. He was educated at the Moravian Seminary at Fulneck, near Leeds. When twelve his parents left him at home to go as missionaries to the slaves of the West Indies, and there in a few years they died.

He refused to become a minister, and chose to be apprenticed as a chandler at Mirfield. Quitting this business, he came to the metropolis to seek his fortune in the fields of literature. At the age of sixteen he was a wanderer in the world. Disappointed, he joined the staff of a Sheffield paper, and, upon the departure of the editor, he took charge of it.

For writing what was considered a seditious libel he was twice sent to York Castle to prison. Here he found material for his first volume, *Prison Amusements: by Paul Positive*, which was issued soon after his release. He wrote stories, squibs, satires, and sonnets, which brought him local fame.

He now devoted himself to literature. Besides editing his paper, and contributing to *The Eclectic Review*, he wrote various volumes of poems. But, while his hymns are remembered, his more ambitious efforts are forgotten.

After conducting the *Sheffield Register* for twenty-five years he resigned his arduous duties; but his pen was never idle. A gift which had been made to him he generously used to re-establish the Moravian Mission in Tobago, which had been abandoned since his father died. It was thereafter known as the "Montgomery Station." He visited various towns to promote the cause of Missions.

Although so generous and missionary in spirit, he passed through, like Cowper, periods of deep despondency and spiritual gloom.

It was, no doubt, this wide experience of the sorrows of the soul that made him meet for the Master's use as a hymn-writer.

The Government—which at one time had put him in prison—cheered his later life by giving him a pension of

£150. In his quiet home, near Sheffield, he gathered a few chosen spirits around him, who were privileged to come in contact with his kindly nature, and listen to his simple and ardent conversation. On his death, in 1854, he received a public funeral.

Most of his hymns were written in the earlier part of his life—some of them in prison, like Bunyan's *Pilgrim's Progress* and Raleigh's *History*. In later years he had less facility in writing verse, although it was near the close that he wrote one of his most lofty pieces :

"For ever with the Lord."

He composed his verses, we are told, "very slowly and only by fits." He "lay in wait for his heart," to catch its highest emotions.

"When seriously ill and advanced in years, he once offered some of his hymns to his attending physician that they might be read aloud to him. But he became very much affected by them, saying that every one embodied some distinct experience, and adding that he hoped they might be profitable to others from this fact."

There is one piece which is sometimes designated a hymn, and even appears in certain books of praise; which, however, is unsuitable for use in public worship. It is the well-known and much-loved piece :

"Prayer is the soul's sincere desire,
Uttered or unexpressed."

Among Christian lyrics there are few things more pure and spiritual. The author has told us that he received more proofs of good having been done by these verses than by any other of his productions. One of its lines was fulfilled in his own experience, for he "entered heaven by prayer."

"O spirit of the living God,"

is one of his missionary hymns; also another, and more widely known, on the same subject:

" Hail to the Lord's Anointed,"

written in 1821, and printed privately as a leaflet for use in a congregation at Fulneck.

The author was addressing a great meeting in a church at Liverpool, and at the close he recited this hymn. Dr. Samuel Clarke, who was present, begged the loan of the MS. and printed it in his illustrious *Commentary* beside the seventy-second Psalm, of which it is a version.

" Sow in the morn thy seed,
At eve hold not thy hand."

Montgomery took a deep interest in the welfare of the young, and he wrote a new hymn for each Whit Monday gathering of the Sunday Schools of the town. Every year, for about twenty-five years, his hymn was sung by twenty thousand children. This is one of the number that he wrote for the Sunday School "Treat." It clearly refers to the "morn" of youth, and the seed sown then—the fruit to be gathered at the eve of life. Originally it consisted of seven stanzas.

" For ever with the Lord"

had, he said, brought more hearts comfort than any other of his verses except those on "Prayer." This hymn was the favourite of the late Earl Cairns, and was sung at his funeral services. As written, it consisted of twenty-one stanzas.

There is another hymn of his which had an interesting origin. In 1849 he received a well-merited honour when the Church Missionary Society, on the occasion of its Jubilee, asked him to write a missionary hymn, which was to be translated into all the languages in which the Gospel had been preached, and which was to be sung, and was sung, at the same time by Christians in all lands under Heaven. The hymn was

"The King of Glory we proclaim."

XI.

EVANGELICAL HYMNS.

1. CHARLOTTE ELLIOTT.

CHARLOTTE ELLIOTT was born at Brighton a century ago. One of her grandfathers was Henry Venn, of holy memory, author of *The Complete Duty of Man*, and honoured for his graces and gifts. The home and surroundings into which she was born were pious, cultured, musical, artistic, and happy.

From a comparatively early age she was a sufferer, and by-and-bye, when forty, became a helpless, incurable invalid.

Dr. Cæsar Malan, of Geneva, was on a visit at her father's house at Brighton, when he became acquainted with her case. He found her trying to work out her own righteousness, only looking to Christ to make up for her failures, unwilling to trust Him entirely. He is reported to have urged her: "Cut the cable; it will take too long to unloose it; cut it; it is a small loss; the wind blows and the ocean is before you—the Spirit of God and eternity."

His visit marked the turning-point in her life, and

his correspondence, carried on till his death in 1864, was a constant source of strength and comfort to her.

She was able to be moved about with care from one place to another, but Torquay, next to Brighton, was her home for the longest period. There she lived fourteen years, and there she wrote many of her hymns, in a harbour overlooking the beautiful bay of Torquay. It was not far off, across Tor Bay, at Brixham, that Lyte wrote his most exquisite lines, "Abide with me," etc.

The place of her birth was the place of her death, which occurred in 1871. Considering her chronic ill-health she attained a great age—eighty-two. She had been a martyr to pain and helpless feebleness for fifty years. Many of her hymns were written during times of suffering, and she seems to have found relief in thus giving poetic expression to her devotion and clinging faith. She says of her illness:

"He knows, and He alone, what it is day after day, hour after hour, to fight against bodily feelings of almost overpowering weakness, languor, and exhaustion, to resolve not to yield to slothfulness, depression, and instability, such as the body causes me to long to indulge, but to rise every morning, determined to take for my motto, 'If any man will come after Me, let him deny himself, and take up his cross daily, and follow Me.'"

But no one can write such verses as

"My God and Father, while I stray,"

without passing through the hot "furnace of living pain." He who would sit on the throne of honour must drink the cup she drank, and be baptized with her baptism of suffering.

In 1836 the *Invalid's Hymn Book* was published, and contained one hundred and fifteen pieces from Charlotte Elliott's pen, including the hymn we all know so well and love so sincerely,

"Just as I am."

It has led many to throw off all self-trust, has enabled others to take the decisive step, has put words into many lips by which the heart has been able to get the true resting-place. It is the actual language of faith. He who can *think* it as he says it is assuredly accepted.

The son-in-law of the poet Wordsworth wrote to her to thank her for her hymn, and to tell her what comfort it had given his wife, Wordsworth's daughter, on her dying bed. "When I first read it," he wrote, "I had no sooner finished than she said, very earnestly, 'That is the very thing for me.' At least ten times that day she asked me to repeat it, and every morning from that day until her decease, nearly two months later, the first thing she asked for was her hymn. 'Now my hymn,' she would say, and she would often repeat it after me, line for line, in the day and night."

Charlotte Elliott's doctor once brought her a leaflet on which this hymn was printed anonymously. "I know," he said, little guessing who was the author, "that this will please you." It pleased her in a way he had not intended, for it could not fail to be a delight to her to find to her surprise that her hymn had been printed, and was thus being circulated and prized.

"A little street waif once came to a New York city missionary, and held up a torn and dirty piece of paper. 'Please, sir,' said he, 'father sent me to get a clean paper like that.' Opening it, the missionary found it was a page leaflet, containing this hymn. He asked where she got it. 'We found it, sir, in sister's pocket after she died. She used to be always singing it while she was ill. Will you give us a clean one, sir? She wanted father to get a clean one and frame it.'"

In the *Sunday at Home* plebiscite, it stands fourth in favour—the first being "Rock of Ages," the second "Abide with me," the third "Jesus, Lover of my soul."

2. BONAR.

The Rev. Horatius Bonar, D.D., is the most prolific writer of first-rate hymns in the present century. He began composing sacred pieces before he was ordained, and has issued various volumes of verse, the best being *Hymns of Faith and Hope* in three series.

While minister at Kelso (1837-66), he did much to revive spiritual life in his country by his *Kelso Tracts*. In the same line he has even done better service in writing two little prose works, called *God's*

Way of Peace and *God's Way of Holiness*. The former is scarcely surpassed as a simple yet thoughtful guide for the heart in its search for peace with God. Christian workers would do well to possess a copy.

At the Disruption in 1843, he followed his old professor (Dr. Chalmers), and Dr. Guthrie in their secession. In 1866 he became minister of the "Chalmers Memorial" or Grange Free Church, Edinburgh, and has since been selected to be Moderator of the Free Church Assembly. In March 1888 his jubilee was celebrated, and in August 1889 he died.

His hymns appear to have no known history. In a courteous and kind reply to a letter of enquiry which the writer sent, his son says:

"There is no publication which contains any account of the history or circumstances connected with the origin of any of my father's hymns. Indeed, my father has kept no record himself of even their dates.

"His 'I lay my sins on Jesus,' about which you ask, was written more than fifty years ago, for the children of a Sabbath School of a Leith church where he was assistant. Some of his best known he wrote in railway trains; others, when sitting by the fireside at night."

Curious that until lately no hymns were sung in his own congregation. While they sang only the Metrical Psalms, Christians throughout the world were singing his hymns with delight.

3. RAY PALMER.

The Rev. Dr. Ray Palmer occupies the place of honour among American hymnists.

His great hymn was written when he was twenty-two years of age, a teacher in a ladies' school, and in training at Yale for the Congregational ministry.

He had been reading a short description in German, in two stanzas, of a suppliant before the Cross. He was struck by it, and made an English translation. He added four stanzas, telling what the suppliant was saying, and these stanzas form the present hymn.

He put the MS. in his pocket-book and forgot it. Two years after, Lowell Mason, the composer, met him and asked him if he had any hymns to contribute to his new hymn book. Palmer produced

> "My faith looks up to Thee,
> Thou Lamb of Calvary,
> Saviour Divine;"

and Lowell Mason begged for a copy. Together they went into a store (in Boston), where the composer took a copy of the young hymn-writer's lines, assuring him of future fame by means of them.

For this hymn, Dr. Mason wrote the well-known tune "Olivet," to which it is wedded.

Ray Palmer said of his production: "I gave form to what I felt by writing, with little effort, the stanzas. I recollect I wrote them with very tender emotion, and ended the last line with tears." Many have sung it as he wrote it.

He was pastor of a church at Albany, N.Y., for fifteen years, and afterwards of a church in New York City. He is described as "a wise teacher, and a simple-minded and devout Christian. He was a healthy, cheerful, buoyant man, loved by everybody who knew him."

> " Take me, O my Father, take me ;
> Take me, save me, through Thy Son ; "

and

> " Yield not to temptation,
> For yielding is sin ; "

are others taken from his considerable number of hymns.

4. Havergal.

Miss Frances Ridley Havergal belongs to our own generation, having died in 1879, at the age of forty-two.

The name of her father, the Rev. W. H. Havergal, is well known by his numerous chants and hymn tunes, as well as by his Cathedral Services and Sacred Songs. Of his tunes "Evan" and "Baca" are widely used.

At his vicarage at Astley, in Worcestershire, Miss Havergal spent the first nine years of her life, when her father removed to Worcester to be Rector of St. Nicholas, and Canon of Worcester Cathedral. She ripened early, and she died while in her prime.

At three she could read and at seven she "lisped

in numbers." Beginning in her school days, she frequently went to the Continent. Although delicate in health, she delighted to climb the Swiss mountains, and revelled in the glory of the white snow.

Early anxious, she was led to Christ by a much-loved school companion. Her life was a close walk with God. At a later stage she was enabled to enjoy what is technically called "the Rest of Faith," and her peace and pleasure in Christ were thereby multiplied.

She acquired languages with great facility. She was versed not only in French and German, but also in Latin and Greek and even Hebrew, and could read both Old and New Testaments in the original.

She had musical genius; could play through Handel and much of Mendelssohn and Beethoven without notes. She also composed much original work; many of her tunes being published in her *Songs of Grace and Glory* and *Loyal Responses*.

Four of her tunes are well known, namely "Hermas," to the words,

"Jesus, I will trust Thee,"

"Epenetus," "Patmos," and "Nymphas."

Her memory was singularly powerful. She knew by heart the whole of the New Testament, the Psalms and Isaiah, and in later years committed to memory the Minor Prophets.

She was equally active in Christian service, in work in Bible Classes, Young Women's Christian Associations, and numerous other Christian agencies.

Hundreds consulted her, personally and by post, on the concerns of the soul.

She wrote much, both in prose and verse. Of her little books in prose, perhaps the best known are *Kept for the Master's Use*, *Royal Commandments*, *The Royal Invitation*, *Swiss Letters*.

She does not profess to meet intellectual needs, or answer the deepest questions of life. She gives highly spiritual teaching in devout language. Some minds find her too mystical, too unhuman, too purely spiritual; others are led by her to a more perfect trust and a more constant joy in Christ.

When twenty-four she was contributing poems to *Good Words*, and thereafter she had applications for sacred pieces from numerous editors. The best known collections of her poems are: *The Ministry of Song*, *Under the Surface*, and *Under the Shadow*.

She could write hymns only when the inspiration came to her: she could not command it at will.

In a letter she says: "I have not had a single poem come to me for some time, till last night, when one shot into my mind. All my best have come in that way, Minerva fashion, full grown.

"One minute I have not the idea of writing anything, the next *I have* a poem; it is *mine;* I see it all, except laying out rhymes and metre, which is then easy work."

Again she says: "Writing is *praying* with me: for I never seem to write even a verse by myself; and feel like a little child writing; you know how a child would look up at every sentence and say, 'And what shall I say next?' That is just what I do. I ask at every line that He would give me, not merely thoughts and power, but also every *word*, even the very rhymes. I can never set myself to write verse. I believe my King suggests a thought, and whispers me a musical line or two, and then I look up and thank Him delightedly, and go on with it. That is how the hymns and poems come."

For five years the gift was suspended or unused; and again, after a long illness, she lost the power to write verse, but it was restored.

She was a frequent sufferer, and was exceptionally sensitive to pain. But her enjoyment of Christ's presence made her, like Paul, glory in her infirmities. She did not *submit to*, so much as *delight in*, what was God's will. Her own description was true of her feeling throughout: "'Thy will be done' is not a *sigh*, but only a *song*."

The sheets of MS. music for *Songs of Grace and Glory* had been prepared at a great cost of personal labour. Soon she heard that the publishers' premises had been burnt down, and the stereotypes of her musical edition destroyed. She sat down with perfect acquiescence, and did the work over again. It was a six months' task, but she took it joyfully as the Divine Will.

Her sufferings prepared her for writing many of her sacred pieces. She wrote only what her own life or heart taught. Hence she is subjective, personal, introspective, dealing with the experiences of the heart.

She died at Mumbles, near Swansea. When told of the approach of death she said, "If I am going, it is too good news to be true."

On her tombstone is carved, at her own request, her favourite text: "The blood of Jesus Christ, His Son, cleanseth us from all sin."

The hymn,

> "Golden harps are sounding,"

was written thus:

Visiting some friends, she walked to the boys' schoolroom, and, being very tired, she leaned against the playground wall, while a clerical friend went in. Returning in ten minutes he found her scribbling on an old envelope; and at his request she handed him the hymn, just pencilled, "Golden harps are sounding."

> "Tell it out among the heathen that the Lord is King! Tell it out! Tell it out!"

was written one day when she was unable to go to church. She had been following the service in the Prayer Book, and had read, "Tell it out among the heathen that the Lord is King." "I thought," she said, "what a splendid first line! and then words and music came rushing in to me. There, it's all written out: words, music, and harmonies complete." The tune usually sung to it, "Epenetus," is her own, the tune referred to.

Among others well known are:

> "I am trusting Thee, Lord Jesus;"
>
> "Jesus, Master, Whose I am;"
>
> "Jesus, Master, Whom I serve;"

and

> "Thy life was given for me,"

which as written began

> "I gave My life for thee"—

the change being made so that the worshipper might address Christ, instead of using words meant only for Christ's lips.

This hymn first appeared in *Good Words*, and was written in Germany, when she was only twenty-two years of age.

"She had come in weary, and had sat down opposite a picture with this motto. At once the lines flashed upon her, and she wrote them in pencil on a scrap of paper. Reading them over, they did not satisfy her. She tossed them into the fire, but they fell out untouched. Showing them some months after to her father, he encouraged her to preserve them, and he wrote the tune 'Baca' especially for them."

Count von Zinzendorf, the head of the Moravian body, said he was led to devote himself to God by the sight of a picture in a gallery at Dusseldorf—a picture of our Saviour crowned with thorns, with the writing above it:

> "All this have I done for Thee:
> What doest Thou for Me?'

Possibly it was some engraving of the same painting that Miss Havergal saw, and that gave rise to this hymn.

> "Take my life and let it be
> Consecrated, Lord, to Thee,"

was written while on a visit to a friend's house. There were ten members of the household, some not Christians, for whom she had long prayed; others Christians, but not able to rejoice in Christ. She prayed that God would give her all in the house. Her prayer was answered: all were blessed. And continuing the description of the event in a letter she says: "The last night of my visit I was too happy to sleep, and passed most of the night in praise and renewal of my own consecration, and these little couplets formed themselves and chimed in my heart one after another, till they finished with

> "Ever, only, all for Thee."

It was her practice to carry out literally the lines:

> "Take my voice, and let me sing
> Always, only, for my King."

She sang sacred pieces only. In this and in other things she overstrained duty. Yet we admire the intensity of her devotion and the thoughtful self-denial of her life.

XII.

OXFORD HYMNS.

1. NEWMAN.

JOHN HENRY NEWMAN has captivated the imagination of religious England more perhaps than any other living character. As the leader of the most important religious movement of the present century, as a pure and lofty personality, as a master of liquid and transparent English, and as a hymn-writer, he has received the admiring and reverent affection of Protestants and Catholics alike.

Born almost with the century (1801), a native of London, the son of a banker, Newman might have been seen, at the age of nine, playing in Bloomsbury with a boy of five, little Benjamin Disraeli.

As a child he was superstitious, used to cross himself in the dark (although in the midst of Protestant surroundings); read the *Arabian Nights* and wished they were true; and delighted in talismans and magical processes.

While in his teens he studied Church history, and learnt to regard the Pope as Antichrist; read *Scott's*

Commentary, and, as he said many years later, passed through a great change of heart as the result of reading it. Of this change, he said only in recent years, " I am still more certain than that I have hands and feet." To Scott " I almost owe my soul."

He went to Oxford and won a high place: met the men—Dr. Arnold, Whately, and others—who were at the time leading a movement towards a more liberal Christianity. But the bent of his mind was in an entirely different direction.

He had become a tutor at Oriel, and one of a circle of kindred spirits consisting of Keble, Pusey, and others. The story of this circle—their influence on each other, of the work they did, of the far-famed *Tracts for the Times* which they issued—is briefly told in connection with Keble's hymns.

Enough to say that *Tract XC.*, a proclamation reminding us as a landmark of Luther's *Theses*, was written by Newman; that it aimed to show that a clergyman might remain in the Church of England while holding many Roman Catholic doctrines, such as the Mass, Purgatory, Invocation of the Saints. *Tract XC.* plunged the author and his friends into a hot controversy, turned the widespread suspicion of the movement into open hostility to it. This tract had such an enormous circulation that the proceeds enabled him to purchase a valuable library.

It was condemned by the authorities, but he refused to retract. He consented, however, to stop its circulation.

He had been Incumbent of St. Mary's, Oxford, and held the chaplaincy of the Church at Littlemore, and from his pulpit preached sermons that left lasting impressions and influences on many of England's future thinkers, teachers, and writers. He was slowly drifting into Roman Catholicism, resigned his Oxford living in 1843 and retired to Littlemore, where he formed a Monastic Brotherhood. He had already retracted publicly all that in earlier years he had said against the Pope. The stories told of the cures and miracles which saints and sacred relics had wrought in mediæval times, he accepted without question.

In 1845 he only took the next natural and logical step when he joined the Church of Rome. Others —Hope Scott, Frederick Faber, two Wilberforces— followed him; and, although there was no secession of large numbers at the time such as formed the Free Church secession in Scotland two years earlier, Newman channelled a course into the Roman Church, and the stream of perverts has been flowing with steady volume ever since.

Since that time Newman's life has been spent mainly at Edgbaston, Birmingham. He there established a school for the sons of Roman Catholic gentry, and at a later period became Head of the Oratory of St. Philip Neri. He gathered round him a number of priests of kindred spirit, among whom was Edward Caswall, also a pervert from the Anglican Church, the author of

"Days and moments quickly flying,"

and translator of

"Jesus, the very thought of Thee" (Bernard of Clairvaux),

"When morning gilds the skies" (original unknown),

"The sun is sinking fast."

In 1879 Newman received the cardinal's hat.

His features are familiar: his keen, ascetic face, the furrows worn deep with thought and self-discipline. No one, whether Protestant or Romanist, but feels the charm of his character, of his clear intellect, of his simplicity of mind and earnestness of belief.

It is remarkable how wide the intellectual separation may be between members of the same family: J. H. Newman a cardinal, his brother, F. W. Newman, at the opposite pole of belief (or unbelief); Hurrell Froude a Tractarian, James A. Froude of undefined negative position; W. R. Bradlaugh a Christian evangelist, Charles Bradlaugh an infidel; George Eliot a Positivist, and her brother a Church of England clergyman.

One thinks of certain words of George Eliot in *Adam Bede:* "Family likeness has often a deep sadness in it. Nature, that great tragic dramatist, knits us together by bone and muscle, and divides us by the subtle web of our brain, blends yearning and repulsion, and ties us by our heartstrings to the beings that jar us at every movement. . . . We see eyes— ah! so like our mother's, averted from us in cold alienation."

Newman's great hymn,

"Lead, kindly Light, amid the encircling gloom,"

was written before he entered on the Tractarian

movement, while he was still a young man, and was only preparing for his life-work. It expresses his premonition and foreboding of a coming crisis.

He had visited the Continent, and was turning his face homeward, full of fierce thoughts and plans. But I had better quote his own account, given in his *Apologia*:

"I began to think I had a mission. When we took leave of Monsignore Wiseman, he had courteously expressed a wish that we might make a second visit to Rome. I said, with great gravity, 'We have a work to do in England.' I went down at once to Sicily, and the presentiment grew stronger. I struck into the middle of the island, and fell ill of a fever. My servant thought that I was dying, and begged for my last directions. I gave them as he wished, but I said, 'I shall not die.' I repeated, 'I shall not die, for I have not sinned against the light.' I never have been able to make out what I meant.

"I set sail for Palermo. Before starting I sat down on my bed, and began to sob bitterly. My servant, who had acted as my nurse, asked what ailed me. I could only answer, 'I have a work to do in England.'

"I was aching to get home, yet for want of a vessel I was kept at Palermo for three weeks. I began to visit the churches, and they calmed my impatience, though I did not attend any services. I knew nothing of the Presence of the Blessed Sacrament there. At last I got off in an orange boat bound for Marseilles. We were becalmed a whole week in the Straits of

Bonifacio. Then it was that I wrote the lines, 'Lead, kindly Light,' which have since become well known. I was writing verses the whole time of my passage."

The original title of this hymn was "The Pillar of Cloud," bearing the motto, "Unto the godly there ariseth up light in the darkness." It is the mirror of the man,—clear, intense, full of pure trust and open-eyed earnestness, as graceful in expression as it is lofty in conception.

He has since been asked to explain the last two lines:

> "And with the morn those angel faces smile,
> Which I have loved long since, and lost awhile."

He has replied that it is no part of a poet's duty to be interpreter of the feelings of years ago.

A fourth verse has been added by Bishop Bickersteth in the *Hymnal Companion*:

> "Meantime, along the narrow rugged way
> Thyself hast trod,
> Lead, Saviour, lead me home in childlike faith,
> Home to my God,
> To rest for ever after earthly strife,
> In the calm light of everlasting life."

This addition is not justified by any vital lack in the hymn as Newman wrote it.

2. FABER.

Frederick W. Faber belonged to Huguenot stock, one of his forefathers having fled from France on the revocation of the Edict of Nantes. At Calverley, in Yorkshire, in his grandfather's vicarage, the future hymn-writer was born in 1814.

At school at Harrow his mind was deeply influenced by Dr. Butler, and still more powerfully by Dr. Longley. He was still young when sorrow after sorrow fell upon him. Within four years he lost first his mother and then his father. He was taken in charge, however, by an elder brother.

From an early period he had displayed the poetic temperament, and while at Balliol College, Oxford, he wrote the University Prize Poem, on a congenial theme, "The Knights of St. John." Here he became a Fellow at the age of twenty-two, and formed some deep friendships. Among these was his intimacy with Sir Roundell Palmer (Lord Selborne), who in after years was to edit the *Book of Praise*.

The one great force at Oxford at the time was John Henry Newman, who was preaching at St. Mary's, and, with his comrades, issuing the *Tracts for the Times*. Faber's nature was one peculiarly liable to fall under such an influence. He became an ardent admirer, "an acolyth" of him, to use his own phrase, and threw himself enthusiastically into the Tractarian movement.

Then after taking Orders, he spent four years in a tour through Europe along with a pupil. Under the influence of the old cathedrals and churches, and of the Roman Catholic Fathers, whose works he studied, he drifted nearer and nearer to Rome.

After officiating for some time at Ambleside, where he made the acquaintance of Wordsworth, he returned to the Continent,* and twice he put on his hat to go to Collegio Inglese to abjure the Protestant faith. On each occasion he was prevented by some accident; and this he attributed to his "guardian angel," whom he fervently and constantly invoked. His anxiety on the subject was the cause of physical infirmities from which he suffered for the rest of his life.

Receiving from his College the living at Elton, he devoted himself with intense earnestness to the reformation of his parish. He found the people intemperate and wicked, and by his personal influence and preaching he led them into habits of thrift and decency.

Here he carried on highly Ritualistic practices. Numbers came to him to confession; others did penance.

One Sunday evening in 1845, he announced to his congregation that he must leave them, and next day he was received into the Roman Catholic Communion, being re-baptized under the name of St. Wilfrid. †

He was led to take this step, he tells us, thus: "He was called to administer the Sacrament of the Lord's Supper to a sick parishioner, when it occurred to him, and the conviction was irresistible, that he was not a priest, and that the Holy Sacrament was

---

* Bowden's *Life and Letters*.
† *Early Life*, by his brother.

nothing in his hands."* But beyond this we know little of his mental history at this period.

A band of eight young men, who had received instruction from him at Elton, followed him to Birmingham, where he founded a community.

In four years he removed to London to take charge of the Oratory of St. Philip Neri at Brompton, where he remained until his death in 1849.

Cardinal Wiseman wrote to him when on his deathbed, referring to his eminent services to the Church, when he said: "This is very kind; but no one knows better than I do that I have no merits of my own, and that my only hope and trust is in the sacrifice of my Saviour."

He was the author of numerous writings, but all are eclipsed by the hymns he left. The latest collection contained one hundred and fifty, corresponding to the number of the Psalms.

He tells us that they were written because there was no collection of hymns suitable for use in Roman Catholic churches and houses. They were meant to take that place among Romanists which the hymns of Cowper, Newton, and Wesley took among Protestants. They were not written mainly to be sung, but, as he tells us in the preface, for private spiritual reading. The majority of them are not suitable for public praise. They are poetic meditations, reflections; or they apostrophize saints and angels.

* *Early Life.*

Curious that Faber had no musical faculty, and yet wrote hymns such as:

"Hark, hark, my soul, angelic songs are swelling,"

which is full of music.

His hymns are divided into different sections, according to the subject treated. They cover the whole round of religious thought, dealing with God and His adorable character, the Trinity, the human life of our Lord at its different stages, the soul's life, and the Sacraments; and many more are devoted to the Virgin Mother, to St. Joseph, St. Michael, St. Raphael, etc., and to the Angels.

The majority, though not all, of his pieces introduce some Romanist idea. It is rare that any hymn of his can be adopted, in Protestant worship, entire and as it stands.

Some seven or eight of Faber's hymns are to be found in most collections, such as

"My God, how wonderful Thou art;"

"O come and mourn with me awhile;"

and

"O Paradise! O Paradise!"

Instead of

"Dear Jesus, ever at Thy side,"

Faber wrote "Dear Angel," addressing it to his guardian angel. His also is

"Sweet Saviour, bless us ere we go."

Faber's hymns are highly imaginative and emotional

They are not sober expressions of worship, but rapturous flights—as in " Angels, sing on, your faithful watches keeping."

In many instances his sentiments are too amorous, too sensuous, too gross, as in a realistic verse of " O come and mourn with me awhile : "

> " Come, take thy stand beneath the Cross,
> And let the Blood from out that Side
> Fall gently on thee drop by drop ;
> Jesus, our Love, is crucified."

Much that he says is neither sober sense nor scriptural truth. Yet his hymns help to expand the soul and fire imagination. We need all kinds, and his with the rest.

3. KEBLE.

John Keble did for the Tractarian movement, fifty years ago, what Charles Wesley did for the Evangelical Revival last century—sang it into the hearts of the people.

He had taken his degree at Oxford, had shown himself a brilliant scholar, and had received the honour of being appointed Examiner for three years; and at a later period became Professor of Poetry at his own University, and, after holding several curacies, became Rector of Hursley, near Winchester. Here he remained until his death in 1866.

He took a large share in originating the Anglo-Catholic, or Tractarian, movement. He had known the leaders of the Liberal Church movement, Arnold, Whately, and others; but their influence over him had been slight.

Hurrell Froude, brother of James A. Froude, introduced him to Newman. These three were joined by Pusey. Froude was gifted, brilliant, dashing, but still immature; he died while still a young man. Keble was a man of beautiful character, yet unconsciously narrow, not only devoted to the Church of England, but unable to see that there was any other Church. He had always been a High Anglo-Catholic.

He did much to encourage Newman. The first Sunday after Newman's return from the Mediterranean, so "full of fierce thoughts and plans," Keble preached the famous "Assize Sermon" on *National Apostasy*, which has been regarded by all as the first decided step in the movement. It was the fan applied to the smouldering fire in Newman and the rest. Soon they issued the *Tracts for the Times*, of which Keble wrote eight.

In course of a few years Keble and Newman parted; the latter to join the Church of Rome, the former to remain in the Anglican Church and follow the *via media*, the "middle path" of Anglo-Catholic Ritualism.

But apart from his famous "Assize Sermon," which flung down the gauntlet, and apart also from the influence he exerted on his comrades, his great contribution to the movement was his *Christian Year*.

The *Christian Year* contains sacred lyrics for each

Sunday and Holy Day in the year. It appeared in 1827, and the author gave consent to its publication only after great pressure from friends. Arnold said of them: "Nothing equal to them exists in our language." Coleridge and Whately also urged their publication. When they did appear they bore no author's name. They are the result of long labour, and as much polishing and revision as Gray put upon the *Elegy*. They are classical in their style, and form a household volume in every English-speaking country to-day. The ninetieth edition was revised by the author. In twenty-five years one hundred and eight thousand copies were issued. In 1873, when the copyright expired—forty-six years after its appearance—three hundred and five thousand five hundred copies had been sold. And since then the circulation of cheap issues has been enormous.

"It is a book," says Bishop Barry, "which leads the soul up to God, not through one but through all of the various faculties which He has implanted in it."

XIII.

HYMNS OF FOUR BROAD CHURCH DEANS.

1. DEAN STANLEY.

FROM Dean Stanley's biography of Dr. Arnold every one knows how as a boy at Rugby he came under the spell of its model head-master.

After a brilliant career at Oxford (Balliol) he became in succession a Canon of Canterbury Cathedral, Professor of Ecclesiastical History at Oxford, and finally Dean of Westminster.

There is a small MS. volume, says his successor, Dean Bradley, written in a boyish but, strange as it may appear to those who knew him later, a singularly clear hand. On the title-page are inscribed the words: POETICAL WORKS OF A. P. STANLEY, Vol. II. " Underneath is a drawing, his own handiwork, of Neptune in his chariot with Amphitrite, and the sea-nymphs sporting around." Some of his subjects are curious: Owls, Humming Birds, Superstition, Forgiveness, Death.

He was only ten or eleven years of age when he wrote the contents of this " Vol. II." They reveal greater originality than his Rugby pieces. His little study was soon named "The Poet's Corner."

He made the acquaintance of many lands and many men, travelled in Sinai and Palestine, and accompanied the Prince of Wales in his visit to Egypt and the Holy Land.

His broad sympathies, his scholarly tastes, his gentle and lovable character, won the homage of sceptic and believer alike.

> " He is gone—a cloud of light
> Has received Him from our sight "—

which, as written, ran

> " He is gone beyond the skies "—

a noble Ascension Hymn, was composed by Dean Stanley for the use of a private family, and first appeared in *Macmillan's Magazine*, where several of his hymns saw the light.

2. Dean Milman.

Milman's best known hymns appeared in Bishop Heber's hymn-book. They are: the majestic Palm Sunday hymn,

> " Ride on, ride on in majesty ; "

the hymn written for the lesson on the Widow of Nain—and hence the reference to "Jesus, Son of Mary "—

> " When our heads are bowed with woe ; "

and

> " O help us, Lord, each hour of need."

It was when Professor of Poetry at Oxford that he wrote his best hymns, and that he composed his great poem, *The Fall of Jerusalem.*

As a Broad Churchman, as the historian of the Jews, etc., as Dean of St. Paul's, but chiefly as a hymn-writer, his name will long remain honoured.

3. Dean Alford.

Dean Alford is known to scholars by his *Greek Testament,* but to the Christian Church at large as the writer of the jubilant and stirring Harvest Hymn:

> " Come, ye thankful people, come,
> Raise the song of Harvest-home;"

of the Christian battle-song:

> "' Forward' be our watchword,
> Steps and voices joined,"

the words and music of which were composed specially for a "Festival" of parochial choirs in the diocese of Canterbury.

His also is

> "Ten thousand times ten thousand,
> In sparkling raiment bright,"

which was sung at the churchyard at the Dean's funeral. The inscription carved on his tomb ran:

> "Deversorium viatoris proficientis
> Hierosolymam"—

" The inn of a pilgrim travelling to Jerusalem."

Many of his hymns were composed in the course of

his solitary walks around Canterbury. The tunes were generally selected, and some indeed composed, at the weekly meeting on Sunday evenings between himself and his coadjutor, Rev. R. Hake. His first object was to initiate and develop Congregational singing in his (Canterbury) Cathedral.

In his *Year of Praise*, a collection of hymns suited to the Church Year, he included several of his own.

4. Dean Plumptre.

The Dean of Wells wrote his fine Hospital Hymn,

"Thine arm, O Lord, in days of old,
Was strong to heal and save,"

for the chapel of King's College Hospital, London. Even finer is his

"O Light Whose beams illumine all
From twilight dawn to perfect day."

The author of *The Spirits in Prison* is a Broad Churchman, a liberal-minded expositor, as well as a reputable poet.

XIV.

HYMNS OF THREE BISHOPS.

1. Bishop Bickersteth.

DR. E. H. BICKERSTETH, for many years the Incumbent of Christ Church, Hampstead, became Bishop of Exeter in 1885.

His hymns he collected and published under the title *From Year to Year*. His most ambitious poetical effort is his *Yesterday, To-day, and Forever*.

As compiler of the *Hymnal Companion*, he had the opportunity—and unfortunately he seized it—of adding a fourth verse to Newman's "Lead, kindly Light." It was both a needless and a presumptuous addition, paralleled only by the Rev. A. T. Russell's addition of an Evangelical verse to "Nearer, my God, to Thee."

Several of Bickersteth's hymns are of the first order, strong, yet refined in tone and taste; for example:

"O God, the Rock of Ages,
    Who evermore hast been,"

founded on the Psalm of Moses (xc.); and

"Peace, perfect peace, in this dark world of sin?"

In their collected form, his hymns have been assigned to their proper Sundays in the Church Year. Two other hymn-writers followed the same method, Bishop Wordsworth and Dean Alford.

2. Bishop Wordsworth.

A nephew of the great Lake Poet, Dr. C. Wordsworth, late Bishop of Lincoln (not of St. Andrews), inherited some of his uncle's poetical gifts. Some of our richest hymns are from his hand, such as:

> "O Lord of heaven, and earth, and sea,
> To Thee all praise and glory be;
> How shall we show our love to Thee,
> Who givest all?"

which was written as an Offertory Hymn.

This is one of a hundred and twenty-seven hymns which he published under the title of *The Holy Year*, being sacred songs suitable for the Sundays and Holy Days of the Church Year. Under the text: "This is the day which the Lord hath made: we will rejoice and be glad in it," appeared the well-loved

> "O Day of rest and gladness!
> O Day of joy and light!"

In a more stirring strain he sings

> "See the Conqueror mounts in triumph,
> See the King in royal state."

Once Head-master at Harrow, finally Bishop of

Lincoln, he will be longest remembered by his *Commentary on the Old Testament* and by his hymns.

3. Bishop Walsham How.

The Bishop who won golden opinions in his diocese in the East End of London, now the Bishop of Wakefield, has also endeared himself to the Christian Church by such hymns as

> " For all the saints who from their labours rest,
> Who Thee by faith before the world confessed ; "

and

> " We give Thee but Thine own,
> Whate'er the gift may be."

"One day he is preaching in a theatre to the working classes : another day he is preaching before the British Association. And such is the fulness of his mind, the richness of his culture, and the wide range of his sympathies that he never fails to put himself in accord with his hearers!"

XV.

HYMNS OF THREE POET-VICARS.

1. MONSELL.

AN Irishman by birth, the Rev. Dr. J. S. B. Monsell spent most of his ministry as Vicar of Egham, and again of Guildford in Surrey.

"Many a time," says Edwin Hodder, "have I listened to the words of life from his lips. Standing there in the pulpit, with a small Bible in his hand, unencumbered with notes or sermon book, the preacher has held his audience spellbound, while in plain, simple language, yet full of tender poetic thought, he has told them the sweet story of eternal love."

His hymns are finding their way in larger numbers into the later hymnals. His best are:

"Worship the Lord in the beauty of holiness;"

"Lord of the living harvest,
That whitens o'er the plain;"

and

"Rest of the weary, Joy of the sad."

It may be interesting to readers to meet with a

piece, not adapted for public praise, but well adapted for nourishing the heart's life :

> "I asked for grace to lift me high
>   Above the world's depressing cares.
> God sent me sorrows. With a sigh
>   I said, 'He has not heard my prayers.'
>
> "I asked for light that I might see
>   My path along life's thorny road ;
> But clouds and darkness shadowed me
>   When I expected light from God.
>
> "I asked for peace that I might rest,
>   And think my sacred duties o'er ;
> When lo ! such horrors filled my breast
>   As I had never felt before.
>
> "'And oh!' I cried, 'can this be prayer,
>   Whose plaints the steadfast mountains move ;
> Can this be heaven's prevailing care ?
>   And oh ! my God, is this Thy love ?'
>
> "But soon I found that sorrow, worn
>   As duty's garment, strength supplies ;
> And out of darkness, meekly borne,
>   Unto the righteous light doth rise.
>
> "And soon I found that fears, which stirr'd
>   My startled soul God's will to do,
> On me more real peace conferr'd
>   Than in life's calm I ever knew."

2. ELLERTON.

The two best of the hymns of the Rev. John Ellerton, M.A., are evening meditations :

> "Saviour, again to Thy dear name we raise
>   With one accord our parting hymn of praise ; "

and
> "The day Thou gavest, Lord, is ended;
> The darkness falls at Thy behest."

Several others have eventide themes:

> "When the day of toil is done;"

> "Now the labourer's task is o'er;"

> "Our day of praise is done."

While a curate at Brighton, he had written some children's hymns for the use of his own Sunday schools and classes.

He became domestic chaplain to Lord Crewe, and took an active interest in the intellectual and social welfare of the artizans at Crewe. For some years he was Vice-president of the Mechanics' Institute, and himself taught several classes.

He succeeded in organizing one of the first choral associations in the Midlands, which has for many years met for its annual rehearsal at Nantwich.

> "Saviour, again to Thy dear name we raise,"

is one of several hymns that were specially written for the Annual Festival of the Crewe Parish Choir.

He is now Rector of White Roothing, Essex.

3. Stone.

The name of the author of two of our most precious hymns,

> "The Church's one foundation
> Is Jesus Christ her Lord;"

and
> "Weary of earth and laden with my sin,
> I look at heaven and long to enter in,"

will always be associated with Christian work in one of London's East End parishes.

When the father of the Rev. S. J. Stone, M.A., went to Haggerston, there was neither church, school, nor vicarage. Where now stands the hymn-writer's church was the receptacle of the rubbish of the neighbourhood. The total endowment of the parish brought in thirteen pounds per annum. But work of strong faith and unflagging self-devotion by father and son has made St. Paul's, Haggerston, a large and rich harvest-field.

The author of the above hymns laboured for eight years at Windsor before undertaking the burden of his father's East End parish.

His hymns were written, a series of twelve, on the topics of the Apostles' Creed. "*I believe in the Holy Catholic Church*" gave Mr. Stone the theme of

> "The Church's one foundation;"

"*I believe in the Forgiveness of Sins*" inspired the lines, so full of humility mastered by faith in the Divine Pity:

> "Weary of earth and laden with my sin."

The former was sung in connection with a Pan-Anglican Synod, by the whole procession of Church dignitaries and clergy as they entered St. Paul's Cathedral for worship.

Another hymn by the same author,
"O Jesus Christ, the righteous!"
was selected by Her Majesty the Queen, out of a large number of hymns specially written, to be sung at the Public Thanksgiving for the recovery of the Prince of Wales.

He may be classed as a High Churchman, but he is first of all, and in all his hymns, evangelical to the core.

XVI.

HYMNS OF AMERICAN POETS.

1. OLIVER WENDELL HOLMES.

IT is curious—unfortunately a surprise—to find the humorist of the *Breakfast Table* books also the author of hymns used in the solemn worship of God. The man who wrote *The Wonderful One Hoss Shay* also wrote these two deeply-devout hymns:

" Lord of all being, throned afar,
   Thy glory flames from sun and star;
   Centre and soul of every sphere,
   Yet to each loving heart how near!

" Our midnight is Thy smile withdrawn,
   Our noontide is Thy gracious dawn;
   Our rainbow arch Thy mercy's sign;
   All, save the clouds of sin, are Thine.

" Grant us Thy truth to make us free,
   And kindly hearts that burn for Thee,
   Till all Thy living altars claim
   One holy light, one heavenly flame,"

which appeared in the *Professor at the Breakfast Table;* and

> " O Love Divine, that stooped to share
> Our sharpest pang, our bitterest tear,
> On Thee we cast each earthborn care;
> We smile at pain when Thou art near."

Both are exquisite both as songs of sacred praise and as works of art.

His versatility is remarkable: professor of anatomy, novelist, essayist, poet, wit, humorist, and the best of talkers. His swift and half-serious, half-humorous analysis of character, his wise wit, his bristling, sparkling points, all captivate the reader. In the pages of his greatest contributions to literature, *The Autocrat*, *The Poet*, and *The Professor, at the Breakfast Table*, we are familiar with the figures of the " Young Man called John," Little Boston, the Schoolmistress, Iris, etc. These characters live, and amuse and instruct us.

His *Elsie Venner* is a study, in novel form, of the law of heredity—too full of points and side reflections to be popular in small lending libraries, but a mine to the thoughtful.

His books are rich in autobiography, in reminiscences of his early years—for example, of "his fears and fancies and superstitions; his first defeat in the moral battle of life; his first love; his first experience of death; the hush at sundown on Saturday evenings, when the crickets and the frogs alone broke the stillness of the Puritan Sabbath."

After the usual curriculum he left Harvard,

> " Armed with his dainty, ribbon-tied degree,
> Pleased and yet pensive, Exite and A.B."

He studied law, but only for a short time. The medical profession became his choice, and he perfected his studies in Paris, where, he thanks God, he "assisted at no scientific cruelties;" where he saw the little girl in her cot in the hospital, the story of whose cruel accident and thrushlike voice thrill the reader with emotion still, as the poor sufferer thrilled the young doctor then.

Dr. Holmes had experience of Puritanic training, such as has made him give many a "cut" at Calvinistic self-complacency. He has tolerance for most people, but not for the "moral bully," who with

". . . his acrid words,
Turns the sweet milk of kindness into curds."

But he is penetrated by a deep religious feeling, displayed in his hymns. He can still sing his *Hymn of Trust* in spite of Science, of which he is a master. He "believes more than some and less than others," and likes "those who believe more, better than those who believe less."

2. WHITTIER.

The Quaker Poet of America, J. G. Whittier, received his earliest inspirations from the songs of Burns, recited to him by a wandering Scotchman. This Scotch packman, says Whittier, "brought with him pins, needles, tape and cotton-thread for my mother; jack-knives, razors, and soap for my father; and verses of his own composing, coarsely printed and illustrated with rude woodcuts, for the delectation of the young branches of the family."

With his rich voice he threw young Whittier into raptures by his singing of "Bonnie Doon," "Highland Mary," and "Auld Lang Syne." His schoolmaster lent him his Burns. "This was about the first poetry I had ever read (with the exception of that of the Bible, of which I had been a close student), and they had a lasting influence upon me. I began to make rhymes myself, and to imagine stories and adventures."

After a time he sent a piece to a neighbouring paper, the *Free Press*, of which William Lloyd Garrison was the editor.

He was at work in the fields of his father's farm when he learned the fate of his first MS. He was assisting in repairing fences, when "the news-carrier stopped his horses, and, opening his bag, drew out a paper and threw it across to the lad, who, eagerly opening it, saw to his delight his own production in print in the " Poet's Corner."

" Some time after, in the summer, a visitor arrived in a carriage, and inquired for Whittier. He was hoeing in his father's cornfield, and immediately leaving his work he hurried in by the back door, and hastily making himself presentable by putting on shoes, waistcoat and coat, he appeared before Mr. Garrison. The young editor had come over to speak a few generous words to the young poet, and to advise him as to his future."

His father was next interviewed, and pressed

earnestly to provide education for a boy with such gifts. It seemed to the farmer that the editor was "putting notions" into the lad's head. But Garrison's words woke ambition in both father and son, and ere long it was decided that the young poet should go to school.

But there was no spare money for education. The way opened, however. "A friendly labourer on his father's farm, who used to spend his winter time in making ladies' shoes, offered to teach the youth his craft, which offer was eagerly accepted, and the following season Whittier earned money enough at the shoemaking to pay for a suit of clothes and his board and tuition for six months." So began his training for a literary life.

His home and surroundings were Puritan. *Uncle Tom's Cabin* appeared in the *Era*, an anti-slavery journal, to which he also became a frequent contributor. Here were published many of his ringing appeals on behalf of emancipation. Every one knows, or ought to know, his ode of triumph, his "LAUS DEO," on hearing the bells ring out upon the abolition of slavery:

> "It is done!
> Clang of bell and roar of gun
>   Send the tidings up and down.
> How the belfries rock and reel!
> How the great guns, peal on peal,
>   Fling the joy from town to town."

On reaching threescore years and ten, in 1877, a banquet of America's greatest citizens was given to him by the publishers of the *Atlantic Monthly*. Emerson,

Longfellow, Oliver Wendell Holmes, were present, and Mark Twain, Mrs. Stowe, and others joined in the celebration.

His hymns deserve a place in every hymnal, and some are admitted into the more recent collections. These are specimen verses :

> "Immortal Love, for ever full,
>   For ever flowing free,
> For ever shared, for ever whole,
>   A never ebbing sea.

> "Our Friend, our Brother and our Lord,
>   What may Thy service be?
> Nor name, nor form, nor ritual word,
>   But simply following Thee."

> "Dear Lord and Father of mankind,
>   Forgive our feverish ways!
> Reclothe us in our rightful mind:
>   In purer lives Thy service find,
>   In deeper reverence, praise."

The language is not drawn from the usual vocabulary of hymns, but do not our hymns need to be re-clothed in fresh phraseology?

3. BRYANT.

William Cullen Bryant, one of America's greatest poets, is the author also of some of America's most pure and finished hymns. A few of these have happily been included in our more recent Hymnals. One is— all are—worth quoting in full, and specially apposite to the great problems of social life now facing the Christian churches:

> "Look from Thy sphere of endless day,
>   O God of mercy and of might ;
>   In pity look on those who stray
>   Benighted in this land of light."

He is probably more extensively known by *Thanatopsis* than by any other of his numerous poems; and it was written when he was in his eighteenth or nineteenth year, although not published till he was twenty-one years of age. Strange that one so young should take Death as his theme:

> "All that tread
>   The globe are but a handful to the tribes
>   That slumber in its bosom."

Bryant has been in succession editor, journalist, and poet. For many years he conducted the New York *Evening Post*, an organ of the Democrats. Among his literary associates were Dana, Bancroft, and Willis.

The story of his baptism when over sixty has a simple beauty which reflects the man.

He had gone to Italy to spend the winter of 1858, and had settled down near Naples. There he met an old acquaintance, the Rev. R. C. Waterston, of Boston. In their rambles round Naples they were frequently together.

One day, says Curtis, his biographer, "after a long walk with his friend on the Bay of Naples, he spoke with softened heart of the new beauty that he felt in the old truth, and proposed to his friend to baptize him.

"With prayer, and hymn, and spiritual meditation, a little company of seven in a large upper room, as in the Christian story, partook of the Communion, and with his good, grey head bowed, William Cullen Bryant was baptized."

This was only a deepening of the religious life in him. He had always been devout, a Bible student and a strict moralist. But at this point the truth of Christianity was "born again" to him.

For eighteen years he was a worshipper in a Presbyterian Church near his home at Roslyn. It was at the request of his minister, Dr. Ely, that he wrote many of his hymns.

The ode sung at the Centennial International Exposition at Philadelphia was written by him.

At the close of the address delivered by Dr. Bellows on the occasion of his funeral, the company of mourners sang his own hymn:

> "Oh deem not they are blest alone
> Whose days a peaceful tenor keep;
> The Power Who pities man hath shown
> A blessing for the eyes that weep."

XVII.

HYMNS OF THREE FEMALE SINGERS.

1. ADELAIDE ANNE PROCTER.

FOR our most perfect songs, as well as for hymns, we are indebted to Adelaide Anne Procter, daughter of Barry Cornwall. In every drawing-room throughout the English-speaking world, mind and ear alike have been charmed by THE LOST CHORD and CLEANSING FIRES, while many have heard Sims Reeves sing THE REQUITAL.

Charles Dickens tells how she first entered upon authorship.

"In the spring of the year 1853 I observed, as conductor of *Household Words*, a short poem among the proffered contributions, very different, as I thought, from the shoals of verses perpetually setting through the office of such a periodical.

"She was one MISS MARY BERWICK, whom I had never heard of; and she was to be addressed by letter, if addressed at all, at a circulating library in the western district of London. Through this channel Miss Berwick was informed that her poem was accepted, and was invited to send another. She complied and became a regular and frequent contributor. Many letters passed between the journal and Miss Berwick, but Miss Berwick herself was never seen. . . .

"We settled somehow, to our complete satisfaction, that she was a governess in a family; that she went to Italy in that capacity and returned. We really knew nothing whatever of her, except that she was remarkably business-like, punctual, self-reliant, and reliable: so I suppose we insensibly invented the rest. . . .

"This went on until December 1854, when the Christmas number entitled *The Seven Poor Travellers* was sent to press. Happening to be going to dine that day with an old and dear friend, distinguished in literature as BARRY CORNWALL, I took with me an early proof of that number, and remarked, as I laid it on the drawing-room table, that it contained a very pretty poem written by a certain Miss Berwick.

"Next day brought me the disclosure that I had so spoken of the poem to the mother of its writer in its writer's presence; that the name had been assumed by Barry Cornwall's eldest daughter, MISS ADELAIDE ANNE PROCTER."

Dickens and Barry Cornwall had been friends of long standing, and she made the brave resolution: "If I send him, in my own name, verses that he does not honestly like, either it will be very painful to him to return them, or he will print them for papa's sake and not for their own. So I have made up my mind to take my chance fairly with the unknown volunteers."*

While still a child, living in her home in Bedford Square, London, she was proving her passion for poetry.

"I have before me a tiny album, made of small note-paper, into which her favourite passages were copied for her by her mother's hand before she herself could write. It looks as if she carried it about as another little girl might have carried a doll."

At twenty-six her religious fervour led her into the fold of the Roman Catholics. But her Christianity was not sectarian nor exclusive: her hymns display no denominational colour, and belong to the Church Universal. Unlike Faber's, it would be difficult to tell from Miss Procter's hymns to what communion she belonged. She spent herself now in visiting the sick, now in sheltering the homeless, and teaching the ignorant; and again, in rescuing those of her own sex who had strayed from virtue.

"Swift to sympathize and eager to relieve, she wrought at such designs with a flushed earnestness that disregarded season, weather, time of day or night, food, rest."

The strain soon told upon her constitution. "She lay upon her bed through fifteen months. In all that time her old cheerfulness never quitted her. She died

---

* Miss Procter's *Legends and Lyrics:* Introduction by Charles Dickens (2nd series),

in the arms of the mother who had copied her chosen verses, and passed away in peace saying: "It has come at last."

2. Jean Ingelow

is a story-teller now in prose and now in verse. A native of Ipswich (1828), her first production, published when she was twenty-two years of age, was *A Rhyming Chronicle*. She early came under the spell of Tennyson and Mrs. Browning. She is best in her narrative pieces, which have lyric form and moral aim. She is introspective and religious in tone, is a minute student of man's inner life and of nature's changing beauties.

Among her most successful novels is *Off the Skelligs*. One of her hymns has become part of our most recent public praise.

"And didst Thou leave the race that loved not Thee?"

3. Harriet Auber.

The story of the origin of Harriet Auber's

"Our blest Redeemer, ere He breathed
His tender, last farewell,"

is told by a writer who assumes the name "Eusebius":

"I happened to pay a visit some nine years since to old Daniel Sedgwick's out-of-the-way shop of hymn-literature, and while there met the late Rev. Dawson Campbell of Ware, Herts, an ardent lover of hymns, who, like myself, had gone to the little shop in Sun

Street in search of hymn-books. In the course of an interesting conversation he told me that he had for some time occupied the house at Hoddesdon, Herts, in which HARRIET AUBER had formerly lived. She had written her beautiful hymn,

> "'Our blest Redeemer, ere He breathed
> His tender, last farewell,'

on a pane of glass in one of the windows with a diamond; and when Mr. Campbell came into possession the pane of glass was still intact. Anxious to have it as a curiosity specially interesting to him, he asked permission of the landlord to remove the pane and put another in its place; but the landlord declined. And so, up to that time—seventeen years after the author's death—the valuable MS. of this sweet hymn remained in its old place.

"Mr. Campbell died, I believe, only a short while afterwards, and I have often wondered what became of that pane of glass—whether it still remains unbroken, or whether some child's elbow, or some street boy's ill-habit of stone-throwing, has made an end of it. Among all the curious forms in which hymn-writers have written their compositions, I fancy this is the only case on record of a hymn written by its author on a window-pane.

"This hymn is one of a number that she wrote for her *Spirit of the Psalms; or a Compressed Version of the Psalms*—a collection of sacred pieces by various writers.

XVIII.

LAST, BUT NOT LEAST.

1. T. T. LYNCH.

LIKE Spurgeon, T. T. Lynch was at one time an usher in a school. He was only twenty-three when he began to preach, gathering poor people together in small companies, but without abandoning his tutorial duties. After taking a short course of study at Highbury College, he undertook the pastorate of a dwindling Independent Church at Highgate. "There are here [Highgate] nightingales and cuckoos as many as one could wish; but Christians and Dissenters are by no means so plentiful." Resigning his dying charge, he ministered to a company of "scattered" and inquiring spirits, first in a small hired room in Mortimer Street, and afterwards in Grafton Street. Mornington Church, an iron building, now no longer a church, in Hampstead, was erected for him by his select admirers, and there he preached for nine years.

He was one of those men described by Henry Ward Beecher: " sharp, glittering swords that cut through the scabbards of the poor flesh holding them." He had strength for only one sermon on Sunday, although for years he wrote a second, which was read to the congregation in the evening by some friend. These sermons were published, after his death, under the half-playful title *Sermons for my Curates*. His congregation consisted mainly of scattered units, gathered from all quarters,—minds generally solitary or perplexed, unable to accept popular theology, and yet earnest and inquiring.

His spirit was singularly pure and devout, his mind independent, and yet intolerant of mere truth-hunting. So peculiar was he in personal appearance that when for the first time he rose at College to address his fellow-students, they greeted him with laughter. But in a few minutes he had them under the spell of his intense thought.

His hymns are gradually finding their way into books of praise. One is well known:

> " Gracious Spirit, dwell with me ;
> I myself would gracious be."

His hymns are connected with a theological controversy which, although almost forgotten now, thirty years ago kept the churches in a "down-grade" ferment.

They are all taken from *The Rivulet: Hymns for Heart and Voice*. Scarcely had they appeared when the *Morning Advertiser*—organ of the *Evangelicals* and the brewers!—fulminated its anathemas on the book.

"Nearly the whole of the hymns might have been written by a Deist, and a very large portion might be sung by a congregation of Freethinkers." Dr. Campbell, editor of the *British Banner*, took up the heresy hunt, banned the *Rivulet* as "Christless," as "deliberately contradicting the Word of God." It "might have been written by a man who had never seen a Bible,"—and so on *ad nauseam*.

A band of fifteen ministers published a protest against the fierce attack made on this delicate and unique spirit. Among his defenders were Thomas Binney, Baldwin Brown, and Newman Hall.

The attack drew from him *Songs Controversial* and *The Ethics of Quotation*, by *Silent Long*, containing poetical replies. The title-page of the latter bore the scathing sarcasm, so unlike his hymns:

> "Quote him to death! Quote him to death!
> Hit him and hear not a word that he saith;
> Shout and cry out, for this is the man
> Out of whose spirit the 'Rivulet' ran.
> What is his soul but a cauldron that brims
> Over and over with poisonous hymns?"

The controversy undermined his ever-feeble health, and laid him aside for a whole year; and no doubt hastened his death.

Twelve years after the first issue of the *Rivulet* he added sixty-seven new hymns to the book. "There came upon me about March, and stayed with me for some time, a spirit of hymn-writing, or rather making, for I

seldom compose verse in hand and paper before me."
"I am issuing a new edition of the *Rivulet* [1868]. Though the Thames has not yet been set on fire, this lesser stream [*Rivulet*] once blazed famously. It will not prove combustible now, I think; and nobody need either fear or loathe to drink of the river, unless he is very 'Egyptian'—that is, very Evangelical—indeed."

He died with these words, so expressive of the yearning of his soul, on his lips: "Now I am going to begin to live."

2. ADAMS.

Sarah Adams, although a Unitarian, has written one of our favourite hymns:

"Nearer, my God, to Thee."

It has been severely criticized because it leaves out all reference to Christ. This criticism is, however, a gun that kicks; for it applies equally to the Book of Esther, which contains no mention of God. But surely the latter reveals the finger of God, and the former the spirit of Christ. Not so thought the editors of the *Baptist Hymn Book*, for whom the Rev. A. J. Russell wrote a concluding verse:

"Christ alone beareth me
    Where Thou dost shine;
Joint-heir He maketh me
    Of the Divine.
In Christ my soul shall be
Nearest, my God, to Thee,
    Nearest to Thee."

Mr. Russell should also be engaged to compose a closing stanza for each of the Psalms; for the name of Christ is not mentioned in them. This addition of Mr. Russell's ranks with the stanza affixed by Bickersteth to Newman's "Lead, kindly Light."

Sarah Flower—afterwards Mrs. Adams—was one of two sisters of great literary and musical capacity. For the hymns of the one, the other sister, whose taste was musical, composed tunes. Thirteen of her Hymns were embodied in the *Hymns and Anthems*, compiled by her minister, who was also the founder of the *Westminster Review*.

Her husband was a London civil engineer of repute, who also possessed considerable literary skill. At her funeral at Harlow, Essex, in 1849, one of her own hymns—said to be

"He giveth sun, He giveth shower"—

was sung by the company of mourners.

3. PALGRAVE.

F. T. Palgrave, now Professor of Poetry at Oxford in succession to Professor Shairp, is a literary and art critic as much as a poet. For a time he acted as secretary to Earl Granville, but his tastes and genius are altogether literary. He has written *Essays on Art*, has made two selections of poetical gems—*The Golden Treasury* and *The Children's Treasury*.

His volumes of verse have all the classical grace of Greek poetry. They are characterized by symmetry and refinement, and an absence of fervent passion. His *Lyrical Dreams* and his *Idylls and Songs* are works of pure art.

His volume of *Hymns* reveals the same qualities of finish and form. We would name one hymn as almost perfect :

> " O Light of life, O Saviour dear,
> Before we sleep bow down Thine ear;
> Through dark and day, o'er land and sea,
> We have no other hope but Thee," etc.

One piece, named *The City of God,* contains two stanzas of beautiful Christian reflection :

> " Where'er the gentle heart
> Finds courage from above;
> Where'er the heart forsook
> Warms with the breath of love;
> Where faith bids fear depart,
> City of God, thou art.

> " Where in life's common ways
> With cheerful feet we go;
> When in His steps we tread
> Who trod the way of woe;
> Where He is in the heart,
> City of God, thou art.

XIX.

RETROSPECT.

THE Romance of the Hymnal is but half told. Very regretfully do we leave untouched the history of the early classic sacred poetry, pictured so exquisitely by George Macdonald in his *England's Antiphon;* the story of *Hymns Ancient and Modern* and Sir Henry Baker, Chairman of the famous "Forty" who compiled that most successful of all Hymnals; "*H. L. L.,*" *Hymns from the Land of Luther*, translated from the German by the two sisters Mrs. Findlater and Miss J. Borthwick; the Fatherless Hymns; and the various versions of the Psalms and Paraphrases. Other names remain: our old friends Josiah Conder, Anne Steele, Olivers, Perronet, Kelly, Robinson; the "saintly" McCheyne, Monod, and Burns; two knights, Sir John Bowring, a Unitarian, and Sir R. Grant.

These, too, have been ministers of grace to our spirits; and we place them in the Legion of Honour of the Christian Church.

PART III.

SOME MODERN HYMN-TUNE COMPOSERS.

BY

F. G. EDWARDS,
Author of "United Praise."

*The fineness which a hymn or psalm affords
Is when the soul unto the lines accords."*
                                   GEORGE HERBERT.

SOME MODERN HYMN-TUNE COMPOSERS.

1. Dr. H. J. Gauntlett.
2. Henry Smart.
3. Dr. E. J. Hopkins.
4. Rev. J. B. Dykes, Mus. Doc.
5. Dr. W. H. Monk.
6. Sir John Stainer.
7. Sir Arthur Sullivan.
8. Mr. Joseph Barnby.

> "The Father spake! In grand reverberations
>   Through space rolled on the mighty music tide;
> While to its low, majestic modulations,
>   The clouds of chaos slowly swept aside.
>
>   *   *   *   *   *
>
> "And wheresoever, in His rich creation,
>   Sweet music breathes—in wave, or bird, or soul—
> 'Tis but the faint and far reverberation
>   Of that great tune to which the planets roll!"
>
> FRANCES S. OSGOOD.

DR. H. J. GAUNTLETT.
1806—1876.

THE period of time intervening between the above dates is one of great interest in the history of English psalmody. In the early part of the century hymn singing, especially in the Established Church, was chiefly confined to metrical versions of the Psalms, sung to tunes crowded with twists, turns, and passing notes, and having repeats which often occasioned more humour than devotion. Readers of George Eliot's *Scenes of Clerical Life*, and Washington Irving's *Sketch Book*, will remember how vividly these delightful authors describe the performances of village choirs in days gone by. The following extract from *Fraser's Magazine*, September 1860, is very droll and highly descriptive:

"The particular choir in our own church we recollect well to this day, and some of their most striking tunes. We used to listen with mingled awe and admiration to the performance of the 18th Psalm in particular. Take two lines as an illustration of their style :

'And snatched me from the furious rage
Of threatening waves that proudly swelled.'

The words, 'and snatched me from,' were repeated severally by the trebles, the altos, the tenors, and the bass voices; then all together sang the words two or three times over; in like manner did they toss and tumble over 'the furious rage,' apparently enjoying the whirligig scurrying of their fugues, like so many kittens chasing their own tails, till at length, after they had torn and worried that single line, even to the exhaustion of the most powerful lungs—after a very red-faced bass, who kept the village inn, had become perceptibly apoplectic about the eyes, and the bassoon was evidently blown, and a tall, thin man, with a long nose, which was his principal vocal organ, and who sang tenor, was getting out of wind—they all, clarionet, bassoon, violoncello, the red-faced man, the tall tenor, and the rest, rushed pell-mell into 'the waves that proudly swelled.' We have not forgotten the importance with which they used to walk up the church path in a body with their instruments after this effort; and our childish fancy revelled in the impression that, after the clergyman, and the Duke of Wellington, who had won the battle of Waterloo a few years before, these singers were the most notable public characters in being."

In town churches the singing, what little there was of it, was mostly confined to the caterwaulings of a few charity children seated around the organ. Charles Dickens, who certainly kept his eyes and ears open, refers to psalmody as if it were only a concern of the charity children. In his *Sketches by Boz* (published in 1836), Captain Purday

"finds fault with the sermon every Sunday; says that the organist ought to be ashamed of himself; offers to back himself for any amount to sing the psalms better than all the children put together, male or female."

No wonder that loud cries of reform came from both pulpit and pew; and, although the Oxford Tractarian Movement is generally credited with being the force which impelled the necessary changes, yet other earnest workers had already begun to sow the seeds of reform, foremost amongst them being the subject of our sketch.

Henry John Gauntlett, the son of a clergyman, was born at Wellington, Shropshire, in 1806. His father shortly afterwards became vicar of Olney, Buckinghamshire, and four of his sons were successively organists of his church—Henry taking the duties at the early age of nine. When he was sixteen, young Gauntlett conducted a performance of the *Messiah*, for which he had copied all the parts with his own hand, and rehearsed all the performers. His father elected to bring him up to the law, and in his twentieth year he was articled to a London solicitor. He practised till 1844, when he relinquished the law and adopted music as his profession.

He studied the organ under "Old Sam" Wesley, but soon became so proficient that Wesley passed the lesson hour in playing to his pupil instead of listening to him. He was organist of St. Olave's, Southwark (1827); Christ Church, Newgate Street; Union Chapel, Islington (1852-61); and St. Bartholomew-the-Less, Smithfield. The high reputation which Dr. Allon's chapel deservedly enjoys for congregational singing is largely due to Dr. Gauntlett's exertions during the thirteen years he directed the musical portion of the services there.

In 1842 he was nominated organist to the King of Hanover; and in the same year received the degree of Doctor of Music from the Archbishop of Canterbury.

The degree had not been conferred by the Archbishop for two hundred years, and Gauntlett was the second recipient of it, the first being Dr. John Blow.

Dr. Gauntlett was a remarkable man in many respects. Mendelssohn said of him, "His literary attainments, his knowledge of the history of music, his acquaintance with acoustical laws, his marvellous memory, his philosophical turn of mind, as well as his practical experience, rendered him one of the most remarkable professors of the age." He was very intimate with Mendelssohn, who specially selected him to play the organ at the production of *Elijah* at Birmingham in 1846, an honour which many an organist might covet. Mendelssohn at that time had written no organ part, so Gauntlett had the anxious task of playing from a full score. In one place he introduced the organ where Mendelssohn had not so intended. "When you began to play in ———," said Mendelssohn to him afterwards, "I ran cold all down my back! I did not intend to have any organ there, but the effect is so fine I shall put it in."

Dr. Gauntlett's life-work may be divided into three portions: his literary work; his introduction of the C or German compass to English organs; and that which was the crowning ambition of his life, the improvement of congregational singing in the churches and chapels of the land.

His literary powers were of no mean order. He had a strong, vigorous style, and expressed his opinions fearlessly. He was full of learning, common-sense, vehemence, and dogmatism. But in pressing his strong opinions he sometimes, no doubt unconsciously, offended delicate susceptibilities, and thus made enemies. He was one of the earliest champions of Beethoven in this country. He was a warm admirer of Bach, whose intense Protestant feeling was doubtless one of the attractions which early led Gauntlett to a study of that master, the fibre of whose choral songs he worked up in his own psalmody.

Dr. Gauntlett was, in his day, an organist of high attainments. He was probably the first advocate in this country for the German system of organ-building, in which the compass of the instrument was altered and extended from G to C, so as to correspond with the orchestral bass. Like most reformers, he encountered the strongest opposition, but finding a valuable auxiliary in William Hill, the organ-builder, he attained his aim, and through his exertions the C organ was firmly established in England. He superintended the construction and re-construction (on his plans) of the organs in Christ Church, Newgate Street; St. Peter's, Cornhill; St. Olave's, Southwark; Dr. Raffles's church, in Liverpool; and the Birmingham Town Hall. It was in reference to the organs of St. Peter's and Christ Church that Mendelssohn made his well-known observation, that "but for him" [Gauntlett] "I should have had no organ to play upon. He ought to have a statue." In 1851 he took out a patent for applying electric or magnetic action to the organ; and proposed a scheme whereby three or four large organs should be erected in different parts of the Crystal Palace, and all be played at the same time from one keyboard by means of electricity; but the proposal was never carried out, owing to its great expense.

Few musicians have done more for church music in England than Dr. Gauntlett, so far as regards hymn-tunes. For the last forty years of his life he was engaged in composing, editing, and publishing psalm-tunes, chants, and anthems; and there is hardly an important collection of church music published within that time, in the preparation of which he was not concerned either as editor or contributor. It is not too much to say that his wide experience, his finished taste, his unceasing and unwearied industry, have assisted in raising English metrical music for public worship to a high rank in Christian song.

Amongst the more important of his works may be named *The Church Hymn and Tune-book* (edited in conjunction with the Rev. W. J. Blew), a model afterwards copied by the compilers of *Hymns Ancient and Modern*, and subsequent hymnals; the *Comprehensive Tune-book*; the *Hallelujah* (with the Rev. J. J. Waite); *The Congregational Psalmist* (with the Rev. Dr. Allon); *Hymns for Little Children*, etc. He also edited the *Church Musician* (a periodical); the *Prayer-book Noted;* a Gregorian, a Cathedral, and a Bible Psalter. A comparison of the above tune-books with those which preceded them will show how much church music is indebted to Dr. Gauntlett for the present style of four-part harmonies, and the exchange of noble simplicity for the shakes, graces, and turns of the old tunes.

It is as a composer of hymn-tunes that Dr. Gauntlett will be best remembered hereafter. He was a most prolific composer. He once said that he thought he must have written "thousands of tunes." He would write a tune while sitting at the table with the same ease as that with which most people pen a letter. Some of his tunes were not written to the words commonly associated with them. For instance, " St. Alphege," sung to hymns of such opposite sentiments as " Brief life is here our portion," and " The voice that breathed o'er Eden," was written for a hymn beginning, "The hymn of glory sing we." This tune (" St. Alphege ") he wrote at the dinner-table while a messenger was waiting, as the proper tune for the hymn had been mislaid or was wanting. Pushing his plate on one side, he said, " Give me some paper," and in a minute or two the well-known tune was written. Another tune, " St. Albinus," was likewise not composed for the words " Jesus lives ; no longer now," etc., usually sung to it. " Angels to our jubilee " was the first line of the hymn for which the tune was written ; and in its original form the tune has the *fifth* note dotted instead of the third, as in some hymnals. His charming tune " Irby," to "Once in royal David's city," a great favourite with children, was originally written as a melody with accompaniment, and not in four parts.

On February 21st, 1876, Dr. Gauntlett, at his house

at Kensington, closed his useful and laborious life. On the morning of his death he wrote seven hymn-tunes before breakfast. On returning from his afternoon walk he sat down in his study, and passed away quietly and very suddenly. The reform of the music of the sanctuary was his unceasing work till the very hour that the Master called him.

HENRY SMART.

1813—1879.

THE name of Henry Smart is well known wherever English hymns are sung. Though his tunes are fewer in number, they almost, if not quite, equal in popularity those by Sullivan and Dykes, and they may be fitly classed as favourites in our "service of praise."

Henry Smart, the son of a musician, was born in London, October 26th, 1813. His uncle was Sir George Smart, a celebrated musician and conductor in his day (also composer to the Chapel Royal), who gave lessons in singing until he was past eighty years of age. As a boy, Henry was passionately fond of engineering, and would spend his half-holidays in rambling through the workshops of organ builders, and of Maudsley's, the well-known engineers. His mechanical drawings at the age of twelve were remarkable, and had means been forthcoming, there is little doubt that our composer would have become an eminent engineer instead of a distinguished musician. Upon declining a commission in the Indian army, he was articled to a solicitor, sorely against his will. After having served four years of his time he learnt enough of law to discover that his articles were informal, not having been properly witnessed, and, greatly to his mother's dismay, he said, " I took up law to please my *relations*, and now I'll leave it to please *myself*." He had extraordinary natural faculties for music, and was to a great extent self-taught. Organ-playing soon became his constant passion, and no scheme of life found favour with him which did not include this fascinating pursuit. His first organ appointment, at the parish church of Blackburn, Lancashire, he obtained at the age of eighteen, by which time he had already become an organist above the average. Pupils soon came to him, but he felt that he himself had much to learn. Late on winter nights he would remain shut up in the church, mastering the difficulties of his instrument, while doubtless the poor blower often wished him in bed. He took a fancy to learning the violin, but the self-inflicted tortures of the scales were too much for him, and in a fit of anguish he threw the unlucky fiddle on the ground and stamped it to pieces. His musical services were often in request for Churches of all communions. Once he conducted Beethoven's Mass in C for the Roman Catholics entirely from memory, *without a copy*, as the score was unaccountably missing. For a missionary meeting of Nonconformists he wrote his beautiful hymn-tune "Lancashire." He trained his own choir to sing *entirely* from memory, as he considered the singers were much more reliable when unencumbered with printed parts.

In 1836 (aged twenty-three), Smart left Blackburn for London. He was organist first of St. Philip's, Regent Street (1836-44), then of St. Luke's, Old Street, City (1844-64), after competition, the judges being Messrs. Turle, Goss, and Topliff. In 1864 he became organist of St. Pancras Church, which appointment he held till his death.

Smart's was a busy life, but, as he kept no diary, and as little of his correspondence has been preserved, the materials for detailed incidents are of the scantiest description. His time was almost entirely occupied with composing and his church duties. He was a great *connoisseur* of organs, for which his musical instincts and engineering proclivities specially qualified him. He was often consulted about, and had much to do with, the planning and erection of organs. To a large extent he drew up the specifications of the large organs in Leeds Town Hall, the City Hall and St. Andrew's Hall in Glasgow. He personally superintended the erection of the last named instrument in every detail, although he was quite blind at the time. He was very severe in his criticism, and fearlessly outspoken in his opinions. Some of the congregation of a chapel in Leeds repeatedly pressed Smart to go and try their (as they thought) " beautiful instrument," and after some persuasion he went. He did not seem to like the flue work, but when he got to the reeds, he uttered a very significant " Bah ! " One of the company said, " Now, Mr. Smart, those are fine reeds, I think," whereupon Smart replied, " Fine, indeed ! are they ? The only sort of sounds I can liken them to is what I have heard in cottages when they're *frying sausages!*"

At an early age our composer suffered from defective eyesight, which became worse until he ultimately lost it altogether. He was therefore obliged to dictate all his compositions to an amanuensis, and it may be readily imagined how severely trying this mode of expressing his thoughts must have been to a sensitive and highly-strung temperament. But his good daughter, Clara, cheered and encouraged him. She devoted herself heart and soul to his interests and work, and spared no pains in writing down every detail of his compositions from his dictation. With ordinary songs, etc., his plan was to have the words read over to him two or three times—they were then firmly fixed in his memory; he would then go to his "den," as he termed his little study, light his pipe, pace up and down the room, or go into the garden, and return to play the piece over on the piano. Calling for his daughter to get out music-paper, pen, and ink, he would proceed at once to dictate the thoughts which were in his mind. The process was very plain and intelligible, though painfully slow. For instance, he would proceed thus :—

"Symphony to a song, key G with one sharp; treble and bass clefs, $\frac{3}{4}$ time; treble, crotchet chord, tail up, D and B below the lines; two quavers, tails up, bound together; G second line, B above; bar. Crotchet, A second space, E below, C below. Two quavers, tails up, bound together; E first line, A second line," and so on, and the result would be

All this trouble just for two bars in the treble only, without bass; but when, instead of a song or organ piece, it came to be an oratorio, written in full score for a large orchestra, solos, chorus, and organ, the wonder is increased, and the labour appears to be altogether herculean.

Smart's vocal music is characterised by freshness of melody and purity of part writing, and is invariably interesting. Although he wrote cantatas and a large number of songs, etc., he is chiefly known by his church and organ music, in which he happily combines the ancient, or strict style, with modern harmonies and modes of musical expression. There is probably no Te Deum more popular than "Smart in F"; and when we consider its grandeur, pathos, and depth of expression, it is no wonder that singers and hearers are thrilled at the soul-stirring strains of this noble setting of the grand Ambrosian hymn. Among many tunes that Smart contributed to various hymnals the following may be considered favourites in "quires and places where they sing": "Heathlands," "Lancashire," "Northumberland," "Regent Square," "St. Leonard," and "Pilgrims"; the last-named is not only the best known, but is a fine specimen of the modern hymn tune with simple harmonies. It is set to Faber's "Hark, hark my soul, angelic songs are swelling," and no other tune suits the words nearly so well.

Space will not admit of detailed reference to Smart's organ music. Suffice it to say that it is the delight of every organist worthy of the name, and that it invariably gives pleasure to those who can appreciate tuneful yet good music when they hear it.

Before closing this brief notice of Smart's life, some reference should be made to his opinions and practices in connection with church music and congregational singing. Smart preferred the old word "Psalmody" to the more modern term "Hymnody," and the stately, dignified, "measured beat and slow" movement of the old psalm tunes was more to his taste than were the more effeminate productions of modern times. Nothing puerile or childish ever met with his approval. "The tunes," he used to say, "which find the most favour nowadays are those which best please the ladies; and the ladies, I hold, are *not* the best judges of what is sound and good in psalmody."

He had no sympathy with Ritualism, and detested Gregorians in any shape or form. On one occasion he met a young high-church curate at dinner who was an enthusiastic admirer of the Gregorian tones. The curate dogmatised too much on the subject to please Smart, who lost his temper entirely. Raising his fine, stalwart figure to its full height, Smart said, "Now, look here! this won't do; who asked *your* opinion, sir, upon musical questions of which you evidently know absolutely *nothing?* You may rely upon it that some day, when you and your friends are shouting those ugly Gregorian chants, Heaven will punish you, and *rain down bags of crotchets upon your heads*, and prevent you from ever singing them again!"

Smart was an advocate of *unison* singing in congregational praise, and his views were admirably put into practice at St. Pancras, where he was so long organist. He had no choir; only about twenty boys from the National School, who practised with him once a week. His accompaniments to the broad voice of the congregational song were masterly. He would frequently alter the harmony to give appropriate colouring to the words. He had a strong aversion to playing the tunes quickly, and said, "I *won't* play them fast, and I tell you why. First, because it is vulgar; second, because it is musically wrong (for all music has its proper time); and third, there is no authority for fast playing. Sometimes I am told that the congregation would like to sing more quickly, but I answer that I am the best judge of their inclinations, and I have a good deal of trouble to keep them up to their present speed." He rightly acknowledged, however, that the St. Pancras service would not do everywhere. There are very few organists who are gifted with the freshness, fertility, knowledge of the various harmonies of which a given melody is susceptible, and mastery of the keyboard, as was Henry Smart.

With his love of congregational singing, and his profound knowledge of harmony, it is not surprising that he was appointed musical editor of *The Presbyterian Hymnal* (used by the United Presbyterian Church of Scotland), which was first issued in 1877.

The following personal reminiscence of Smart is taken from Mr. J. Spencer Curwen's interesting *Studies in Worship Music* (1st Series). Mr. Curwen says:—
"On one occasion he invited me to sit with him on a Sunday evening in the roomy organ pew at St. Pancras Church. Mr. Smart was so companionable and chatty that he liked to have friends with him at his organ, and indeed I believe he was seldom alone. As the service opened he beckoned me to come and sit on the stool beside him. At the 'Cantate Domine' the people began to make themselves heard. 'Do you hear that?' he said, as the sound rose from nave and gallery; 'that, to my mind, is finer than any choir!' And he played away, revelling in the massive unison which he was accompanying. He managed to give expression to the hymn in this way [it should be remembered that he was then quite blind]: The youth who was his amanuensis and companion would read the words to him, while he listened with head bent, drinking in, as it were, the spirit of the poet. Then, when the time came for singing, he was ready. But now and then in the progress of the hymn he would forget, and ask, 'What's the next verse about?' changing the character of his accompaniment to suit the words. 'Hark at that,' he said to me, as he played an old tune which he admired, 'there's a fine line. Regular German that. *Could you take that faster?*'"

The following amusing anecdote relating to Henry Smart may prove of interest. It was formerly the custom for the organist to play a few chords by way of interlude between *each* verse of the hymn. In Smart's early organist days there were some grumblers (the race is still in existence) who adversely criticised his playing in the service. Smart said nothing, but waited his opportunity. It came when "Miles' Lane," to "All hail the power of Jesu's Name," was to be sung. He started it in the usual key, B flat. All went well at the first verse. In the interlude between verses one and two he modulated, almost imperceptibly and very cleverly, into B, a semitone higher; between verses two and three he modulated into C, when it was found that the high notes on "Crown Him" did not come so easily; between verses three and four a semitone higher still, and so on, until the high notes of the remaining verses must have silently followed those of the "Lost Chord," and it may be that only in heaven we shall hear those lost high notes. Needless to say that the young organist effectually silenced (in two ways) his critics by this masterly display of skill. The moral of this incident is that organists, be they young or old, are only human beings, and cannot please everybody at the same time.

Smart died after a short illness, literally in harness, at his house near Primrose Hill, London, on July 6th, 1879, at the age of sixty-seven. On his deathbed he received the news that, upon the recommendation of Lord Beaconsfield, the Queen had been graciously pleased to grant him a pension of £100 per annum from the Civil List. He never lived to enjoy this reward, but was much gratified at this Royal acknowledgment of the services he had so faithfully rendered to musical art. He was buried in the picturesque cemetery of Hampstead, in the same "parcel of ground" where three other of Music's gifted sons—Joseph Maas, Walter Bache, and George Alexander Macfarren—sleep "the sweet sleep of death."

DR. EDWARD JOHN HOPKINS.

1818—

IT is Easter Sunday. Following the example of Dr. Johnson, "let us take a walk down Fleet Street." Proceeding eastward we soon arrive at the narrow entrance to Inner Temple Lane. Entering the half-open gateway we find ourselves in the region of law and lawyers. All is calm and still, but should the strains of

"*Brief* life is here our portion"

strike our ears, we should appreciate its appropriateness. A few steps and we reach the portal of the celebrated Temple Church.

The history and monuments of this church are very interesting. It is a beautiful Gothic stone building, and was founded by the Templars in the reign of Henry II., who built it in imitation of the Temple of the Holy Sepulchre at Jerusalem. It practically consists of two churches in one. The circular portion (one of the four round churches in England) is Transition and Early English, and was consecrated 1185; the choir (or "square" portion) is pure Early English, and was consecrated in 1240. Some of the

Crusaders are buried here, and Oliver Goldsmith's remains rest in the churchyard.

Lawyers and musicians have, perhaps, not much in common, unless it is in their mutual acquaintance of the *bar*. Yet the music at the Temple Church has long been famous. The organ is of historical interest. About 1683 the Benchers were desirous of having a first-class organ. Bernard Schmidt (a German who afterwards swelled the roll of the English Smiths, but with the prefix "Father") competed with John and Renatus Harris for the honour of supplying the instrument. Each builder erected an organ in the church. Smith's was in a gallery at the west end of the square portion, and Harris's on the south side of the communion table. The two instruments were used on alternate Sundays. Drs. Blow and Purcell performed upon Smith's organ, while Harris employed Draghi, organist to Queen Catherine, to play upon his. Ultimately, both organs were played at the same services, and after repeated trials the Benchers, at the end of 1687, or the beginning of 1688, decided to accept Father Smith's organ on the ground of its greater strength and depth of tone. The original specification included three full sets of keys and quarter notes ("great, choir, and Ecchos"), four hundred and one pipes, and twenty-three stops, among which were some German stops hitherto unknown in England. The organ has been frequently added to, and entirely reconstructed. It now contains four manuals and a pedale, 3,643 pipes, and seventy stops. Here, seated at the key-boards of this fine instrument, we find the subject of this sketch very much "at home."

Edward John Hopkins was born at Westminster, June 30th, 1818. He is one of a musical family. His brother, John Hopkins, is at the present time organist of Rochester Cathedral, and his cousin, John Larkin Hopkins, was organist of Trinity College, and also to the University of Cambridge. Like Sir Arthur Sullivan, he was a chorister of the Chapel Royal, St. James's. In 1834, Master Hopkins, then "a youth of sixteen, in a light blue jacket-suit of clothes with gilt buttons," aspired to the vacant organist's seat at Mitcham Church. Turle (then organist of Westminster Abbey) knew of this, and one day contrived that Hopkins should play a service at Westminster Abbey in the hearing of an influential Mitcham amateur. The competition took place, and No. 7 (Hopkins) was chosen; but his sixteen years, to say nothing of his "jacket-suit," were against him, and the committee hesitated. Then spoke up the influential amateur, who quoted Turle: "Tell them" (the committee), "with my compliments, that if they fear to trust Hopkins to accompany chants and hymns at Mitcham Church, Mr. Turle does not hesitate to trust him to play services and anthems at Westminster Abbey." That, of course, settled the question, and Hopkins was duly appointed. After Mitcham he was organist successively of St. Peter's, Islington, and St. Luke's, Berwick Street.

On Sunday, May 7th, 1843, Mr. Hopkins, at the request of the Benchers, played his first service at the Temple Church. There were a great many candidates for the post, but the contest ultimately lay between him and the late George Cooper. In the following October, Mr. Hopkins, then twenty-five, was duly elected organist, and shortly afterwards choirmaster as well. At that time there were but three surpliced choirs in London—St. Paul's Cathedral, Westminster Abbey, and St. James's, Chapel Royal. When the beautifully restored Temple Church was reopened in 1842, the Benchers decided to establish a choral service in their celebrated fane. In the old days, the organ filled the arch between the round and the square churches (it is now in a specially constructed chamber at the north side), and the only music was that of a mixed quartet, who sat in front of the organ and revealed themselves by withdrawing a curtain as the time for each psalm-tune came round. The rest of the service was said, not sung.

Mr. Hopkins soon revolutionised the musical service, which he has raised to a very high standard of excellence. The singing of the boys is faultless, and causes envy in the breast of many a choirmaster. Every afternoon he spends an hour and a half with his little men, practising with the piano only, and on Saturdays there is a full rehearsal with organ in the church. Mr. Curwen truly says, "At the Sunday service, the ear of the listener is arrested by the smoothness and blending of the general effect. It is the purest art. Mr. Hopkins knows the power of soft music over the emotions, how the spirit of the worshipper yields to the still, small voice when thunder and declamation fail to touch. With a choir of twelve boys and six men he realises his ideal of 'quality, not quantity.'"

Dr. Hopkins, who received his degree from the Archbishop of Canterbury, is no less famous as an accompanist than as a choirmaster. "In accompanying," he says, "the organ should be the background; and the remedy for indecision and flattening in choirs is not more organ, but better choir-training." In this respect he practises what he preaches. It is a lesson to any organist to listen to the exquisite taste of the Temple organist's accompaniments:—varied, refined, illustrative, delicate, and always in perfect sympathy with the words. The chanting alone is worth going many miles to hear—no gabbling, every syllable clearly enunciated, punctuation duly observed, emphasis natural, intonation true, and the accompaniment a model to be imitated.

As a composer Dr. Hopkins is favourably known. His anthems, services, hymn-tunes, and organ pieces are much sung and played, and have a high reputation. In his compositions for the church he favours the warmth and emotional freedom of the modern style, without altogether disregarding the traditions of the English school of church music. His great desire is to draw music and words into closer sympathy, and not allow the words to be a mere peg on which to hang the music. "Music," he says, "should so reflect the words that a foreigner, ignorant of our language, and coming into the church, should be able to tell the character of the words from the character of the music."

"In his hymn-tunes" (again quoting from Mr. Curwen) "Dr. Hopkins has fed his taste upon the old psalmody, though his tunes are many of them modern in character, and his popular tune to 'Saviour, again to Thy dear Name we raise,' shows that he is abreast of the movement of the times." (This tune should always be sung in *unison*, with varying organ harmonies, as originally written by the composer.) "It is interesting in another respect. Dr. Hopkins has formed the design of reviving the old church modes in the construction of hymn-tunes. 'Saviour again,' but for one inflected note at the end of the second line, is in the Mixo-Lydian mode—the mode of the fifth of the scale—that in which 'Scots, wha hae' is composed. It was designedly written in this mode by Dr. Hopkins, and the melody derives much of its freshness and charm from this novel construction."

Dr. Hopkins rightly objects to adaptations from the great masters for hymn-tunes. "The tune," he says, "should be the offspring of particular words, and should be consecrated to them." In this way he himself composes, taking care to write for the hymn as a whole, and not for the first verse alone. One great charm of his tunes is the purity and singableness of the inner parts, as well as the melody. In many of them the alto or tenor part runs the soprano very close in point of tunefulness. Happy are the altos and tenors when they have to sing a tune by Hopkins!

Dr. Hopkins enjoys a high reputation as musical editor of modern hymnals. In addition to his own *Temple Service Book*, he has edited *The Wesleyan Hymn-book, Free Church of Scotland Hymnal, Hymnal of the Presbyterian Church of Canada, Church Praise* (Presbyterian Church of England), and the *Congregational Hymnal*. So that various denominations, in different parts of the world, reap the benefit of his experience and refined taste. Mention must also be made of a literary work of great value, which is a standard book of reference on the great subject of which it treats: *The Organ: its History and Construction*, by Drs. E. F. Rimbault and E. J. Hopkins. Speaking of this valuable work, the late Sir G. A. Macfarren said, "Dr. Hopkins has made known what might be called the physiology of the instrument."

Dr. Hopkins has now been organist of the Temple Church for forty-six years, and, speaking in 1884, he said, "During forty-one years I can hardly call to mind more than twenty occasions of absence." Although past "threescore years and ten," he is still active, and delights in his congenial work. His many friends will heartily wish that he may live to celebrate the jubilee of his organistship of the Temple Church.

REV. J. B. DYKES, M.A., Mus. Doc.
1823—1876.

IT has been said that the tunes best suited for congregational use are those composed by amateurs, and not by professional musicians; and, judging from those so largely contributed by Dr. Dykes, there appears to be some truth in the assertion. That "the shoemaker should stick to his last" is unquestionably sound advice; and, as a rule, ministers are better sermon makers than hymn-tune manufacturers. But whereas some musicians (not many, perhaps) might write and deliver an excellent sermon, a clergyman might be so gifted as to compose hymn-tunes which, by their devotional fervour and fitness for worship, would excel those produced by the sons of Jubal. Such a clergyman-composer there has been, and he forms the subject of this sketch.

John Bacchus Dykes (strange second name) was born at Hull on March 10th, 1823. He was the son of Mr. W. H. Dykes, and grandson of Rev. Thomas Dykes, LL.B., for many years incumbent of St. John's Church, Hull. His grandfather was a strict Evangelical of the old school, whose views in matters theological contrasted strongly with those subsequently held by his musical grandson. Both grandfather and grandson have found a place in that literary Walhalla, Mr. Leslie Stephen's *Dictionary of National Biography.*

As a child John Dykes showed a remarkable talent for music, which seemed to come to him by instinct. He really needed little instruction, and could catch any air or play from ear long before he was able to play from note. At the early age of ten he was accustomed to play the organ in his grandfather's church at Hull; and it is stated that one of the greatest punishments which could be inflicted upon him was to debar him for a time from his favourite pastime of organ-playing. This was always in after years one of his greatest delights, and those who heard him extemporise on the instrument, or accompany the service in his own peculiar, delicate way, will scarcely forget the charm which he seldom failed to throw over them.

In October 1843, at the age of twenty, he matriculated at St. Catherine's Hall, Cambridge, and a few weeks after was elected Yorkshire scholar of his college. Previous to his arrival at Cambridge, a small musical society had been formed at Peterhouse, and this was shortly afterwards merged into a larger one, called the Cambridge University Musical Society, of which Mr. Dykes and Sir William Thompson, F.R.S., were the leading members. Mr. Dykes was unanimously chosen conductor of the society, and under his able management it very greatly prospered. The founders of the society had probably little idea what an important place it would assume amongst English musical institutions, or foresee the good work it would do for high-class music in this country. An account of the first concert of the society, on May 1st, 1844, is interesting and amusing. Haydn's "Surprise" symphony was performed. "Then Mr. Dykes, who also presided during the evening at the piano, sang a pretty little ballad, which, we believe, was his own composition. Most deservedly was he encored, when he threw the whole room into fits of laughter by an imitation of John Parry in two of his humorous songs. The whole style of this gentleman's performances stamps him at once as a thorough musician."

For the undergraduate singer of comic songs to develop into the learned theologian and composer of devotional hymn-tunes is a species of evolution somewhat strange, but nevertheless true. His musical attainments caused him to be much sought after by both Town and Gown, though, to his credit be it said, he did not neglect his studies. The amount of steady reading he accomplished was extraordinary. Though he had to prepare his college lectures, as well as his work for his private tutor, he always found time daily for a certain amount of exegetical and devotional study of the New Testament and the Psalms. And even so early in life, he was very fond of striving to unravel the mysterious prophecies contained in the books of Daniel and the Revelation. *Newton on the Prophecies* he looked upon as a sort of relaxation from harder study, just as in after life the composition of hymn-tunes and other sacred music was felt by him as a great relief from his parochial and other arduous duties. The delight he found in meditating on these books of Holy Scripture has been fully shown by some of the learned papers he wrote in the *Ecclesiastic*, from the year 1852 until he undertook the charge of the parish of St. Oswald, Durham.

In January 1847 John Dykes took his B.A. degree in Honours, being classed among the Senior Optimes. He was ordained deacon by the Archbishop of York in the same year, and licensed to the curacy of Malton. In 1848 he took priest's orders. In July 1849 he was appointed by the Dean and Chapter of Durham to be Minor Canon and Precentor. This was due to his musical skill and his success as conductor at Cambridge. He found matters at Durham in a neglected state. A collection of chants was in use which paid no regard to the character of the Psalms, and which led to the singing of jubilant words to plaintive music, and *vice versâ*. He took the greatest interest in his new office. Its duties were not heavy, and he had leisure to devote himself to composition. He began his more important musical works by contributing an anthem, "These are they which came out of great tribulation" (for All Saints' Day), to the late Sir Frederick Ouseley's collection of anthems for special occasions. And for use in the cathedral he wrote a burial service and other music. This was also a most productive period in regard to hymn tunes.

In 1850 Mr. Dykes married. Of his family of six

children, one of his sons, Mr. John A. Dykes, has studied music under Madame Schumann, and has made a successful appearance in public as a pianist and composer.

In 1861 the University of Durham conferred upon Mr. Dykes the degree of Mus. Doc. in recognition of his musical talent. In 1862 he was presented by the Dean and Chapter to the Vicarage of St. Oswald's, a parish church in Durham. Here for fourteen years he discharged his duties with an earnestness and love that won for him the affection of many and the respect of all who came into contact with him. A local obituary notice records, "The parish has lost one of the most kind, generous, and hard-working pastors that has ever presided over a flock. He was a model parish minister."

Life was not all smooth and peaceful, however. As already stated, Dr. Dykes belonged by descent to the Evangelical party in the Church of England; but during his University career the Oxford movement was in progress, and it had penetrated the sister University. The sermons of Dr. Mill and the lectures of Professor Blunt on the duties of a parish priest made a deep impression upon the scholarlike and theological mind of the young student, and he adopted the views of the new school. Through life he maintained them with, if possible, increasing fervour, and valued highly the advanced ceremonial so characteristic of High Church services. Dr. Dykes' ritualism provoked the displeasure of his Bishop, who prosecuted him in the Ecclesiastical Courts. The Bishop further refused to license him a curate, so he strove single-handed to supply to his people all the ministrations to which they had been previously accustomed when he had the assistance of a curate to share his work. Under the weight of this labour and the deep anxiety which it entailed, he completely broke down. He went to St. Leonards to recover, but died there on January 20th, 1876.

At his death a "Memorial Fund" for the benefit of his family was started, and in response over £10,000 was contributed, a proof of the extent to which his beautiful tunes had touched the hearts of the nation. The Rev. Dr. Allon, a well-known Nonconformist minister, who could hardly be expected to sympathise with Dr. Dykes' ritual, wrote, "I shall deem it a great privilege to contribute, as an expression of common gratitude for his rich and precious contributions to the worship-song of almost all English-speaking congregations."

Dr. Dykes' character was very sweet and attractive. His daughter says, "His nature was bright, sunny, and joyous, and he had a power of making friends, inspiring ardent friendships. He was a most amusing and delightful companion, and one whom all loved and courted. His great charm was, however, his deep and most sincere religion. This seemed to be the hidden spring of all his outer life."

Dr. Dykes wrote upwards of two hundred and fifty hymn-tunes and carols, which have appeared in various hymnals. Many of his best tunes seem to have come to the words to which they were composed as inspirations, and for this reason he always preferred keeping them to these. He used to write them quite independently of the piano, sometimes during a solitary walk, or in a railway train. The tune to "Hark, hark, my soul" was composed as he was ascending Skiddaw. His children often used to sing over some of his new tunes on Sunday evening, and not unfrequently their critical suggestions were adopted. He used to say that he always made a practice of offering some short prayer before writing anything.

Dr. Dykes may well be called the Apostle of the modern hymn-tune. The old tunes, such as "Melcombe," "London New," etc., have a rigidity about them which is in strong contrast to the warmth and deep feeling of, for instance, Dr. Dykes' "Hark, my soul, it is Lord," or "The King of Love my Shepherd is."

"Dr. Dykes' tunes," wrote his friend Sir Henry Baker, "are just like himself; he was so full of feeling, so gentle, so unselfish." They are so well known and universally loved that it is not necessary to enlarge upon their beauties. They are for the most part very congregational. In fact, the present writer's experience in congregational singing at three large churches in London is that they are more heartily and *feelingly* sung than those of any other composer. Dr. Dykes was a great advocate of congregational singing, and often urged it in his sermons.

Many of our most popular tunes are by him. "Hark,

my soul, it is the Lord"—notice how happily the dotted notes accent important words; "Jesu, Lover of my soul"—how tenderly it breathes the spirit of Wesley's hymn; "Fierce raged the tempest"—with its change from the surging C minor opening to the "calm and still" close in E flat; "The day is past and over"—how soothing and restful the feeling it produces; and many others are equally beautiful and full of tenderness.

Mention must be made of a most beautiful setting of Ellerton's funeral hymn, "Now the labourer's task is done," which is touchingly pathetic, and when sung for the first time by a large congregation in London was known to bring tears to the eyes of many of the worshippers. Another favourite tune must also be referred to, "Eternal Father, strong to save," one of the most popular of all, in which the hymn "for those at sea" has a perfect setting. In the last line but one of each verse the inflected note (F sharp) gives to the word "cry" a piercing and plaintive emphasis, and yet its introduction seems so natural and unrestrained.

Dr. Dykes wrote a fine setting of the *Te Deum* in the key of F, which is not only admirably suited for congregational singing, but, like all his church music, is worthy of the great hymn to which it is set.

Let all lovers of church music be thankful for the labours of one who has provided so much that is beautiful, melodious, and inspiring in the service of song in the house of the Lord.

WILLIAM HENRY MONK, Mus. Doc.
1823—1889.

*H*YMNS *Ancient and Modern* is known wherever the English language is spoken. Upwards of *twenty-seven million* copies have been sold since its first issue in the year 1861. What has been the cause of such extraordinary popularity? Surely not its doctrinal points, for we find the book in nearly every home among Nonconformists, who would have little sympathy with its theological tenets. May it not lie in the excellence of its music rather than in the merits or demerits of its theology? Although of making many hymnals there seems to be no end, yet *Hymns Ancient and Modern* remains unapproachable from the musical point of view, whether considered practically or æsthetically. The responsibilities of the musical editor of this hymnal must have been very great. To learn what kind of man he was, let us take a brief glimpse into his life and work.

William Henry Monk was born at Brompton, London, in 1823. His first musical impressions were derived from the concerts of the Sacred Harmonic Society, at which for many years he was a constant attendant.

He studied music under Thomas Adams (*the* organist of his day), J. A. Hamilton (of dictionary fame), and G. A. Griesbach. He was organist successively of Eaton Chapel, Pimlico; St. George's Chapel, Albemarle Street; and Portman Chapel, Marylebone. All these are chapels-of-ease belonging to the Church of England. In 1847 he was appointed director of the choir of King's College, London; in 1849 organist; and in 1874, upon the resignation of John Hullah, professor of vocal music in the college. Monk apparently had no objection to pluralities. In 1852 he became organist and choirmaster of St. Matthias, Stoke Newington, and he held this appointment concurrently with that at King's College till his death. He was therefore "chief musician" in these two churches for the long periods of forty-two and thirty-seven years respectively.

Dr. W. H. Monk (the degree of Doctor of Music was conferred by the University of Durham) would possibly have remained a comparatively unknown musician but for one important circumstance. About the year 1850, the influence of the Tractarian movement was rapidly making itself felt in the services of the Church of England. Many of the clergy became dissatisfied with the existing hymnals, and steps were taken to produce a hymn-book which should be acceptable to the large and growing section of the high church party. In 1858, the late Sir Henry Baker enlisted the help of some twenty clergymen, including several who had published or projected similar works, and laid the foundations of that important hymnal *Hymns Ancient and Modern.* A working committee of hymnologists was formed, with Sir Henry Baker as chairman, and in 1860 the first edition (words only) came out. Dr. Monk was appointed musical editor. He had the sole musical initiative and veto on the original edition, and no other musical counsel was called in until the position of the book had been made, and an enlarged edition was called for; indeed, *Hymns Ancient and Modern* in its early days was often called " Monk's book." The first music edition came out in 1861.

The success of the book has been extraordinary and unprecedented, and, in spite of the inevitable competition of these times, and the prejudice in some quarters against its doctrinal basis, it still holds the field. An average sale of *one million* copies *per year* since its introduction is a practical proof of its popularity and fitness for congregational singing.

Dr. Monk's musical editorship was not, however, confined to the book which made his name. He compiled a series of tune and anthem books for the Church of Scotland, and supervised the new edition of Dr. Allon's *Congregational Psalmist.* Moreover, he contributed tunes to several other hymnals, so that various sections of the Church have benefited by his sound judgment and artistic taste. Dr. Monk, in addition to being a high churchman, was a strong purist in Church music, and could not tolerate anything which savoured of irreverence or secular influences. He had a preference for Gregorian music, believing it to be not only ecclesiastically correct, but better suited for congregational purposes, on account of its simplicity and of being sung in unison. At St. Matthias he had ample opportunity for carrying out his views. He did his utmost to bring the musical part of the Church service within the range of the worshipper, and refused to be led away by the modern tendency to confine the music to the choir. This ideal he strictly carried out in every bar he wrote. Simple, devotional, and pure are stamped on all his compositions; and as he only wrote one song to secular words, his life and works were thus devoted to the cause of congregational worship-music.

Dr. Monk was a singularly modest and reserved man, and led a retired life. His home ties were strong and particularly sweet. He was fond of his garden, and loved to watch the growth of plants and flowers. He had a strong deep love for nature, and was an enthusiastic pedestrian. His hymn-tunes, of which he must have written nearly a hundred, are a reflex of his home life; some of them, such as "Abide with me" and "Sweet Saviour, bless us ere we go," are sung by Christians of many denominations everywhere, and are not likely to be superseded. How delightful it is to think that music soars above all sectarian differences! In his hymn-tunes he possessed such power in fitting appropriate music to words that it would in many cases be almost a sacrilege to dissociate them. He would sometimes get out of his bed to write down a tune. The tune to "O perfect life of love" was composed in this manner, and that to "Thou art coming, O my Saviour," was written in a railway train. His best known tune, "Eventide," to "Abide with me," was composed under peculiar circumstances. He told a friend that when he (Dr. Monk) and the late Sir Henry Baker were once going out, they suddenly remembered that there was no tune for hymn 27, "Abide with me," and that he sat down, and, undisturbed by the noise of a piano lesson which was then going on, wrote that excellent and popular tune in ten minutes.

Dr. Monk held very strong opinions on the sacredness of the church musician's office. He maintained the principle of gravity, solemnity, and reverence in church music. He insisted on a high conception of the great object of worship. Rowland Hill used to say that it was a pity the devil should have all the good tunes, and therefore did not disapprove of adaptations from secular as well as sacred works. This doctrine Dr. Monk could not tolerate; yet it was a strange irony of fate that when his house was full of manuscripts, offered by correspondents for insertion in *Hymns Ancient and Modern*, the tune of which he received the greatest number of copies was an adaptation of the opening chorus in Weber's *Oberon*, sung by fairies as they trip about the stage, which is known in many hymn-books by the name of "Weber" (7s, in key F).

As an organist Dr. Monk held a high place. He once said he did not feel quite comfortable on the question of organ recitals in churches. He held that the organ should only be touched as an adjunct to worship; if used as a solo instrument its utterances must be so solemn as to minister to true religious thought. He not only preached this doctrine but practised it. "He was," says the *Church Times*, "a church musician literally to his fingers' ends, for there was no part of his work which so thoroughly manifested his real ability and devotion as his organ accompaniments. Solemnity without dreariness, feeling without the eccentricity which so often passes for that quality,—these were the elements that will always be remembered as his chief characteristics. The organ was to him an instrument, not for the display of skill, but for touching the souls of men; and probably some of the most powerful sermons preached in St. Matthias have come from the organ chamber." His vicar, in his memorial sermon, said, "He had wonderful power in playing our devotional hymns. He could make a single word speak with a deep pathos. At times he appeared under a kind of inspiration, the infection of which touched the hearts of all. He taught many to praise God who had never praised Him before; he taught others to praise Him more worthily than hitherto."

Dr. Monk was a truly just and good man, and died literally in harness on March 1st, 1889, deeply loved and much lamented.

The following advice which he once wrote to a near and dear friend is full of wisdom, and may fitly close this brief record of his career:—" Two things I would wish to say to you: 1. Be honest in your convictions and act up to them. 2. Believe others who may differ in opinion or in action to be the same. As far as I know 'the world,' the great sin towards others is the contrary of (2), and the imputation of motives. There are times when you hardly know what to do yourselves, and are anxious for and pray for guidance. Believe that others do the like; and, above all, have 'fervent charity among yourselves.'"

SIR JOHN STAINER, M.A., Mus. Doc.

1840—

"THE little chorister who became organist of his cathedral, and was afterwards made a knight," would be an appropriate sub-title for one of those "very nice" little books written for the purpose of inculcating lessons of perseverance into the youthful mind. Yet this is the true life-story of the eminent musician whose name appears above. Such a pleasing outline suggests pleasanter " fillings in," full of interest to lovers of sacred music. We have stretched the canvas, and the figuration now proceeds.

John Stainer, son of a schoolmaster, was born in London, June 6th, 1840. He became a chorister in St. Paul's Cathedral when only seven years old: at that age, however, he could already play Bach's fugue in E major, and the overture to *Acis and Galatea*, besides being no mean performer on the organ. He sang solos at St. Paul's till after he was sixteen, with the result that when he entered manhood he had "no more voice than a crow." At the age of fourteen he was appointed organist and choirmaster of St. Benedict and St. Peter's, Paul's Wharf. Through the liberality of Miss Hackett, the choristers' friend, he received a course of lessons on the organ from George Cooper at St. Sepulchre's. At the same time, he learned harmony from Mr. Bayley, master of St. Paul's boys, and counterpoint from Dr. Steggall, who delights in telling the following incident in connection with his gifted pupil. In 1852 Dr. (then Mr.) Steggall took his degree at Cambridge, and it is the custom for the musical exercise for the Doctor's degree to be performed before the University. Dr. Steggall asked Mr. Bayley (of St. Paul's) to send him one of his boys to sing the solo part at Cambridge. He sent a bright-faced, curly-headed little fellow, who charmed his hearers by taking a top C as clear as a bell. "That boy," says Dr. Steggall, with a radiant smile, "was John Stainer."

Young Stainer at this time, though still a chorister, used often to take the organ at St. Paul's. One day both Goss and Cooper, the organist and deputy, were absent, and Chorister Stainer was officiating at the organ. "It was a fortunate thing for me," he says, "that these great lights were extinguished for the day. The late Sir Frederick Ouseley had come to ask whether either of them could recommend a young organist for his recently founded college at Tenbury, and he came up into the organ-loft, where he found me getting on very comfortably, and so, in the evening of that day, he wrote me a very kind letter, asking if I would play his organ." The invitation was accepted, and his work at Tenbury, where the late Sir F. Ouseley possessed the finest musical library in the world, was not only very congenial but most valuable to the young musician.

His boy friend, Arthur Sullivan, a chorister at the Chapel Royal, paid a visit to Tenbury at the time Sir F. Ouseley was putting up a large and fine organ in his church and experimenting in pipes, pneumatic apparatus, etc. Stainer and Sullivan got the idea that guttapercha would make a cheap and resonant substance for organ pipes! Guttapercha was scarce, and their financial resources limited, but they got together a few old guttapercha shoes, and set to work with ardent enthusiasm. To their great regret they were stopped in their experiments, because the horrible smell which they made poisoned the whole building, and Sir Frederick arrested them in the initiative stage. But they could not help thinking that there was a bit of jealousy in his prohibition of their inventive faculties!

His promotion in the profession was very rapid. He remained at Tenbury only three years, and in 1859, at the age of nineteen, became organist of Magdalen College, Oxford, after six months' trial. In the same year he had matriculated at Christ Church, Oxford, and taken the degree of Mus. Bac. He then entered at Edmund Hall as a resident undergraduate, and, while discharging his duties at Magdalen, worked for his B.A. degree, which he took in Trinity term 1863.

Meantime he had been appointed organist to the University, and was conductor of a flourishing College Musical Society and of another association at Exeter

College. But nothing interfered with his duties a Magdalen, where he raised the choir to a very high state of efficiency. In 1865 he proceeded to his Mus. Doc. degree, and in the following year to M.A.

Dr. Stainer's name will long be remembered in Oxford as the founder of the Philharmonic Society, and as the reviver of the Choral Society, both of which still exist and remain in a flourishing condition.

It is with expressions of gratitude that he speaks of the kindness he received from everybody in Oxford, not only from fellow-musicians, but also from the college dons. It must have been particularly gratifying to him to know that his efforts for the better cultivation of music were thoroughly appreciated. A substantial recognition of his zeal, taking the form of a magnificent suite of Sèvres ornaments, now adorns his drawing-room mantelpiece; and to this testimonial the whole college, from dons to undergraduates, subscribed.

Dr. Stainer's next step in life—at the age of thirty-two—was of no ordinary kind, being his unsolicited appointment as organist of St. Paul's Cathedral, the largest church of the largest city in the world. It is possible that his selection may have been partly due to his old association with St. Paul's as a chorister; but undoubtedly it mainly arose from the fact that an active administrator as well as a musician—one, too, who was versed in modern music—was sorely needed. Under his predecessor, Sir John Goss, the general choral music had arrived at a crippled, if not moribund condition, owing chiefly to the lack of interest shown in the music by the Cathedral authorities. Goss made frequent attempts to improve the services, but he was too tender-hearted, and not sufficiently tenacious of his purpose. Two stories will illustrate his difficulties. Sydney Smith, the wit, when Canon at the cathedral, caused some difficulty by saying one day, "Mr. Goss, about that chant this morning." "The minor one, do you mean, sir?" said Goss. "Yes. Have no more minor chants, and no more minor music, while I am in residence, if you please." Whereupon Goss explained the importance of the minor key, and that much of the best music was written in that way. But Sydney Smith was inexorable, and no more minor music was given. After a time the order was withdrawn, but only reluctantly. Goss received the following letter: "MR. Goss,—Since you make it a point of conscience to have music in the minor key, I give way.—SYDNEY SMITH." Another story told of him in connection with the same Canon was respecting the organ. Goss pointed out that the organ was getting very antiquated, and needed improvements in stops, etc., as it certainly did in those days. Sydney Smith only said, "You have a bull stop and a tom-tit stop, and what on earth more do you want?"

Dr. Stainer came as a reformer. He received strong support from the Dean and Chapter in the work of re-organisation. Moreover, he possessed a large reserve of tact, an essential qualification in the management of a choir; and very soon St. Paul's became as conspicuous for the high character and attractiveness of its musical services as it had formerly been for their dulness and slovenliness. The music at St. Paul's has been part of a great revival in things pertaining to worship music, and it has exerted an influence that has been felt throughout the kingdom. Dr. Stainer, like every organist who is well supported by his choir, has been much indebted to his excellent singers, though he says, "Often at the close of a very beautiful anthem or creed, I have been more inclined to say, 'Thank God,' than 'Thank you, gentlemen of the choir.'" The thanks of all lovers of sacred music are due to Dr. Stainer for introducing into St. Paul's oratorios with the accompaniment of a full orchestra. Those who have heard Bach's *Passion* or Mendelssohn's *St. Paul*, sung to vast congregations filling the great cathedral, will not easily forget the effect of such sublime music so beautifully rendered amidst such appropriate surroundings.

After sixteen years' splendid service in the Metropolitan Cathedral, Dr. Stainer resigned his appointment in 1888, owing to impaired eyesight. Nothing but universal satisfaction was expressed when the Queen conferred upon him the honour of knighthood at Windsor, on July 10th, 1888.

Sir John Stainer's constant engagements for many years have left him little time for composition. However, he has already written sufficient to make his name memorable as a composer; and now that he is enjoying comparative leisure at his home at Oxford, he will not have just cause or impediment for neglecting his awakening muse.

Sir John's compositions have been almost entirely sacred. His anthems—*e.g.*, "Lead, kindly Light," an exquisite setting of Cardinal Newman's words; the bright Christmas anthem, "The morning stars sang together," written in his nineteenth year; and the well-known and effective "What are these?"—are all imbued with deep devotional fervour and skilful musicianship. His services—in E flat and A—are performed to enraptured congregations wherever choral services are known, whether in England, in the Colonies, or in America. His cantata, "The daughter of Jairus," is full of pathos and beauty, and is the delight of choral singers everywhere; and a subsequent work, "St. Mary Magdalen," is strikingly descriptive. Mention must be made of the "Crucifixion," a setting of the Passion-music within the capabilities of church choirs, and with organ accompaniment only. The writer will not easily forget the solemn effect of this beautiful music at its first performance in Marylebone Church, when it was conducted by the composer.

Sir John Stainer is a good Hebrew scholar: so it is singularly appropriate that he should write *The Music of the Bible* (Cassell & Co.), a book which is full of interest to all students of sacred music. His hymn-tunes, though not very numerous, are very good. His setting of Keble's "Hail, gladdening light," "Holy Father, cheer our way," "There is a blessed home," etc., breathe the spirit of devotion, and are thoroughly congregational. Sir John, although accustomed to a cathedral service all his life, is much interested in hymn-tunes. He thinks that all our hymn-singing is much too fast, and, in large churches especially, that slowness should be cultivated. He thinks the clergy are much to blame in this matter for not permitting their organists, as is frequently the case, to use their own judgments in determining the proper rate of speed. He says that each tune has its own particular *tempo*, depending upon its date and its special characteristics, and that it would be just as absurd to insist on singing all Schumann's songs at one and the same speed as to do so with all hymn-tunes. Speaking at the Musical Association on the subject of *modern* hymn-tunes, he said: "The fact of the matter is, that a very large number of them are very weak and sentimental; but on behalf of composers—and being one of the humble scribblers of tunes myself occasionally—I must say that tune-writers are very much at the mercy of the writers of words. If you give a man a stupid, sentimental subject, it is impossible that he can sit down and rise to the occasion, and turn out a tune of strength and dignity. It is a very difficult thing to write a good hymn-tune. I have had many thousands pass through my hands when I worked with Dr. Monk and the late Dr. Dykes in the revision of *Hymns Ancient and Modern*. We worked very hard, and it gave me a great insight into hymn-tunes. I think very few editors can tell, sitting in their room, or even playing it on the pianoforte, what will be the success of a tune. I have long given up hopes of being able to decide it. It is like the old Latin proverb, *solvitur ambulando.* You must put it into the mouth of the people, and see if it answers when it is used; there is no other test. . . . As regards passing notes, I think, although I am a great Radical in some things, I am very conservative in others, and I am often very sorry to find the old notes and twists that my dear mother used to sing to me are turned out of such tunes as 'Rockingham' and 'Wareham.' When we have them in St. Paul's, I hear a number of the congregation putting them in just as they used to do in old days."

Although Sir John Stainer's name is chiefly associated with his good work at St. Paul's, he has held important public offices. He was principal of the National Training College for Music, and organist to the Albert Hall (now Royal) Choral Society. He has been decorated with the French *Legion d'honneur*, and is Her Majesty's Inspector of Music in the Education Department. In July 1889, he was appointed Professor of Music in the University of Oxford (in succession to the late Sir Frederick Ouseley); a well-deserved honour, which practically places him at the head of his profession in this country.

As an organ accompanist Sir John is unrivalled. It is a source of regret with his brother organists in London that his retirement from St. Paul's deprives them of the pleasure and privilege of listening to his masterly treatment of the organ in accompanying the Cathedral services. As a man he is beloved and esteemed by all who know him. "He is the most perfect gentleman that comes into this place," once remarked a music-seller's assistant to the writer. "A thoroughly good-hearted, genial, splendid fellow," is the verdict of all who come in contact with him, and right well he deserves it. Long may he be spared to further enrich our store of sacred music.

We conclude with a story. At the recent (1889) annual gathering of the College of Organists, the President, a distinguished organist and musician, addressing his fellow-organists, said: "I was one Sunday walking at some seaside place, and on turning a corner I heard a number of Sunday School children singing a hymn I had composed. I thought to myself, 'I want no higher reward than this for all my work.' I can only tell you that I would not exchange it for the very finest monument in Westminster Abbey." The man who can give utterance to such sentiments as these is a *great* man, and draws out our esteem, our respect, our love. The speaker was none other than Sir John Stainer.

SIR ARTHUR SULLIVAN.

1842—

ARTHUR SEYMOUR SULLIVAN, the son of a musician, was born in London, May 13th, 1842. At the age of eleven he became one of the children of the Chapel Royal, St. James's. "His voice was very sweet," says the Rev. Thomas Helmore, master of the children, "and his style of singing far more sympathetic than that of most boys." During his choristership he wrote several anthems, one of which was sung at an ordinary service, and so pleased the Dean (also Bishop of London) that he sent for the youthful composer to come into the vestry after the service, and rewarded him by patting his black curly head to the accompaniment of half-a-sovereign. One of the friends of his boyhood was John (now Sir John) Stainer, at that time a chorister at St. Paul's Cathedral. The two lads when off duty were wont to delight in trips together on the penny steamboats on the Thames, their enjoyment of which was considerably enhanced by a copious consumption of nuts and oranges. In 1856, the Mendelssohn Scholarship (in memory of the illustrious musician of that name) was brought into active existence, mainly through the exertions of that estimable artist and lady the late Madame Jenny Lind Goldschmidt. In July of that year Sullivan, in competition with nineteen others, carried off this important musical prize. Without leaving the Chapel Royal, he began to study at the Royal Academy of Music, under John Goss for harmony, and Sterndale Bennett for piano. In the autumn of 1858, under the terms of the Scholarship, he entered the Conservatorium at Leipzig, amongst his teachers being Moscheles, who thirty-four years previously had given pianoforte lessons to Mendelssohn. On his return to London, Sullivan brought with him his music to Shakespeare's *Tempest* (his *exit opus* from the Conservatorium), which was performed at the Crystal Palace on April 5th, 1862, to the contentment of Charles Dickens, and repeated the following week. This beautiful composition made a great sensation in musical circles, and our composer at once made his mark. At his first concert in St. James's Hall Jenny Lind came from her retirement on purpose to sing for him. Never was a composer more auspiciously launched into London musical and fashionable society. During the early part of his career Mr. Sullivan was organist and choirmaster of St. Michael's, Chester Square, and of St. Peter's, Onslow Gardens; but in 1871 he entirely relinquished his Sunday engagements.

It is beyond the province of this notice to trace his career step by step. Suffice it to say that success has accompanied his progress in an extraordinary manner. Nearly all the productions of his pen — symphony, overtures, oratorios (*The Prodigal Son, The Light of the World*), *Festival Te Deum* (on the recovery of the Prince of Wales from his illness in 1872); cantatas (*The Martyr of Antioch, The Golden Legend*); operas, songs, part-songs, anthems, hymn tunes, etc., have fared alike, in having sustained an almost unbroken record of brilliant achievement. Of late years Sir Arthur has struck upon a new vein of musical works, the comic operas which are inseparably associated with his name, and which have met with unprecedented success. His songs and part-songs are, perhaps, as widely known as his other works. They are generally of a tender or sentimental cast, and some of them stand in a very high rank. Many have attained a wonderful degree of popularity, and have hit the public taste in a remarkable manner. Such, for instance, as "Will he come?" "The Lost Chord," "The Distant Shore," and "O, hush thee, my babie."

From our composer's early training in the Chapel Royal, and his subsequent organ appointments, it is not to be wondered at that his church music attains a high standard of excellence. His anthems and hymn-tunes are as popular and tuneful as his secular compositions. If congregations were asked to vote upon their favourite tune, Sullivan's "St. Gertrude," to "Onward, Christian soldiers," would head the list with a very large majority. (It will be noticed that the *tenor* of the first four bars of this tune becomes the *melody* of the next four bars, and *vice versâ*.) Most of his tunes were written between 1867 and 1874, and were principally contributed to *The Hymnary* and *Church Hymns*. Of the latter he was musical editor, and contributed to it twenty-one original tunes, most of which have found their way into other collections, and are sung with enjoyment by various sections of the Christian community.

Mr. Sullivan was Principal of the National Training School for Music from 1876 to 1881. He received the honorary degree of Doctor of Music from the University of Cambridge in 1876, and Oxford in 1879. In 1878 he was decorated at Paris with the *Legion d'honneur*, and he bears the Order of Saxe-Coburg and Gotha. In 1883, in company with the late Professor G. A. Macfarren, he received the honour of Knighthood at the hands of the Queen.

Sir Arthur Sullivan's music—vocal and instrumental alike—is characterised by melodiousness and exquisite refinement. He possesses the rare gift of being able to satisfy the critical instincts of the trained musician and the natural longings of the musically uncultured at the same time. In his compositions he never fails to be interesting; he is always tuneful and never dull. Everything that he puts his hand to is sure to meet with success, whether it be a child's simple hymn-tune —*e.g.*, "Brightly gleams our banner"—or an elaborate chorus with brilliant orchestral colouring. The sound schooling in the traditions of the English Church composers which he received at the Chapel Royal is manifested in many of his works; indeed, it is no uncommon thing to find specimens of this strict ecclesiastical style in several of his compositions that can hardly be classed as serious. To the excellent vocal training imparted to him during his choristership may be traced that easy flow of the voice parts in his part music that makes it so delightful and pleasant to sing. Judging from his latest works, the stream of melody seems to be almost perennial; there is no sign of its becoming in the least degree parched, for it flows on as freshly, as copiously, and as joyously as ever.

Unlike most of his craft, Sir Arthur has had little experience of the joys and sorrows of teaching. He says: "When I began the study of music I was determined to live by my pen, if it were possible, and I resolved not to teach if I could help it; and I was for several years a church organist living on £80 a year, that I might devote all the time I could to composition."

Sir Arthur resides on A flat (*a natural* abode for a musician) in Victoria Street, Westminster, where he hospitably entertains his numerous friends, among whom is no less a personage than the Heir Apparent. He is naturally a prominent figure in London Society, and his vivacious manner and cheerful temperament make him an exceptionally pleasant companion. He composes at a time when most other people are composed in slumber, viz., in the small hours of the morning—to use his own words, "When postmen cease from troubling, and omnibuses are at rest."

MR. JOSEPH BARNBY.
1838—

YORKSHIRE is the "county of many acres" and of many singers. One Yorkshire voice is equal to about two and a half London voices, and the perfection of choral singing may be heard in our largest county. It seems quite natural, therefore, that one of our best choirmasters and most skilful conductors should hail from this very musical region.

Joseph Barnby was born at York, August 12th, 1838. He was the youngest of seven brothers, all of whom have displayed musical talent. At the age of seven this "Benjamin" (albeit named Joseph) of the family became a chorister in York Minster. Music came to him instinctively, and he cannot remember ever having learned the alphabet of his art—it was in his blood. He became an organist at the age of twelve. Four years later he came to London, and, entering the Royal Academy of Music, became a fellow-student of Sir Arthur Sullivan. When the Mendelssohn Scholarship was instituted in 1856, the two friends had a neck-and-neck race for the first scholarship. There was a dead heat, and at the final trial Barnby became a very good second.

He was organist successively of St. Michael's, Queenhithe; St. James-the-Less, Westminster; and St. Andrew's, Wells Street. It was during the palmy days of the St. Andrew's choir, which was then engaged in developing the modern style of cathedral music, that Mr. Barnby succeeded in advancing its efficiency till it was second to none in London.

His engagements became so pressing, that in 1871 he was compelled to resign this post, where week-day as well as Sunday duties occupied him, for the less arduous duties of St. Anne's, Soho. There he introduced, for the first time in England, Bach's smaller *Passion of St. John*, which was and is still performed every Friday during Lent, and it has been characterised as scarcely less impressive than the Ober-Ammergau Passion Play.

Since 1875 Mr. Barnby has been precentor and director of musical instruction at Eton College—a position he still worthily holds. The advantage of having a musician of his experience and attainments to develop the musical taste in this historic school is obvious; and, as the study of music in all the lower forms is now compulsory, the influence which he wields amongst the scions of the aristocracy should leave its effect on the art of music in the highest circles in the land.

From 1861 to 1876 Mr. Barnby held the responsible post of musical adviser to the great firm of Novello, Ewer, & Co. But perhaps his chief claim to the niche of fame is his skill as conductor of large bodies of singers and players. Owing to his success with his church choir, and backed up by Messrs. Novello, he raised a larger one to sing at St. James's Hall, which soon became known as "Barnby's Choir." Its performance constituted his first great success as a conductor, and that, too, in the face of considerable misgivings on the part of the profession, who thought it would be impossible to get an amateur choir to sing without professional leaders. But Mr. Barnby persevered. As he observes, with considerable feeling, "I had myself trained my choir, I believed in its capabilities, and I was not disappointed. On the opening night, as I raised my bâton, the choir burst forth into song like one voice. I have never obtained a finer start." So delighted and astonished were Benedict and Sims Reeves, that at the conclusion they hurried up to congratulate him. It is worthy of remark that Mr. Barnby has gained all his choral successes, from that time to the present, by means of amateur singers, without any admixture of the professional element. The secret of his triumphs must be ascribed to the possession of an indomitable will, a frank good-nature, and a power of keeping the minds of his singers concentrated on their work. Another secret of his success is his insisting upon having the words clearly enunciated, so that anyone can understand what is being sung without having the words before him. The writer well remembers the attention paid to this important feature at the earliest rehearsals of the choir in a small hall near Oxford Street, and recalls with gratitude the many lessons he received on a point so frequently overlooked by choirmasters.

Mr. Barnby revived several neglected but fine works of the old masters, notably Handel's *Jephthah*, till then never heard in England since Handel's time; and Bach's greater *Passion of St. Matthew* for double orchestra and double choir. The latter proved a brilliant success. Macfarren asserted that it was so perfect that he would gladly rest his memory for ever on that one performance; while Dean Stanley was so impressed by its grandeur, sublimity, and beauty that he sanctioned its introduction at Westminster Abbey, and no words can adequately describe the unprecedented effect of this marvellous music rendered by a surpliced choir of three hundred and fifty voices within the walls of the grand old Abbey. Those who were present assert that no more impressive musical performance has ever been heard.

In 1871 Mr. Barnby succeeded Gounod as conductor of the Royal Albert Hall Choral Society, now the Royal Choral Society, with what success it is hardly necessary to say.

As a composer Mr. Barnby has been very successful. Every admirer of Church music is familiar with his service in E, the favourite service of Charles Kingsley, who, whilst Canon of Chester, always had it performed for the benefit of any distinguished visitors who might happen to be attending. A friendship and a reciprocated admiration existed between the Canon and the composer, fostered by their mutual love of music. Mr. Barnby gives an interesting account of his first sight of Kingsley on his own hearthrug at Eversley. He was dressed in a quaint unclerical "get-up" of knickerbockers, high-lows, velveteen shooting coat, and a wisp of black ribbon around a shirt-collar much opened at the throat. Mr. Barnby also relates how agreeably he spent his first evening under the Canon's roof, swinging in a hammock, while Kingsley, seated close by, read Shelley aloud as only he could do.

One of his most popular compositions is the part-song "Sweet and Low" to Tennyson's words. This lay buried for some time under a heap of manuscripts at a music publisher's, when Mr. Barnby one day called upon the firm and unearthed his music, and would have taken it away; but when the publishers heard him play it over they eagerly accepted it. His cantatas, *Rebekah* and *The Lord is King*, with the motett "King all glorious," are favourably known; while of anthems, who does not know his setting of "O Lord, how manifold"? Of his secular songs, "When the tide comes in" may be instanced as a composition of singular beauty.

Mr. Barnby has largely contributed to our ever-increasing stock of hymn-tunes. He edited the *Hymnary*, and enriched it with many choice tunes. His setting of the "Endless Alleluia," "When morning gilds the skies," and "Jesu, my Lord," are widely known and always admired. A unison tune to "Jesu, Lover of my soul" (composed in 1866) is full of pathos, and illustrates the depth and expression of Charles Wesley's words with remarkable beauty and appropriateness. Indeed, his compositions possess a flow of beautiful melody, and there is also evident a richness and originality in the harmony which has rarely been surpassed by English writers.

Mr. Barnby is a strong Radical in Church music, and especially in regard to hymn-tunes. He has no sympathy with those who plead for the " severe but pleasing simplicity of Tallis and other old writers." Nor does he approve of confining his writings to any one style or period, but believes in composing tunes in a style that will be the natural expression of his feelings. But we will let him speak for himself, in the preface to his collection of *Hymns and Tunes* (1st series, 1869):—

" The terms effeminate and maudlin, with others, are freely used nowadays to stigmatise such new tunes as are not direct imitations of old ones. And yet it has always appeared strange to me that musicians should be found who, whilst admitting that seventeenth century tunes were very properly written in what we may call the natural idiom of that period, will not allow nineteenth century ones to be written in the idiom of that day. You may imitate and plagiarise the old tunes to any extent, and in all probability you will be spoken of as one who is 'thoroughly imbued with the truly devotional spirit of the old ecclesiastical writers,' but you are not permitted on any account to give your natural feelings fair play, or, in short, to write spontaneously. The strangest part of the argument, however, is that whilst you are urged to imitate the old works, you are warned in the same breath that to succeed is altogether without the bounds of possibility. The question then naturally arises, Would it not be better, though at the risk of doing feebler things, to follow your own natural style, which at least would possess the merit of truth, and to leave the task of endeavouring to achieve an impossibility to those who prefer it? For my part, I have elected to imitate the old writers in their independent method of working rather than their works."

We shake hands with our composer over this "confession of faith," and bid our readers "Farewell."

INDEXES.

INDEX I.

PSALMS MENTIONED.

	PAGE		PAGE
iii., iv	58	lvii.	6
vii.	31	lx.	10
viii	16	lxviii.	38
xiv.	6	lxx.	6
xviii.	38	lxxii.	5, 6, 67
xix.	16	lxxvi.	79
xxii.	10	lxxxiv.	86
xxiii.	16	lxxxix.	5
xxiv.	38	xc.	5, 7
xxix.	16	c.	10
xxxii.	47	ci.	38
xl.	6	cii.	86
xlii., xliii.	5, 6, 86	cvi.	5
xlv.	10, 67	cviii.	6
xlvi.	79	cxiii.-cxviii.	11
xlviii.	79	cxv.-cxviii.	99
li.	47	cxix.	9
lv.	58	cxx.-cxxxiv.	38, 99
lvi.	10, 31	cxxxvii.	86

INDEX II.

HYMNS MENTIONED.

	PAGE
A safe stronghold our God is still	151
Abide with me! fast falls the eventide	164
All glory, laud, and honour	146
All praise to Thee, my God, this night	166
All things bright and beautiful	122
And didst Thou leave the race	264
Angels and supernal powers	127
Art thou weary, art thou languid	140
Awake, my soul, and with the sun	166
Awake, my soul, to meet the day	178
Before Jehovah's awful throne	173
Begone, unbelief	206
Behold the glories of the Lamb	171
Brief life is here our portion	146
Brightest and best of the sons of the morning	122
By cool Siloam's shady rill	122
Children of the Heavenly King	124
Christ, Whose glory fills the skies	189
Come, Holy Ghost, our souls inspire	139
Come, let us join our cheerful songs	171
Come, Thou Holy Spirit, come	147
Come, ye sinners, poor and wretched	125
Come, ye thankful people, come	243
Creator Spirit, by Whose aid	158

	PAGE
Day of wrath, O day of mourning	149
Days and moments quickly flying	230
Dear Christian people, now rejoice	152
Dear Jesus, ever at Thy side	237
Dear Lord and Father of mankind	258
Do no sinful action	122
Eternal Beam of Light Divine	190
Far from the world, O Lord, I flee	199
Father, I know that all my life	126
Fear not, O little flock, the foe	153
For all the saints who from their labours	247
For ever with the Lord	213
For thee, O dear, dear country	146
"Forward" be our watchword	243
From Greenland's icy mountains	209
Gentle Jesus, meek and mild	121
God moves in a mysterious way	198
Golden harps are sounding	225
Gracious Spirit, dwell with me	267
Hail, gladdening Light, of His pure glory	131
Hail to the Lord's Anointed	213
Hark, hark, my soul, angelic songs	237
Hark how the adoring host above	172
Hark the glad sound! the Saviour comes	179
He giveth sun, He giveth shower	270
He is gone—a cloud of light	242
Holy, Holy, Holy, Lord God Almighty	209
Holy, Holy, Holy, Lord God of Hosts	129
How are Thy servants blest, O Lord	160
How doth the little busy bee	174

	PAGE
I am trusting Thee, Lord Jesus	226
I do not ask, O Lord, that life may be	126
I think when I read that sweet story of old	121
Immortal Love, for ever full	258
Jerusalem the golden	146
Jesus, I my cross have taken	164
Jesus, I will trust Thee	222
Jesus, Lover of my soul	191
Jesus, Master, Whom I serve	226
Jesus, Master, Whose I am	226
Jesus shall reign where'er the sun	175
Jesus, the very thought of Thee	145
Jesus, Thou art the Rose	128
Jesus, Thou joy of loving hearts	145
Jesus, where'er Thy people meet	198
Just as I am, without one plea	217
Lead, kindly Light, amid the encircling	231
Let dogs delight to bark and bite	120
Let us with a gladsome mind	158
Lo! on a narrow neck of land	190
Look from Thy sphere of endless day	259
Lord Jesus, think on me	133
Lord of all being, throned afar	253
Lord of the living harvest	248
Much in sorrow, oft in woe	161
My faith looks up to Thee	220
My God and Father, while I stray	216
My God, how wonderful Thou art	237
My heart is resting, O my God	126
My very thoughts are selfish	124

	PAGE
Nearer, my God, to Thee	145
Now thank we all our God	154
Now the labourer's task is o'er	250
O come and mourn with me awhile	237
O conscience! conscience! when I look	128
O day of rest and gladness!	246
O deem not they are blest alone	260
O for a closer walk with God	197
O for a thousand tongues to sing	191
O God of Bethel, by Whose hand	180
O God, the Rock of Ages	245
O happy band of pilgrims	143
O happy day that fixed my choice	179
O help us, Lord, each hour of need	242
O Jesus Christ, the righteous!	252
O Light of life, O Saviour dear	271
O Light Whose beams illumine all	244
O Lord of heaven, and earth, and sea	246
O Love Divine, that stooped to share	254
O Paradise! O Paradise!	237
O sacred Head once wounded	145
O spirit of the living God	213
Object of my first desire	183
Of the Father's love begotten	136
Once in Royal David's city	122
Our blest Redeemer, ere He breathed	264
Our day of praise is done	250
Peace, perfect peace, in this dark world	245
Praise God from Whom all blessings flow	166
Prayer is the soul's sincere desire	212
Rest of the weary, Joy of the sad	248

	PAGE
Ride on, ride on in majesty	242
Rock of Ages, cleft for me	184
Safe home, safe home in port	143
Saviour, again to Thy dear Name we raise	249
Saviour, visit Thy plantation	205
See, the Conqueror mounts in triumph	246
Shepherd of tender youth	130
Sometimes a light surprises	197
Sow in the morn thy seed	213
Sweet Saviour, bless us e'er we go	237
Take me, O my Father, take me	221
Take my life, and let it be	227
Tell it out among the heathen	225
Ten thousand times ten thousand	243
The Church's one foundation	250
The day is past and over	137
The day Thou gavest, Lord, is ended	250
The King of Glory we proclaim	214
The Lord delights in them that speak	120
The spacious firmament on high	161
The Sundays of man's life	128
The sun is sinking fast	231
There is a dreadful hell	120
There is a green hill far away	122
There is a land of pure delight	174
Thine arm, O Lord, in days of old	244
Throughout the deep Thy footsteps shine	188
Thy life was given for me	226
Yield not to temptation	221
Your harps, ye trembling saints	183
Wake, awake, the night is flying	153

	PAGE
We are but little children weak	122
We give Thee but Thine own	247
Weary of earth and laden with my sin	251
What if His dreadful anger burn	119
When all Thy mercies, O my God	160
When Israel of the Lord beloved	161
When I survey the wondrous cross	174
When morning gilds the skies	231
When our heads are bowed with woe	242
When the day of toil is done	250
Where'er the gentle heart	271
Worship the Lord in the beauty of holiness	248

INDEX III.

HYMN-WRITERS MENTIONED.

	PAGE		PAGE
Adams	269	Ellerton	249
Addison	159	Elliott, Charlotte	215
Adolphus, Gustavus	153	Ephraim the Syrian	131
Alexander, Dr. J. W.	145		
Alexander, Mrs.	122	Faber	124, 233
Alford	243		
Ambrose	134	Gerhardt	116
Anatolius	137	Gregory the Great	137
Auber, Harriet	264		
		H. L. L.	272
Bardesan	131	Hart, Joseph	124
Bernard (Clairvaux)	143	Havergal	125, 221
Bernard (Cluny)	146	Heber	122, 207
Berridge, John	128	Herbert, George	128
Bickersteth	233, 245	Holmes, O. W.	253
Bonar	218	How, Walsham	247
Bowring	272		
Bryant, W. C.	258	Ingelow, Jean	264
Cennick, John	124	Keble	238
Clement of Alexandria	130	Ken	166
Cowper	195		
		Luke, Mrs.	121
Doddridge	176	Luther	113, 150
Dryden	158	Lynch	296

Lyte	163
Milman	242
Milton	158
Monsell	248
Montgomery	210
Neale	116, 146
Newman	228
Newton	200
Nicolai	153
Olivers	114
Palgrave	270
Palmer, Ray	220
Plumptre	244
Procter, A. A.	126, 261
Prudentius	136
Rinckart	154
Robert II. of France	147
St. Cosma	140

St. John Damascene	140
St. Joseph of the Studium	143
St. Stephen the Sabaite	141
Scott, Sir Walter	161
Stanley	241
Steele, Anne	114
Stone	250
Synesius of Cyrene	133
Tate, Faithful	127
Taylor, Ann	121
Taylor, Jane	121
Theodulph	146
Toplady	181
Waring, A. L.	126
Watts	118, 170
Wesley	121, 186
White, Kirke	161
Whittier	255
Wither, George	123, 127
Wordsworth, Bishop	246
Xavier	116

INDEX IV.

HYMN-TUNE COMPOSERS MENTIONED.

	PAGE
Barnby, J.	332
Dykes, J. B.	302
Gauntlett, H. J.	277
Hopkins, E. J.	295
Monk, W. H.	310
Smart, H.	285
Stainer, J.	317
Sullivan, A. S.	327

INDEX V.

HYMN-TUNES MENTIONED.

	PAGE
Aber ("O perfect life of love")	313
Benediction ("Saviour, again")	300
Beverley ("Thou art coming")	313
Dominus regit me ("The King of Love")	308
Endless Alleluia	336
Epenetus	122, 225
Eventide ("Abide with me")	313, 314
Heathlands	289
Hermas	122
Hollingside ("Jesus, Lover of my soul")	309
Irby	283
Lancashire	289
Laudes Domini ("When morning gilds the skies")	336
London, New	308
Melcombe	308
Melita ("Eternal Father, strong to save")	309
Miles' Lane	293
Northumberland	289

	PAGE
Nun danket .	155
Nymphos	122
Olivet ("My faith looks up to Thee").	220
Patmos	122
Pilgrims (Smart) .	289
Regent Square	289
Requiescat ("Now the labourer's task is done").	309
Rockingham	325
St. Aëlred ("Fierce raged the tempest")	309
„ Albinus .	283
„ Alphege .	283
„ Anatolius ("The day is past and over")	309
„ Bees ("Hark, my soul")	308
„ Chrysostom ("Jesus, my Lord") .	336
„ Fabian ("Jesus, Lover of my soul")	336
„ Gertrude .	329
„ Leonard .	289
„ Matthias ("Sweet Saviour, bless us") .	313
„ Theresa ("Brightly gleams our banner")	330
Sebaste ("Hail, gladdening Light") .	323
The blessed home	323
Vesper ("Holy Father, cheer our way") .	323
Vox angelica ("Hark, hark, my soul")	308
Wareham	325
Weber	314

www.ingramcontent.com/pod-product-compliance
Lightning Source LLC
Chambersburg PA
CBHW020234240426
43672CB00006B/518